RAYMOND J. LEARSY

Oil and Finance

The Epic Corruption

From 2006 to 2010

iUniverse, Inc.
Bloomington

Oil and Finance
The Epic Corruption

Copyright © 2011 Raymond J. Learsy

iUniverse books may be ordered through booksellers or by contacting:

iUniverse
1663 Liberty Drive
Bloomington, IN 47403
www.iuniverse.com
1-800-Authors (1-800-288-4677)

ISBN: 978-1-4620-1809-3 (sc)
ISBN: 978-1-4620-1810-9 (hc)
ISBN: 978-1-4620-1811-6 (e)

Library of Congress Control Number: 2011906881

Printed in the United States of America

iUniverse rev. date: 5/11/2011

My thanks to my wife, Melva, who was my editor-in-chief and who graciously put up with me these past many months. My thanks also go to Beth Rybczyk for her thoughtful and cheery assistance and to Stefan Beck for all his help.

Believe what you see, and lay aside what you hear.

ويعتقد ما نرى، وتضع جانبا ما تسمع

–Arabic proverb

Contents

Introduction

This book is about the ongoing saga of oil, specifically focusing on the events of the past five years. It is about the manipulation of oil by producers and their allies, its malign interrelationship with the financial sector, and the dangerously benign or neglectful policies of our acquiescent government. Oil, as an industry and mind-set, has become the canary in the coal mine of so much that has negatively affected the way we live today—environmentally, economically, politically, and morally. Oil has seeped into parallel sectors of the economy, especially into the world of finance, in a way that is speeding us toward disaster. The gulf oil spill is a belated wake-up call to each and every one of us, alerting us to the extent of the catastrophes that have been building and to what may lie ahead.

These writings are real-time commentaries on a series of events and issues casting the oil industry and its many facets in sharper relief. It is a compilation of selected and redacted posts that I contributed to the *Huffington Post* during the past five years. The posts emanate from personal experience and knowledge gathered during a quarter of a century in the commodity trading field and dealing in a wide array of physical materials, ranging from oil and gas (liquefied natural gas) to basic commodities for the chemical and chemical fertilizer industry, shipping cargos of these commodities throughout the world. I have also authored the pointedly focused *Over a Barrel: Breaking Oil's Grip on Our Future*. The posts are organized chronologically within thematic subcategories.

The book, then, is meant to access the real-time response of the blogosphere as an instructional encounter with what happened as it happened. As you read, please understand that these posts were written in response to live issues as they evolved; consequently, some repetition of information was unavoidable as a means of keeping things in context.

I hope to provide the reader with a better understanding of where we find ourselves today and of how we got there, as well as with contemplations, reactions, and solutions suggested by the flow of events. I also hope to impart an understanding of how the system has worked and of the degree to which it has been manipulated to the benefit of the few at the expense of the many.

For example, the recent oil spill disaster in the Gulf of Mexico has not only taken lives but also destroyed the livelihoods of thousands and thousands of people. It is an environmental catastrophe reaching biblical proportions. And yet it is also the direct result of the corporate culture of an oil industry—and more specifically an oil company, BP—whose performance over the past years has been dismal, as set forth in posts dating as far back as August 2006.

The history of the oil business looks like variations on a theme, be that theme oil production; oil pricing and attendant speculation and manipulation; the politics of oil and its impact on our nation and our security; the influence of oil on our government policies, both foreign and domestic; the menacing environmental impact of oil; or oil's effects on our infrastructure, from the demise of our railroads to the crippled state of our mass transportation facilities.

This book, in chronicling the corruption of a commodity that is essential to the world's economic well-being, should also be taken as a forewarning of and a wake-up call to what lies ahead when core commodities are subject to political, monopoly, marketing, and financial manipulation.

The events of these past years will serve as prologue to what can be expected to emerge in the decades ahead, as encroaching food shortages become acute in the face of the compelling need to double the world's calorie production by 2050, driven by population growth and changes in dietary habits. This projected dramatic leap in the world's need for food once again risks providing trading windfalls to the few while placing millions, perhaps billions, at grave risk of malnutrition and possibly starvation.

This book further deals with the perverse success of the Organization of Petroleum Exporting Countries (OPEC), which culminated in driving crude oil prices to the precipitous height of $147/barrel (hereafter abbreviated "bbl") in July of 2008. Just how was this economically devastating feat accomplished? OPEC, a group of twelve countries (Algeria, Angola, Ecuador, Iran, Iraq, Kuwait, Libya, Nigeria, Qatar, Saudi Arabia, the United Arab Emirates, and Venezuela) that controls some 40 percent of the world's oil production and is led in large measure by Saudi Arabia conspires to manipulate and control the supply and hence the price of oil.

I also discuss OPEC's interface with our government in recent years—including the shameful acquiescence of the Bush administration to OPEC's manipulations—and OPEC's policies and public declarations. I will shine a light on our somnambulant media; the glaring speculation on our trading exchanges; the lack of oversight by our regulatory agencies; and the abject opportunism of our financial sector, especially of large banks abetting and grossly profiting from rising oil prices much to the detriment of households struggling with escalating heating bills and gasoline costs.

Perhaps most importantly, these writings delve into the issue of national security and the challenges wrought by what has become, together with climate change, the greatest threat to our nation and to the world—the transfer of literally trillions of dollars of the nation's wealth to oil interests and terror-sponsoring despots around the world. These trillions have helped to destabilize today's world, lubricating the clash of civilizations and making it possible for billions upon billions to be spent by Middle East oil producers to radicalize the young and vulnerable in all corners of the globe with the destructive ethos of jihad and intolerance.

Raymond J. Learsy
December 31, 2010

SECTION I

Enemies Foreign

PART I

OPEC, the Saudis, and Our National Security

Cheney, in Saudiland, Don't Hold Abdullah's Hand!
January 6, 2006

Vice President Dick Cheney is about to visit Saudi Arabia, where he will be meeting with King Abdullah. Beware! No hand-holding, please.

The last time Abdullah's hand was held was during his April 25, 2005, visit with President George W. Bush at the Crawford Ranch. Then—as now—oil prices and supply were a topic of discussion. At the time of the Crawford barbecue, the price of oil hovered around $48/bbl, near to and breaching levels that had never before been achieved in the oil market—and nearly 50 percent above prices from the year before. Whatever was said at the time and in spite of the widely reproduced images of President Bush and then-Prince Abdullah holding hands in fraternal companionship, the net result bordered on disastrous.

Abdullah left Texas reassured with little concern that the already egregious price of oil had reached the limits of American tolerance. Within four months of the visit, the price of oil continued its aggressive spiral upward, reaching $65/bbl—this before Katrina's sweep—a staggering increase of some 35 percent. Prices have hovered around these levels since the summer of 2005, costing Americans, who consume more than twenty million bbl of oil a day, an additional $340 million in increased daily disbursements to OPEC and to the bottom line of the oil industry.

Vice President Cheney, in his discussions with the king, might determine whether Saudi Arabia and its OPEC cartel brethren can supply more oil to the marketplace to break the fevered advance of crude oil prices. To put the current situation in proper context, the OPEC cartel, led by Saudi Arabia, currently supplies fewer than thirty million bbl of oil a day to the world market.

In 1979—I repeat, in 1979—the OPEC cartel pumped thirty-one million bbl per day. Today OPEC tells us that they are at the virtual limits of their pumping capacity. The Vice President should be clear in his discussions that this claim (that the OPEC cartel and Saudi Arabia have not added to their pumping capacity in more than a quarter of a century) is either dubious or an attempt to disguise a willful constraint of production, undertaken to manipulate prices.

In any event, our vice president should restrain himself, no matter his impulse, from walking hand in hand with King Abdullah. The last time this came to pass, it cost us dearly. A similar percentage jump in prices from today's levels would cost us all an additional $440 million a day. Vice President Cheney, hands in pockets, please.

Oil Company Profits and Our National Security
January 26, 2006

Not long from now, oil companies will be reporting their year-end profits. They will show massive gains over the past year. This week ConocoPhillips reported a jump of 66 percent in earnings to $13.5 billion. As ExxonMobil, Shell, BP, and others report their profits, this story will be strikingly reinforced.

A simple fact needs be stated and understood. The greater the profits of these oil companies, the greater the risk to our national security. The logic behind this is straightforward. Higher oil company profits go hand in hand with higher oil prices (now in excess of $65/bbl). Higher oil prices result in a massive transfer of wealth to hostile nations that fund the dissemination of hate-filled preaching calling for the demise of the United States and the West. Higher oil prices enable the activities of dysfunctional governments that are tyrannical to their own populations and, in an era marked by the proliferation of weapons of mass destruction, are increasingly dangerous to the world at large.

We are led to believe by the oil patch pundits that company profits are a fair reflection of free markets at work. They are not. The market for oil, more so than for any other major commodity, is rigged, and the oil companies are riding the coattails of this manipulation to ever greedier levels. They do this, in effect, by taxing us, the public, by selling us back the nation's natural resources of gas and oil at profit levels that have little or no connection to the cost of production.

How is this possible? The royalty system as enacted by the US government in the Federal Oil and Gas Royalty Management Act of 1982 is the patchwork of an oil-friendly administration and the influence of K Street lobbyists. It permits oil and gas extraction on public lands and coastal waterways at minimal benefit to the public—the presumptive owners of these resources—and maximum benefit to the oil companies and their shareholders. The public gets hit twice. The transfer of title to the resources is tantamount to a giveaway at today's prices. Then the public has to buy back the resources at rigged market levels.

The rigging of prices is done outside the purview of our present laws and to the enormous benefit of the oil patch. To achieve high prices and profits, international oil companies and our own need not collude. If they did, they would be subject to civil and criminal prosecution under our antitrust laws. But they have a better method. The OPEC cartel takes care of matters for them, by restraining production or making the public believe that the members of OPEC have reached the limits of their capabilities.

What our oil patch has done is piggyback on OPEC's machinations while being the cartel's greatest cheerleader and convincing us, the gullible public, that the cartel is simply a kindly group of nations struggling to meet our energy needs and that its prices are the manifestation of market forces. While prices go up, oil companies increase their profits without adding any economic value to their product. A gallon of gas takes your car only so far, whether you pay $1.50 or $2.75 for it.

If you are an oil producer as well as a refiner, as many oil companies are, the difference is pure gravy, hence these earnings reports we are seeing now. Take the oil patch to Las Vegas, and these guys would be railroaded out of town.

OPEC Agonistes
January 29, 2006

OPEC will meet in Vienna, Austria, this week. Even with crude oil prices near all-time highs, Iran and Venezuela are pressing for a reduction in production quotas from current levels of twenty-eight million bbl per day (excluding Iraq, which is barely producing one million bbl per day in addition). Meanwhile, the Saudi oil minister, Ali al-Naimi, is quoted in a statement to the private Indian NDTV television channel, as reported by Pat Boyle of the *Irish Independent* on January 24, 2006, as saying "Unless the market changes significantly between now and the meeting, there is probably no real reason to do anything different."

Bolstering al-Naimi's air of "reasonableness," we have OPEC song masters—such as Matthew Simmons, the author of *Twilight in the Desert: The Coming Saudi Oil Shock and the World Economy*—predicting that oil prices will approach $190/bbl by the end of winter in 2006 and the often-quoted oil analyst Philip Verleger predicting that "[w]e'll see prices well over $100 a barrel before the end of the year."

To round out the chorus, there is our own energy secretary, Samuel Bodman, who claims regular contact with oil producers. "By and large, they seem to be understanding that there needs to be more oil rather than less oil in the world," he was quoted last week as having said in the *New York Times* (Jad Mouawad, "OPEC expected to reject Iran's and Venezuela's push to cut output," January 27, 2006). His supplications must be extremely well-mannered. Back in 2000, when Bill Richardson was secretary of energy and placed a call to the then-president of OPEC, Iranian officials waxed indignant at the thought that one of their robbery victims might have a say in the matter. "In the forty-year history of OPEC," they fumed, "there has never been a case of the secretary of energy calling OPEC ministers in the middle of a meeting.[...] We are very upset and disappointed at the external pressure. We don't like it" (Edmund L. Andrews, "Reluctant Iran Falls in Line with OPEC Production Rise," *New York Times*, March 30, 2000). It was as though fixing quotas to manipulate prices had become a divine right.

We have learned our lessons well since then. We have learned to say thank you to the Saudis for holding the bad guys (Iran and Venezuela) in check, all the while paying through the nose (now over $67/bbl) for a product that costs them less—in many cases, considerably less—than $1.50/bbl to produce (speech by Saudi Minister of Petroleum and Mineral Resources Ali Al-Naimi in Huston, Texas 1999). If General Motors and Ford had such margins, they could sell their Chevy Blazers and Tauruses for three hundred thousand to four hundred thousand dollars each.

What Mr. Bodman should be saying to his interlocutors at OPEC is this: "Listen, my good friends, as you are fully aware, the price of oil today is at levels that are far beyond any economic justification. I have seven hundred million bbl of oil in my strategic petroleum reserve, and the industry is holding a further 310 million in reserve in commercial stocks that are now 10 percent higher than a year ago.

"We are also members of the International Energy Agency, which holds an additional seven hundred million in its strategic oil reserves (http://www.iea.org/stats/oildata.asp?COUNTRY_CODE=US).

Together, we hold a total of 4.1 billion in reserves both strategic and commercial. If you cut production, we will begin to introduce these reserves into the market to stabilize availability and price, and you, my good friends at OPEC, will be losing your equivalent market share. By the way, are you listening, Iran?

What we would really like you to do is increase the availability of oil so that the price returns to levels that make economic sense and reflect free market conditions. And please don't tell me you are doing all you can by pumping twenty-nine million bbl a day (including Iraq). For those of you who keep a diary, turn to 1979 when you will see that you were producing thirty-one million bbl a day. Here we are, more than a quarter of a century later, and you tell me you can't do better? C'mon, guys, give me a break. I've got a job to keep here, and you can't make me look that dumb.

OPEC to Bush: "Drop Dead";
Texas to the Rest of Us: "Say Please"
February 3, 2006

President Bush runs the risk of alienating the world's biggest source of oil with his plan to end America's oil addiction. So proclaimed OPEC delegates and oil ministers yesterday. His plan was neither "achievable nor prudent and could make investment in the industry more difficult. He has not heeded the call to give producers a road map of future demand" (Carola Hoyos et al, "Bush misfires in drive to end 'oil addiction'" *Financial Times*, New York edition, February 2, 2006) to help petro-states decide how much to spend on future capacity. This complaint came from members of the same cartel that has steadfastly stonewalled any attempt to solicit its reserves and production capacities for outside audit, thus preventing consumer nations from planning their energy needs intelligently with real data instead of with OPEC press releases.

Saudi Arabia's ambassador to Washington, Prince Turki al-Faisal, expressed further puzzlement about President Bush's singling out of the Middle East in his State of the Union address. "Is that a declaration that the US is going to work to be independent of Canadian oil, Mexican oil, and Venezuelan oil? I see no threat to America from receiving its oil from the Middle East" (Elisabeth Bumiller, "State of the Union: Energy; Bush's Goals on Energy Quickly Find Obstacles," *New York Times*, February 2, 2006).

Keep in mind that al-Faisal made this outrageous statement as a representative of the nation that gave us fifteen of the September 11, 2001, hijackers, a nation that, to this day, provides the largest number of foreign suicide bombers in Iraq, to say nothing of the billions of its dollars going to anti-Western Wahhabi madrassas and mosques throughout the world.

The commedia continues with Secretary of Energy Samuel Bodman's craven backtracking at the first sign of Saudi and OPEC displeasure. His conciliatory gesture was to state to reporters in a conference call on Wednesday, February 1, 2006, that the president's mention of Middle East oil was "purely an example" (Elisabeth Bumiller, "Make Industries' Tax Breaks Permanent, President Urges," *New York Times*, February 3, 2006). This must have been a thank you to Saudi Arabia for holding the line against Iranian and Venezuelan pressures at the ongoing OPEC meeting to push oil prices even higher than the current excessive level, having Bodman's Department of Energy subscribe to and give public credence to the fiction that oil is a freely traded commodity.

A depressing insight into where the government really stands on energy issues was provided by Joe L. Barton, republican from Texas and chairman of the powerful Committee on Energy and Commerce. Upon hearing the President's address, Barton advised us that "America runs on energy that is both abundant and available at prices we can afford to pay" (Elisabeth Bumiller, "State of the Union: Energy; Bush's Goals on Energy Quickly Find Obstacles," *New York Times*, February 2, 2006). I did not make that up. May I suggest we send our heating bills to Representative Barton's Texas address? And, of course, let's not forget to send thank you notes to the oil patch in Texas and to the ministers of the OPEC nations for making it all so affordable.

OPEC Pushing to Refine Our Addiction
February 18, 2006

As its latest favor to Western consumers, OPEC plans to increase refinery capacity in the Persian Gulf by 60 percent over the next decade.

If we want to lower oil prices, said Saudi oil minister Ali al-Naimi just a few days ago, "Build, build, build more refineries!" (Javier Blas and Kevin Morrison in Vienna and Carola Hoyos in London, "Opec urges nations to build more refineries," *Financial Times,* June 16, 2005, http://www.ft.com/cms/s/0/699e2966-de63-11d9-92cd-00000e2511c8. html#axzz1HGVpBJjk).

Al-Naimi reminds me of Tom Lehrer's "The Old Dope Peddler," because the peddler was spreading joy wherever he went and building tomorrow's business by giving the kids free samples.

Led by al-Naimi, OPEC has been claiming for several years that it is a lack of refining capacity (among other scapegoats) that is to blame in driving oil prices higher. This argument is transparently false. A shortage of refineries could certainly account for higher prices of refined product—gasoline, diesel oil, jet fuel, and the like—but it would not push up the price of crude oil. In fact, if crude oil were flowing freely and there weren't enough refineries, it would tend to drive *down* the price of crude. The reverse is happening. Yet again, OPEC simply wants to hide the fact that it is manipulating the oil market with phony shortages and artificially high prices.

It's true enough that we are pushing the limits of refinery capacity in the United States. There hasn't been a new refinery constructed in this country in three decades, primarily due to environmental concerns and the understandable not-in-my-backyard reactions of local communities. Existing refineries, however, have been expanded and modernized, and we have been importing enough refined product, mostly from Latin America and the Caribbean, to keep up with demand.

If we don't want refineries in our backyards, the OPEC nations will be happy to build their own refineries in situ, exporting not only crude oil but also downstream production as well. But this sample from the peddler will have two main effects. First of all, it isn't really free. The producers will keep the refining profits on top of the roughly $60/bbl they already get for their crude—an enormous windfall. Secondly, and more importantly, the Persian Gulf will become the world's biggest source of refined product, and it already makes up the major portion of OPEC's 40-percent share of the world's crude production.

Put simply, even as President Bush vows to reduce America's

dependence on Middle Eastern crude by 75 percent, we would become even more deeply and dangerously addicted.

Have a snort, kiddies. It's really cool!

Oil-Funded Influence, Al-Arabiya, and Our Port Security
February 22, 2006

Dubai is a "country that plays by the rules ("Bush Backs Transfer of U.S. Ports to Dubai Firm," MSNBC.MSN.com, accessed 4/12/2011, http:// www.msnbc.msn.com/id/11474440/ns/us_news-security/). This was one of the reasons given by President Bush for his decision to veto any attempt by Congress to stop the transfer of control of major American port facilities to Dubai Ports World (DP World), an entity owned by the government of Dubai in the United Arab Emirates.

Meanwhile, incitement to murder was the offense specified by the Iraqi administration in its decision to ban, temporarily, the Al-Arabiya Television Network (Dexter Filkins, "Revising Report, Army Denies Throats of 2 G.I.'s Were Cut," *New York Times*, November 25, 2003). The US State Department spokesperson Philip Reeker has called Al-Arabiya's coverage of news events in Iraq "irresponsible in the extreme" (Peter Feuilherade, "Profile: Al-Arabiya TV," *BBC News*, November 25, 2003, http://news.bbc.co.uk/2/hi/3236654.stm). Defense Secretary Donald Rumsfeld has called the network "hostile to American interests" (Peter Feuilherade, "Profile: Al-Arabiya TV," *BBC News*, November 25, 2003, http://news.bbc.co.uk/2/hi/3236654.stm). Over time, Al-Arabiya has begun to clean up its act, but that cat has clearly shown its stripes.

Dubai, which "plays by the rules," also happens to be the seat of and has extended hospitality and support to the Al-Arabiya Television Network. Now this putatively law-abiding country wishes, through its subsidiary, to run our ports. Permit me a slightly strained analogy: This would be like turning our port facilities over to the Pakistani Intelligence Services, which is purportedly our friend but known to be rife with admirers of Osama bin Laden. I think you'll understand what I mean.

Given Dubai's support of Al-Arabyia, it would appear to be sheer madness to entrust them with probably the most sensitive and vulnerable aspect of our port security, namely the loading, shipping, discharging, and terminaling of containers and container traffic. The reach of Peninsular and Oriental Steam Navigation Company (P&O, the company to be taken over) extends far beyond its facilities in US ports, where they range from New York to New Orleans. Their control extends to many of the major shipping ports outside the United States, so that Dubai would have de facto control of not only what is received at our ports but also what is loaded out at the port of shipment.

Stewart Baker of the Department of Homeland Security put it bluntly (unlike his boss, Michael Chertoff, who has been off the ranch, peddling the deal to the public) that this was the first-ever sale involving US port operations to a state-owned company. "In that sense this is a new layer of controls," (Ted Bridis, Associated Press writer, "Bush Shrugs Off Objections to Port Deal," msnbc.msn.com, February 21, 2006, http://www.msnbc.msn.com/id/11474440/ns/us_news-security/). Has anyone determined what these new layers of control would entail, at what and whose cost, including the diversion of resources and focus from other priorities at this time of great risk?

According to Chertoff, the administration wants this deal to happen in order "to support a robust world trading system" (Brian Knowlton, "Lawmakers Increase Criticism of Dubai Deal for Ports," *New York Times*, February 19, 2006). Too often, with our government, that translates to supporting the vested interests of oil money in whatever form that money presents itself. Dubai spreads its riches and reach to K Street and beyond. Sadly, our security too often plays a secondary role. Secretary of State Condoleezza Rice just recently complained about Venezuelan President Hugo Chavez's oil-funded influence in Latin America. She needn't have gone that far afield.

President Eisenhower, Secure Our Ports
February 27, 2006

Upon leaving his presidency, Dwight D. Eisenhower warned the nation about the danger to its future in the gathering power and influence of what he called the military-industrial complex. He wanted to add Congress to his admonition, but he decided to drop it at the last moment.

Turning over our port terminals to DP World is perhaps the latest and certainly among the most brazen examples of that influence, which today could be amended to "oiligopoly-government complex." Oil money is corrupting the good sense of our government.

The influence it brings to bear recalls and brings new meaning to Eisenhower's warning that the democratic process risks losing its voice when lined up against the power of these corrupting interests.

Is it coincidence that—according to a report by Christine Romans, the CNN correspondent on CNN's *Lou Dobbs Show* that aired on February 22, 2006—the Carlyle Group, an investment firm known for close links to Middle Eastern money, has a significant stake in P&O and that ex-President George H. W. Bush is a former senior advisor of the Carlyle Group? There is nothing improper or nefarious in this, but it does point to a mentality and an amalgam of influence that is cause for concern. One might well assume that the principals of P&O and the principals of DP World share a mutual trust and speak much the same language. But it is not so much the principals that are of concern, be they the governments of Dubai (owner of DP World) or the United Arab Emirates.

The concern, rather, is the radicalized elements within those societies from the two citizens of the Emirates who were among the perpetrators of the September 11, 2001, attacks to the bankers who transferred funds to al Qaeda operatives to the managers of the Al-Arabiya Television Network with its virulently anti-American coverage of Iraq to the port terminal operatives who permitted the transfer of Pakistani nuclear components to North Korea and Iran. These are not issues for the dealmakers, but they should be of grave concern to our government, which is charged with providing our security.

Here is where the oiligopoly-government complex manifests it grip, smoothing out these concerns through highly placed lobbyists and K Street functionaries, persuading responsible government officials through mollifying arguments or well-focused political contributions to look the other way. Too often there is nobody asking the truly difficult questions.

Yes, it is understandable that commentators like the *New York Times*'s Thomas L. Friedman ("War of the Worlds," February 24, 2006) would take a conciliatory posture toward the DP World takeover in the name of setting an example of international civility and tolerance.

Unfortunately, it is also a step away from the current realities of the world. We are dealing with an implacable enemy who will try to exploit any weakness. Our ports are recognized as highly vulnerable, and container cargo traffic is among our weakest links. To say that port security is the responsibility of the coast guard and let it go at that is nonsense. The coast guard's vigilance, because of limitations on funding and manpower, extends to but a small fraction of the tonnage moved. The port terminal operators play a key role in establishing the essential work ethic motivating their personnel to be on the lookout for any discrepancies. That can only come from the top down.

The downside of one mistake, one nuclear device detonating in one of our ports, is too horrible to contemplate. But that, and nothing less, is the danger. This is neither the time nor the place to set an example of international political correctness or to accede to Mr. Chertoff's rationale "to support a robust world trading system." The potential for disaster is too great.

And for those too young to remember, Eisenhower was no lefty.

President Bush's Most Respectful Letter to King Abdullah on Energy Cooperation
June 22, 2006

A few days ago, Saudi Ambassador Turki al-Faisal, in conversation with the press, advised that President Bush had sent a letter to Saudi Arabia's King Abdullah reaffirming his commitment to the agreements reached at the ranch at Crawford, Texas, in April 2005. It was a sort of belated penance for the comments in his State of the Union address and his concurrent call to cut oil imports from the Middle East. Herewith, some rumination on what President Bush might have written in his letter.

> Your Royal Highness,
> I have such fond memories of your visit to Crawford last year. Strolling along hand in hand was truly a highlight of my days at the ranch. A few questions have come to mind. Permit me, Your Highness, to set them forth below.
> When you visited in April 2005, the price of oil was in the upper $40s/bbl. A few months later, it jumped to some

13

$70/bbl, where it remains today. Laura asks me nearly every day what it was that I said to you that encouraged you to persuade your brethren in OPEC to allow prices to jump that high—and so quickly after our visit. I know there was Katrina (which I hear a great deal about from my friends in the oil business) but to stay there still after all this time.... A near 50 percent jump in price almost immediately after our meeting really isn't good for my image, though I must tell you, my friends in the industry are delighted.

That you agreed to increase your production capacity to 12.5 million bbl from some ten million bbl per day by 2009 really impressed me. That you were going to commit fifty billion dollars to expanding your production was a gesture I found especially moving, as I told you at the time. But since then, I've been doing some arithmetic, and I've begun to realize it's a little thin. Fifty billion by 2009 to help bring the world economies and oil production into closer balance ...well, at today's prices and your current announced production levels ($70/bbl times ten million bbl shipped daily), that's barely two weeks of oil revenues a year each year through 2009. That's not very much, given the dimensions of all that is at stake. I won't go into comparisons with our commitments elsewhere.

It is only natural that we agreed to cooperate, because we have so many interests in common. You are a major source of energy for us and the world. We are, in large measure, the de facto guarantors of your independence (Remember Gulf War I and Saddam Hussein? Now think of Iran on your left flank and al Qaeda on your right). Yet we know so little about your true production capabilities. We are happy to provide, through our Department of Energy, whatever information you may wish to have about us on crude production, known reserves, refinery capacity, transportation infrastructure, and energy generation in all its manifestations (coal, nuclear, wind, hydroelectric, and so on), or through the Department of Commerce, should you wish to have additional data on consumption and distribution. Yet your reserves, your production capacity, remain a mystery to us. Your resources are the world's largest currently known—I'm sure you are aware that only 10 percent of Iraq's landmass has been prospected for oil, so there's no telling what one might find there if the Sunni insurgency abates. But we are flying blind on specifics. If we are to cooperate, you must be more open with us and with the rest of the world. We have major responsibilities in planning future steps for our economies, for which we need facts and not hearsay on energy capabilities. Transparency on your part would be helpful as well. It would make our cooperation more fruitful and convey a greater sense of shared mission in the economic realm.

Oh, Your Highness, one last question: Back in the 1970s, Saudi Aramco brought out a study calling for Saudi Arabia to increase its oil production capacity to twenty million bbl per day. Do you happen to have a copy of that study?

Your Highness, With My Highest Esteem,
President George

Al Qaeda in the Service of OPEC?
October 30, 2006

OPEC is desperately trying to keep oil prices above $60/bbl. The cartel's members have made fevered attempts to keep the price of oil from falling further by cutting production targets some 1.2 million bbl per day and threatening further cuts during their scheduled December meeting. Yet, surprisingly, prices continued to erode in the face of the announced cuts last week.

A temporary blip occurred on Wednesday when storage levels for crude oil at Cushing, Oklahoma, the traditional benchmark for US inventories, showed a surprisingly large drawdown, resulting in a knee-jerk pop in prices. When it was widely realized that the drawdown was due to temporary technical difficulties in offloading tankers at gulf coast ports rather than to heightened consumption, prices began to decline again.

Early in the trading day on Friday, October 27, 2006, as oil prices were beginning to slip under $60/bbl once more, a *Reuters* news flash hit the wires as if on cue: UK forces were being sent to Saudi Arabia's Ras Tanura oil terminal. Ras Tanura has a loading capacity of six million bbl per day, making it the largest offshore loading facility in the world. The US naval forces central command in Bahrain advised that coalition naval forces were taking "prudent, precautionary measures" (Associated Press, "Warships Deploy around S. Arabia Oil Facilities," msnbc.com, October 27, 2006, http://www.msnbc.msn.com/id/15442751/ns/world_news-terrorism/#); the US central command in Florida cited "recent threats to oil infrastructure" (Stefano Ambrogi, "Navies Help Keep Guard on Saudi Oil Facilities," *Reuters*, October 27, 2006, http://uk.reuters.com/article/2006/10/27/us-energy-saudi-threat-idUKL2783708620061027). As this story broke, the price of oil immediately spiked back up to more than $60/bbl.

Al Qaeda was in all likelihood the source of the "recent threats," given that the group has threatened repeatedly to attack the oil shipping and production infrastructure. But the timing of this threat raises some curious questions.

Was it merely fortuitous that al Qaeda's threat helped OPEC play on the consuming world's supply anxieties, exacting, in effect, a propitiously timed fear premium? Perhaps. In the recent round of OPEC negotiations, Saudi Arabia had taken the lead in cutting production in order to ratchet up prices. Though Saudi Arabia and al Qaeda are purportedly avowed enemies, individual Saudi ties to the terrorist group run deep. Could there be an intersection of interests there? The higher the price of oil, the more money is available to fund Wahhabi clerics, mosques, social centers, and madrassas (Muslim educational institutions often associated with a mosque inculcating the very young)—all feeding into the culture of al Qaeda and of Islamic radicalism in general.

Far-fetched? Again, perhaps. But given the nature of the dangers at hand, the time for linear thinking has passed.

One last thing: While Saudi Arabia and OPEC plot to manipulate the price of oil to extortion levels, it is not the Saudi navy that is protecting Saudi ports but the navies of the coalition forces (read, the United Kingdom and the United States). In offering such protection, the coalition permits Saudi Arabia and its OPEC cohort to safely and blatantly jump prices and thumb their noses at American and global consumers.

All this is being done at enormous cost to US taxpayers. According to Amy Myers Jaffe, an analyst at the James A. Baker Institute for Public Policy at Rice University, it was estimated that the US military alone is spending some eighty million dollars per day to guard OPEC against terrorist attack ("United States and the Middle East: Policies and Dilemmas," bipartisanpolicy.org, November 17, 2004, http://www. bipartisanpolicy.org/sites/default/files/United%20States%20and%20 the%20Middle%20East-%20Policies%20and%20Dilemmas.pdf). Remember, the gouging begins at the well, long before the oil reaches the gasoline pump.

Saudi Realpolitik: Political Blackmail & Oil Price Extortion
December 17, 2006

Some two weeks ago, according to the *New York Times* (Helene Cooper, "Saudis Say They Might Back Sunnis If U.S. Leaves Iraq," December 13, 2006), Saudi King Abdullah issued a warning to Vice President Cheney during Cheney's one-day summoned visit to Saudi Arabia. His nation would provide financial support to Iraqi Sunnis if the United States pulled its troops out of Iraq, thereby helping to safeguard the Sunni minority from Iraq's larger contentious Shiite population.

This report has been denied both by the Saudis and White House spokesman Tony Snow, who said, "[T]hat's not Saudi government policy" (Associated Press, "Saudis Warn Against US Pullout," *Washington Post*, December 13, 2006, http://www.washingtonpost.com/wp-dyn/ content/article/2006/12/13/AR2006121300144_pf.html). Yet, what if it *is* true? Duplicity is not an unknown feature of discourse with our Saudi friends. Just last month, Nawaf Obaid, a senior advisor to Prince Turki al-Faisal, the Saudi Arabian Ambassador to the United States, wrote in the *Washington Post* ("Stepping Into Iraq; Saudi Arabia Will Protect Sunnis If the U.S. Leaves," November 29, 2006), quoting from a speech al-Faisal gave the month before: "[S]ince America came into Iraq uninvited, it should not leave uninvited."

A personal aside: No mention was made of the fifteen Saudis on the three planes that set off this disastrous chain of events.

Obaid went on, "If it does, one of the first consequences will be massive Saudi intervention to stop Iranian-backed Shiites from butchering Sunnis [...] As the economic powerhouse of the Middle East, the birthplace of Islam, and the de facto leader of the world's Sunni community [...] Saudi Arabia has both the means and responsibility to intervene." Shortly thereafter, Obaid was summarily dismissed. Barely two weeks later, Prince Turki al-Faisal resigned as ambassador to the United States. Was candor their sin of commission?

If so, it would be blatant political blackmail to threaten the American government with the following Hobson's choice: Either you maintain your presence in Iraq at the expense of your soldiers' lives and at a cost of billions and billions in treasure, or we, the Saudis, will initiate policies all but guaranteeing a massive riposte by Iran and the descent of the region into a conflagration of war and savagery. It will certainly result in impaired access to, or possibly even destruction of, the region's oil and gas infrastructure, pushing the world's economies into deep crisis.

This implicit threat underscores the grave dilemma in which we now find ourselves. Whether to stay in Iraq, and for how long, has become a matter of urgent debate for the American public. But it is clearly in the vital interests of the Saudis that we stay. Yet, in classic "heads, I win; tails, you lose" fashion, the Saudis have taken the lead within OPEC at this crucial moment in initiating the first series of production cuts in two and a half years to further drive up the price of oil.

This comes at the very beginning of the winter heating season, and with the price of oil already some 300 percent higher than at the start of the invasion of Iraq, it provides "cold comfort" for a risk-prone global economy, according to the Oil Market Report that the International Energy Agency released on December 13, 2006. Before OPEC's decision, Energy Secretary Samuel Bodman, together with the head of the International Energy Agency, Claude Mandril, called on OPEC (read, Saudi Arabia) to wait until next year before deciding on additional production cuts. Their call fell on deaf ears. While we are engaged in Iraq, looking after interests that include those of fundamental importance to the Saudis, they are happily stabbing us, and the rest of the world, in the back.

Only this past week, Saudi Arabia successfully bought the British government. Britain's Serious Fraud Office decided to drop a corruption probe into a transaction (British Aerospace Electronic [BAE] Systems's Al Yamamah arms deal) with Saudi Arabia. The Saudis threatened to pull out of negotiations to purchase seventy-two fighter jets from the British and to buy French jets instead unless the probe was brought to an end. Sure enough, with Tony Blair's blessing, Attorney General Lord Goldsmith announced that he was dropping the probe. He added that the decision had been made in the wider public interest, which had to be balanced against the rule of law.

Are we far behind the British? It would be highly interesting to shine a bright light on the interface between our elected officials, our government agencies, and the moneyed influence of the Saudis, beyond the Bush White House and the Baker law firm. Saudi Arabia's current relationship with the United States is perhaps summed up in a phrase: "Ask not what we can do for you; ask what you can do for us." And it is high time that changed.

Saudi Arabia's Oil? Sovereign Responsibility Trumps Sovereign Rights!
January 15, 2007

Late in December 2006, the subjects of King Abdullah's Saudi Arabia received what others elsewhere might have termed a Christmas present. The king decreed that a planned 25 percent increase in the price of regular gasoline would be canceled ("Saudi King Orders Petrol Price Hike Cancelled," Gulfnews.com, December 24, 2006, http://gulfnews.com/business/oil-gas/saudi-king-orders-petrol-price-hike-cancelled-1.271759). Oil Minister Ali al-Naimi, who was in the vanguard of recent efforts to bring about the first OPEC production cuts in two and a half years (in a collusive effort to support a world price of $60/bbl), took time enough off from chirping about high inventory levels to proclaim in that same article, "This order is the latest of [Abdullah's] initiatives which aim to contribute to the welfare of the Saudi people."

The Saudi people are very fortunate indeed. Keeping the price at

0.60 riyals per liter for 95-octane gasoline is the equivalent of 60.6 US cents per gallon; 91-octane was priced at 0.45 riyals per liter or 46 US cents per gallon. A nice tankful, if you can get it.

One can assume that crude oil constitutes some 60 percent of the price of gasoline, so on the basis of 60 riyals per liter, the crude oil cost basis is about $15/bbl. This is a far cry from what world consumers are paying for the same commodity, ranging this past year from $78/bbl to the current roughly $55/bbl.

The discrepancy is so great that one must ask whether Saudi Arabia, as the current custodian of the world's greatest natural resource, its largest reservoir of crude oil, is fulfilling its responsibilities to the larger world. Our globe, its societies, its politics, and its economies have become so interdependent that perhaps the time has come to demand sovereign responsibility corresponding to sovereign rights.

The oil under Saudi Arabia's suzerainty is being made available to the world at large virtually without consideration of need or equity. Furthermore, Saudi Arabia has breached its fiduciary trust and delivered this vast, important resource to the larcenous OPEC cartel in order to extort the maximum possible lucre, irrespective of the enormous economic distortion it creates. The kingdom has wrested the means to build palaces and yachts from the backs of the miserably poor on the Asian subcontinent, in Africa, and throughout the world. The Saudis attain these riches without producing anything of value, without entrepreneurship or inventiveness—simply by the serendipity of finding themselves with so-called sovereign rights to one of the world's key economic engines.

An entire nation of otherwise competent people has been anesthetized by oil wealth and government boondoggles. This is to say nothing of the sinister billions upon billions being funneled to teaching facilities and prayer halls worldwide that preach or rationalize irredentist extremism and enable the social, political, and economic chaos it engenders (David B. Ottaway, "U.S. Eyes Money Trails of Saudi-Backed Charities," the *Washington Post*, August 19, 2004).

In today's world, sovereign rights can no longer go unchallenged if they do not entail sovereign responsibility (think of Sudan). Saudi Arabia has used its patrimony to enrich itself not through free and open markets but through the willful distortion of price and supply. This is an affront to the rules of the World Trade Organization (WTO); those rules explicitly ban conspiracies to rig markets and prohibit WTO members from setting quantitative restrictions on imports and exports.

Saudi Arabia's custodianship is further placed into question by its dismissal and stonewalling of calls to share with the world—in other words, its customers—information on production and reserves to enable world economies to plan their future energy determinants. Saudi Arabia is generally understood to have crude oil reserves of 264 billion bbl, according to the US Energy Information Administration. Yet, in an unguarded moment in December of 2004, Saudi oil minister, Ali al-Naimi volunteered that this amount could readily be increased by two hundred billion bbl. That a nation at the fulcrum of the world's economic health could be so cavalier in its lack of candor, its lack of accountability to its worldwide markets is appalling. Given the critical importance of the resource for which the Saudis are custodians, it becomes an act so fundamentally self-serving that it should not be tolerated.

In addition, this sovereign state is unable to protect the treasure lode that has served it so well. An international task force of warships navigates the Persian Gulf off the Saudi coast (at a cost of more than one hundred million dollars a day, paid for by the citizens of the coalition), riding shotgun on Saudi oil shipments and at the ready to fend off any impediment or attack. One wonders if, rather than being a short hop away at sea, it makes more sense to have the coalition secure the oil fields themselves in the interests of global economic well-being.

Why not turn the administration, production, and distribution of this resource over to an international agency, such as a newly reformed United Nation or, better yet, to the International Energy Agency? The agency's mandate would be to distribute this treasure in keeping with the world's social and economic needs and not in a manner dictated by the priorities of the OPEC coven.

Certainly, Saudi Arabia's interests could be looked after as well but not to the extortionist degree we currently tolerate. Sovereign rights and sovereign responsibilities—where does one draw the line? Perhaps the time has passed for considering sovereign rights sacrosanct; perhaps it is time that this issue be opened to scrutiny and public debate. We might all be the better for it, and that includes the Saudis themselves.

Taking a Page from John D. Rockefeller: Foreclosing America's Energy Security
January 22, 2007

Our energy neck is in a tightening noose. One can glean from information found at the International Energy Agency's website (http://www.iea.org/stats/index.asp) that between 75 and 90 percent of the world's oil and gas reserves are held by national oil companies that are partially or fully controlled by their governments. As such, the distribution and marketing of oil has become so highly politicized as to cripple the power of market forces to ensure access to and security of supply.

What must we do to guarantee that our nation's energy needs will continue to be met? Simply this: We have to become independent of foreign sources and the consequent political misadventures and fiscal extortion such dependence causes. No more ill-conceived entanglements in the Middle East, no more shakedowns by OPEC and its cronies—we must become fully self-reliant. We must look to our own producers to supply the energy our economy requires and to support our social and environmental well-being through alternatives to fossil fuels. Many of these alternatives are being proposed, discussed, and acted upon, and all of them hold out significant domestic possibilities. The literature on ethanol, biodiesel, wind, solar, hydro, nuclear, hydrogen, clean coal, and so on is extensive.

Though alternative fuels have great potential, we must nonetheless recognize that more than 60 percent of our current petroleum needs are met through imports. Even with massive changes and more rational policies of consumption, we would still need to tap additional domestic sources of fossil fuel for decades to come. Fortuitously, we have oil reserves measuring in the trillions of bbl locked in our oil shale deposits and significant potential reserves in deep-well reservoirs offshore, not to mention the oil left in capped marginal onshore wells. We have access to well over a hundred years of coal reserves and the technology to convert it into clean energy. The trouble is that these sources are relatively high-cost sources compared to what the world's national oil companies pay to bring their oil out of the ground.

More to the point, these national oil companies are not fools. They are keenly aware of their cost advantage, and their deeds make it clear that they wouldn't hesitate to follow the teachings of the master, John D. Rockefeller, to protect their advantage. Rockefeller, you see, brought competitors to heel by giving them what he called "a good sweating," meaning that his Standard Oil would cut prices until a cheeky rival couldn't withstand the operating losses. Sadly, at this juncture, we have no way to fight back against such tactics. Our antitrust laws have been rendered ineffectual by the sovereign exemption, which prevents us from reaching across borders to deal with the collusive practices of the national oil companies. And we have no Teddy Roosevelt to stand up against the oil cabal.

Nor do we have a congress willing to enact another kind of remedy. On April 9, 2002, Senator Kay Bailey Hutchison (a republican from Texas) pleaded with her colleagues in Congress to establish a floor price of (then-modest) $15/bbl for oil. She wanted to give small drillers an incentive to reopen their wells. "They are not going to reopen a well if they do not have a floor to help them stay in business [...] that is the reason so many of the wells that were closed when the price was $11 a barrel have not reopened [...]. If we could get all the marginal wells pumping in this country, we will equal the amount we import from Saudi Arabia every day" (Congressional Record, V. 144, pt. 14, September 9, 1998 to September 21, 1998).

Of course, nothing happened. Four years later, the Saudis and their handmaidens in OPEC had ratcheted up the price to $78/bbl. Then, predictably, once prices started to come back down, the cartel moved to cut production in an attempt to stabilize the world market price at $60/bbl—nearly fifty times greater than their average production costs. But you can bet that the minute we seriously invest to produce more on our own, they will do their utmost to "sweat" those major capital investments out of existence. Having accomplished that, they would work just as assiduously to ratchet up the price again, knowing that we had all learned an expensive lesson.

We have much to contend with in these times. We have the brazenness of the Saudis in maximizing the price of oil while instructing our president in how to conduct his Middle East policies. We have last week's lovefest between Venezuelan President Hugo Chavez and his Iranian counterpart, Mahmoud Ahmadinejad, who are bound by their declared enmity to the United States. We have the political instability in Nigeria. We have the broken rule of law in Libya, which, in a craven mockery of justice, sentenced Bulgarian nurses to death for allegedly infecting children with HIV. We have the shameless wielding of petropower by Russia against its neighbors and European customers. We have Ecuador's confiscation of international oil assets. We have, of course, the lingering trauma of Iraq. Finally, closer to home, we have the troubling fact that even our northern neighbor, Alberta, Canada, has threatened to review its oil export policies if we don't lift our mad-cow–related embargo on Canadian cattle and beef.

In light of all these challenges, it has become ever more evident that, for reasons of national security and even national independence, we need to develop our own energy resources and to protect their economic viability over the long term.

Senator Hutchison had the right idea with her suggestion of guaranteeing our domestic oil and gas industry a floor price to allow the development of higher-cost fossil fuel sources—not so we can consume more but rather to maintain an adequate supply and to begin weaning ourselves off of imports.

Simultaneously, we must impose a tax on all fossil fuel imports— crude oil, diesel oil, heating oil, gasoline, and the like—to reduce overall consumption and force ourselves onto the difficult but necessary path of energy self-reliance. In return, the oil industry will have to give up depletion allowances and tax credits, while also revisiting the structure of royalty payments to bring them more in line with less one-sided national programs such as those governing Britain's North Sea production. If these actions raise US fuel costs, so be it. At the very least, we will be paying out our dollars to domestic producers to cover domestic costs rather than shipping billions overseas to those who wish us ill.

It's time to fight back against OPEC-inspired John D. Rockefeller wannabes who would slavishly drop the price of crude and related products to prevent us from developing a competing domestic industry, thus holding us in their thrall, dancing to their tune. Our national security is paramount. All the same, should this program reduce the consumption of fossil fuels because of their cost or accessibility thereby significantly reducing carbon dioxide emissions, then so much the better for our polluted environment.

Saudi Arabia's Oil Plot Arrests: Targeting al Qaeda or Our Congress?
May 1, 2007

On April 27, 2007, it was reported by Sean Alfano of CBS/Associated Press ("Saudis Nab 172 Suspected Militants") that Saudi security forces had arrested 172 Islamic militants in an advanced stage of readiness to attack energy and high-impact targets, according to the Saudi interior ministry. "They had the personnel, the money, the arms," said spokesman Mansour al-Turki. Quick cut to Saudi television broadcasting images of neatly lined up rapid-fire armaments, ammunition clips, and orderly stacks of Saudi riyals. Real life or stage props? Please be reminded of the comments Nawaf Obaid, senior adviser to the then-ambassador Prince Turki al-Faisal, made indicating that Saudi Arabia had the means and responsibility to intervene with the Iranian-backed Shiites on behalf of the Sunnis.

On April 27, the Senate passed a bill seeking the exit of our troops from Iraq. Just a few days later, Saudi security forces, after a year of limited activity, announced this arrest of 172 militants. The world was immediately, clearly reminded of Saudi Arabia's vulnerability. Of course, the price of oil shot up right after the announcement. Along with the announced arrests, there were statements by Saudi analysts linking the militants to events in Iraq. "The chaos in Iraq has fueled radical ideology among the region's youth while providing an environment for militants to train." They also said, "It is the beginning of jihadi operations leaking out of Iraq" (Michael Slackman, "Saudis Arrest 172 in Anti-Terror Sweep," *New York Times*, April 27, 2007).

Is the nexus of Iraqi-inspired jihadist operations targeting oil installations in Saudi Arabia and the congressional vote to exit Iraq a coincidence or proof of a successful, cleverly staged reminder to our government of the degree of chaos into which the Middle East could plunge, with its inevitable disruption of the supply of oil and its dramatic impact on the global economy?

One must remember that we are dealing with the relationship between two key sets of players—our government and the Saudi hierarchy. Here we have the Bush administration so in thrall to the Saudis that were the Saudis to put on so much as a puppet show, our administration would be obligated to pass it off as real-life drama. Only a few days ago, the *New York Times* could write ("As Saudi Steps Surprise US, A Prince Is Sounding Off-Key," April 29, 2007) about Prince Bandar's influential relationship with the Bush family and the current administration. Prince Bandar is Saudi Arabia's former longtime ambassador to Washington, and he remains a frequent visitor to the Oval Office. I quote, "Prince Turki [al-Faisal] was never able to match the role of Prince Bandar, whom the president, vice president, and other officials regularly consult on every major Middle East initiative—from the approach to Iran to the Israeli-Palestinian peace process to Iraq" (Helene Cooper and Jim Rutenberg, "Saudi Prince Tied to Bush Is Sounding Off-Key," *New York Times*, April 28, 2007).

So how real are these arrests? Perhaps it's better to ask how real the arrested players are. Was this a setup meant to communicate to our Congress that it may be playing with Saudi fire if it really plans to take American troops from Iraq before the country's civil and sectarian war has been stabilized, before the last American soldier has been sacrificed and the last bit of American treasure spent?

To put the issue in context, we must inquire into the nature of our relationship and cooperation with the Saudi government and its security services on matters pertaining to terrorism. Sadly, the answer is not good. Other than soothing lip service, cooperation and transparency are problematic at best. To take one example, after the bombing of the Khobar Towers on June 25, 1996, which took the lives of nineteen US servicemen, it took until 2001 to bring an indictment against fourteen perpetrators, some of whom had time to seek safe haven in Iran. In large measure, this disgraceful delay was caused by the recalcitrance of the Saudis in refusing Federal Bureau of Investigation (FBI) interrogations of the suspects for several years.

The FBI director, Louis Freeh, who was then at the end of his mandate, officially thanked the Saudis for their help in bringing about the indictments. At the same time, Kelli Arena, *CNN*'s White House correspondent in an interview with CNN anchor, Lou Waters, stated that "[i]ntelligence sources have told *CNN* that, while the Saudi government was cooperative, they were cooperative to a point. That there was much more that could have been done to help them come up with more concrete evidence and more suspect names; that they could have completed this task, perhaps, a little earlier. After all, it did take five years to come to this point" ("U.S. Indicts 14 for Khobar Towers Bombing," Lou Waters interview with Kelli Arena, *CNN Live Event/Special*, aired June 21, 2001, http://edition.cnn.com/TRANSCRIPTS/0106/21/se.05. html). If faint praise can be damning, here's a sample that deserves a blue ribbon.

Is the current roundup real or just theater? I don't know. Perhaps our intelligence services can speak to this issue. But it does raise some very disturbing questions in the realm of realpolitik. Is it sensible for a nation of twenty-two million (half of whom, as women, are completely disenfranchised), who are vulnerable to the vicissitudes of regional politics and sectarian bloodshed, politically brittle, and incapable of viable self-defense to be the guardian of 10 percent of the world's oil production, whose product it doles out to the world's economies at extortionist OPEC-structured prices?

After all, the resources over which the Saudis currently reign and from which they profit limitlessly are essential to the well-being of the hundreds of millions in Southeast Asia (Pakistan, Bangladesh, India, and Malaysia) and in the Eastern Asia (China, Vietnam, Cambodia, and on and on)—essential, indeed, to the global economy. This issue must be taken up not only by the United States but also by the entire community of nations.

Oil Price Follies: This Week Starring OPEC!
September 10, 2007

Like *The Perils of Pauline* serial of times past, the OPEC serial meetings come at us with heightened drama and bombast. With OPEC, it isn't Pauline tied to the rails with a steam engine barreling down the track toward her but rather us and the world economy being held over a barrel. Whereas in Pauline's case we could count on a rescue just in the nick of time, with OPEC, every meeting portends slipping further into the quagmire of oil patch hegemony.

Last Friday's job data, which showed the first drop in four years, underlines a growing consensus that the economic recovery is veering precipitously toward recession. It is therefore troubling that not a single official voice has been raised to point to the price of energy as a key component in the deteriorating economic situation.

The subprime debacle is playing a major role in the economic events of the moment, but this nation—as the world's largest oil consumer, which is experiencing a 50 percent increase, since the beginning of the year, in the price of an economically crucial commodity—faces a particularly staggering blow. It represents an additional outlay of more than five hundred million dollars a day or the equivalent of a transfer tax of more than 150 billion dollars a year to oil interests based on the difference in price from January to September alone. This has a debilitating effect on discretionary spending and business expenditures and investment.

Where is the outrage or even mere concern from Treasury Secretary Henry Paulson, Energy Secretary Samuel Bodman, and most especially, that great advocate of the free market, President George W. Bush? The president has seen oil prices climb some 300 percent during his time in office, with nary a chastisement for either the oil industry or its friendly comrades-in-arms, the Saudis and other members of OPEC.

If ever a Freudian slip made its point, it was President Bush's at the Asia-Pacific Economic Cooperation meeting in Australia last week, when he expressed gratitude for having been invited to the OPEC summit and while reviewing the Australian brigade commended the *Austrian* soldiers; the OPEC meeting takes place tomorrow in Vienna, Austria.

While the price of oil is nearing all-time highs and OPEC is gathering in Vienna this week, we are being treated to the same blather that precedes all of these witches' covens—oily palaver meant to lull us into believing that OPEC is doing all it can to supply the world's oil needs in responsible fashion.

In sharp contrast with OPEC's public face and the administration's apparent acquiescence to OPEC extortion, the International Energy Agency clearly stated to OPEC that the world needs more oil and that it should increase production to ease price pressures. Oil in the neighborhood of $70/bbl was too high, said the International Energy Agency, and a decided threat to the world economy (Ed Crooks, "Energy Watchdog Urges OPEC to Lift Output," *Financial Times*,

August 28, 2007, http://www.ft.com/cms/s/0/a41e4d80-5591-11dc-b971-0000779fd2ac.html#axzz1G2VNdoFU).

OPEC, meanwhile, issued its oily explanations. Only yesterday, Mohamed bin Dhaen al-Hamli, United Arab Emirates oil minister and OPEC's president, advised that "[c]urrent supplies to the petroleum market are sufficient" ("Oil Supplies Sufficient: OPEC President," *The Economic Times/India Times,* September 9, 2007, http://articles. economictimes.indiatimes.com/2007-09-09/news/28411987_1_official-production-quota-opec-president-dhaen), following up on comments made last Thursday, when he said, "I think the market is very well balanced. There is no shortage of supplies.[…] If you think prices are high in nominal terms, they are almost close to what they were in the 1970s" (Reuters, Dalian China, "OPEC president says oil market well balanced," *Reuters.com,* September 6, 2007, India edition, http://in.reuters.com/article/2007/09/06/idINIndia-29368320070906), as if to justify today's vertiginous prices.

In keeping with al-Hamli's comments, within the past fortnight Abdullah al-Badri, secretary general of OPEC, opined that the group was unlikely to raise production levels when its ministers meet. "You cannot convince any member to add more crude oil to the market because we have enough crude," he told Bloomberg and other news agencies during a visit to Angola as reported by Ed Crooks ("Energy watchdog urges OPEC to lift output," *Financial Times,* August 28, 2007). Really? Since the beginning of the year, OPEC has held back 1.7 million bbl of crude a day from the market. The group's production was some thirty million bbl per day—30.37 million bbl per day in August—all near the lowest levels in the past four years. To underline the patent nonsense in OPEC's claim that it hoped to "achieve supply and demand equilibrium," (OPEC, "Keeping an Eye on Everything," OPEC Bulletin Commentary, August 2007, http://www.opec.org/opec_web/en/press_room/842.htm). its production in 1979 was thirty-one million bbl per day, and that was at a time when its stated and acknowledged reserves were far less than those acknowledged today.

An oft-repeated refrain has been that we have to consider the weakness of the dollar as a rationalization for increasing prices. One must remember that, since January, the dollar has decreased in value by less than 10 percent and only against certain currencies. Meanwhile, the price of crude has increased 53 percent.

OPEC's friends in the oil patch are always happy to chime in with their expertise to assuage our anxieties at the outset of these meetings. This time around there was Christophe de Margerie, chief executive officer of the French oil giant Total, telling us and the *Financial Times* last week that "definitely the price will remain high, and we have to build our strategy on this" (Ed Crooks and Javier Blas, "Oil Price Tests an All-Time High," *Financial Times*, September 6, 2007); he also insisted that biofuels would not provide an answer to the world's energy needs. One would imagine that this unfettered third-party opinion would provide some cover for whatever excess comes out of the meeting. Could it be that de Margerie's current negotiations on a ten billion-dollar gas project with Iran make him so amenable to OPEC's point of view?

Then there is OPEC's ongoing contention that oil inventories are adequate and that, therefore, nothing much needs to change. This, of course, is a red herring. OPEC does not meet to determine stock levels as its first order of business but rather to determine the level of tolerance that will be accepted by its customer base (are you reading this, Mr. Bush?) in order to maximize price.

Since January, OPEC has been successful in raising that price by more than $25/bbl—the price per bbl of oil at the beginning of the George W. Bush presidency. Likely owing to this administration's incestuous ties to the oil industry, this dramatic increase has been tolerated with little or no pushback. OPEC will feel at liberty, therefore, to drive prices higher. Oh, and excuse me for bringing this up: where are our congressional leaders and presidential candidates on this issue?

Is Saudi Arabia Waging Resource Aggression Against the American People and the World Economy?
November 8, 2007

Imagine waking up to the following nightmare headline: "Canada Interdicts the Headwaters of the Missouri and Mississippi Rivers, and All Water Flows from Its Territory into the Great Lakes." One's reaction to such a blatant act of resource aggression would not be passive, and nor would our government's. If you'll permit a glib interjection, any argument to the effect of "well, it's water on their side of the border" would not hold up whatsoever. The deterioration of relations between the United States and Canada would be immediate, grave, and threatening.

Yet, to a degree, this is the current status of our resource relationship with the Saudis. Consider what follows. On March 5, 2007, in a front-page article entitled "Oil Innovations Pump New Life into Old Wells," Jad Mouawad of the *New York Times* reported that Nansen G. Saleri, the head of reservoir management at the state-owned Saudi Aramco, disclosed that Saudi Arabia's total reserves were almost three times higher than its officially published figure of 260 billion bbl. He estimated its resources at 716 billion barrels. Mr. Saleri continued that he wouldn't be surprised if Saudi Arabia's ultimate reserves reached a trillion barrels. The world daily oil consumption is eighty-seven million bbl; the United States averages twenty million bbl.

This amazing revelation from the reservoir manager of Aramco underlines the degree to which the Saudis have perverted the current world oil market. The Saudis are the putative leaders of OPEC, and their capabilities and objectives determine OPEC's policy goals. It is clear, as the International Energy Agency said in their recent report, that "[t]he greater the increase in the call on oil and gas [...] the more likely it will be that they will seek to extract a higher rent from their exports and to impose higher prices [...] by deferring investment and constraining production" (IEA/WEO 2007, Executive Summary, "China and India Insights," http://www.worldenergyoutlook.org/docs/weo2007/WEO_2007_English.pdf).

Given its enormous reserves, Saudi Arabia could readily produce significant additional quantities of oil in order to abate the steep run-up of oil prices. At these price levels, the fact that they and OPEC are maintaining the major portion of their production cuts made at the beginning of this year—OPEC's production cut of 1.7 million bbl per day altered by a production increase of only five hundred thousand bbl per day starting this month—is smoking-gun evidence of their extortionist intent. By holding oil that they clearly have in ample supply off the market, they are gouging the world's economies and pricing their product at levels that have no market rationale whatsoever. They are preying on the world's need for oil. It is an act of resource aggression against the world's consumers, much like Canada's hypothetical interference with the headwaters of our major waterways would be an act of aggression against the United States.

Please note that I referred to waging resource aggression against the American people in my title. The government was not mentioned, because in this imbroglio, our administration is in effect Saudi Arabia's—as well as OPEC's and the oil patch's—greatest ally. In the near seven years of this presidency, virtually nothing has been done to constrain Saudi Arabia's policies. On the contrary, our president and vice president are so wedded to the oil industry's interests that the enormous increase in oil prices during their tenure can well be ascribed to a willful lack of any forceful policies to counter the Saudi extortion. This has manifested itself in many ways. Let me cite just a few:

- In the near seven years of the Bush presidency, virtually no serious steps have been taken to significantly abate demand for fossil fuels.

- The nation's strategic petroleum reserve has been used to underpin escalating prices by continuing to make purchases even as prices explode, thereby signaling the government's acceptance and approval of these price levels. Worse, the administration announced the doubling of the strategic petroleum reserve just as crude oil prices were retreating to $50/bbl earlier this year.

- The administration has not made Saudi Arabia understand, either through "friendly persuasion" or as a Dutch uncle, that its price and production policies are intolerable. This even as we serve as the protector of the Saudi coastline and Saudi Arabia itself as an enormous cost to US citizens. This serves as a bulwark against Shia Iran, which would give free rein to its designs against Sunni Saudi Arabia in our absence.

- Our high government officials have shown nothing but obsequiousness toward Saudi officialdom. Prince Bandar enjoyed open access to the Oval Office while he was ambassador in Washington and thereafter. And don't forget President Bush's symbolic holding of then-Prince Abdullah's hand at the Crawford Ranch meeting, an encounter whose coziness resulted in an almost immediate upward ratcheting of oil prices.

The administration's oil industry buddies are ecstatic at the windfall the entire oil sector has reaped by the quadrupling of prices to levels undreamed of before the advent of this presidency. Meanwhile, many of the nation's citizens are having their household budgets ripped to shreds in order to pay their home heating bills this coming winter. Rarely, if ever in the history of the United States, has there been such a divergence between the nation's needs and the aims of the vested interests that form the administration.

Bashing Hugo Chavez, Kowtowing to OPEC
December 5, 2007

Poor Hugo Chavez. He threatened to cut off oil supplies to the United States if we dared exert so much as a whisper of influence on last weekend's Venezuelan referendum to amend 69 articles of the 2007 Venezuelan constitution. In return, he's had all manner of opprobrium visited on him by Americans of all stripes—from politicians to editorial writers to private Joes and Janes like the rest of us. All this after the indignity of being told to shut up the week before by King Juan Carlos of Spain at the Ibero-American summit in Chile and receiving a further dressing down by Spain's prime minister, Jose Zapatero. Then, to top it all off, Chavez suffered a stunning rebuke to his bizarre attempt to remove the imposed term limits in an effort toward his becoming president for life, by a roused and valiant Venezuelan electorate refusing to be cowed by his bombast and threats.

Compare Chavez's unhappy state of affairs with that of our government's and press's coddling of OPEC and its media stars. The cartel is scheduled to meet today and will undoubtedly regale us once more with platitudes about its diligence and its concern for our well-being. Its helplessness in the face of monstrously high oil prices will be played up to the point that much of its audience, especially in the media, will pity the poor cartel. The media will present OPEC's dilemma with such poignancy that one will imagine that only the Salvation Army could properly intervene.

OPEC dazzles us with such pithy nonsense as its Secretary General Abdullah al-Badri's comment implying that they will add more oil if it goes to refineries but not if goes into stocks, which makes as much sense as would Campbell telling us, "if you put more than three cans of baked beans in your cupboard, we'll stop delivering the beans."

An alert and responsive energy department would respond by promptly desisting from making further additions to the strategic petroleum reserve. This should be done loudly and clearly, to signal our outrage at this ongoing theater and to underline our grave displeasure at OPEC's efforts to present the current vertiginous price levels of $80/90 or more/bbl as the new norm. At these levels, there is no longer any reason whatsoever to hold back production while presiding over spare capacity generally understood to be some 2.5 million bbl per day.

But the nonsense doesn't stop there. One can always count on Saudi oil minister Ali al-Naimi for a *bon mot*. He simply denies that short supply of oil has anything to do with recent price increases. "There is absolutely ample supply," he told us last Friday from Singapore. "The price movement has nothing to do with fundamentals of the market" (Jad Mouawad, "OPEC's Tough Call: Raise or Hold Oil Supply," *New York Times*, December 3, 2007, http://www.nytimes.com/2007/12/03/business/worldbusiness/03oil.html). Well, there you are. Only the OPEC public relations department could come up with such a fantasy and have the good fortune to employ an al-Naimi to deliver it with a straight face. He went on to say that there is a "mismatch" between high prices and oil supplies. "Anyone that tells you otherwise is wrong." (Jad Mouawad, "OPEC's Tough Call: Raise or Hold Oil Supply," *New York Times*, December 3, 2007, http://www.nytimes.com/2007/12/03/business/worldbusiness/03oil.html).

But wait, just wait. Maybe there is something to what al-Naimi is saying, something he knows that we don't. The price of oil today is not set by trading physical product, actual bbl of oil, which was how it was purchased and sold some years ago. Back then, prices for physical product were set at posted levels and contracted accordingly, or each cargo was negotiated separately between buyer and seller—that is to say between oil producer and end user or, on occasion, by traders who served as intermediaries and took physical possession of the oil.

Now, oil is traded in a virtual world by buyers and sellers trading contracts on commodity exchanges. They rarely take possession of the oil; many—I would venture to say even most—have never seen or touched a bbl of oil. These commodity markets are worldwide, and the trading is enormous. But the markets are also opaque; anyone can trade, sometimes through straw men or companies, without revealing himself. There is little oversight there and virtually none in exchange platforms overseas. This is an invitation to mischief or, better put, manipulation. It takes a lot of wherewithal to tinker with these markets, but it can be done if one has specific goals and the resources to achieve them.

Who is best positioned to push prices ever higher on the commodity exchanges, especially given that the exchange prices today determine the prices of actual transactions for the physical product? I'll give you one guess. Right. OPEC. With the cartel's goal of driving prices up, they certainly have the means, given the avalanche of cash flooding their coffers at the rate of some $2.5 billion every day. Hypothesis? Perhaps. But let me go back a few years to 2004. On December 12 of that year, our peripatetic Ali al-Naimi made an astonishing prediction. He was reacting to a surprise drop in prices even though OPEC had just voted to reduce production by 4 percent. Speaking to *Arab News* about the price of oil, al-Naimi said, "Watch what happens tomorrow. I will tell you, it will go up tomorrow" (AFP, "Naimi Expects Oil Prices to Rise," *Arab News*, December 12, 2004, http://archive.arabnews.com/?page=6&section=0&article=55949&d=12&m=12&y=2004). And, hocus-pocus, indeed they did. One assumes that the only way al-Naimi could have predicted the price move with such assurance was if he, through OPEC or its agents, was manipulating the oil futures market. If it happened then, how many times and how effectively has it happened since?

While poor old Chavez takes it on the chin, where is the condemnation of al-Badri and al-Naimi and their blather? Perhaps it is time for Congress to wake up and give the Commodity Futures Trading Commission the power to really smoke out the oil trading cabal on the commodity exchanges.

Questions Congress Needs to Ask Before Authorizing Bush's See, Hear, and Speak No Evil Saudi Arms Deal
January 21, 2008

Upon his recent visit to Saudi Arabia, Bush reaffirmed his close personal relationship with King Abdullah. That close personal relationship culminated in the proposed sale to the Saudis of twenty billion dollars' worth of highly sophisticated military equipment, including bomb guidance kits with built-in satellite and motion-sensing navigation systems. This is fully in keeping with Bush's fawning, subservient see-no-evil,-hear-no-evil,-speak-no-evil posture toward the Saudis, a posture that has been massively detrimental to our nation's well-being.

The arms sale will require Congressional approval and is now under discussion. Before authorizing the sale of some of our most sophisticated military hardware to what is, at best, a fair-weather friend, to the nation from which, after all, the majority of the September 11, 2001, hijackers sprung, a number of questions should be asked and answered. Let me list but a few of them:

- Has the Saudi Arabian government stopped financing the Sunni insurgency in Iraq, through charity fronts and otherwise, and how will this interdiction be monitored?

- Has Saudi Arabia taken the necessary steps to end the flow of Saudi nationals into Iraq, where they have enlisted in the insurgency and become the largest group of foreign fighters engaged as suicide bombers?

- How will Saudi Arabia monitor its 814-kilometer border with Iraq and make it impenetrable to the clandestine movement of equipment, men, and funding in support of those interests intent on sabotaging the Iraqi government and imperiling coalition forces?

- What steps will the Saudis take to eliminate the rhetoric of jihad and hate directed at Western and American society, Christians, Hindus, Shiites, and Jews, from the state-supported imams and religious centers in Saudi Arabia and the Saudi-funded madrassas, mosques, and religious centers around the world?

- A few weeks ago, Saudi Arabia released 1,500 al Qaeda operatives from detention within the kingdom. According to Saudi officials, those individuals had been counseled and seemingly purged of their takfir ideology, which holds that there are separate rules that allow believers to lie to, steal from, and even kill nonbelievers. As a condition of their release, they were required to sign a statement promising to refrain from jihad *within the Arabian Peninsula*. Does this mean they have permission to attack cities elsewhere around the world, including within the United States?

• What long-overdue steps will the Saudis take to liberalize their society, starting at the very least with enfranchising and imparting civil rights to female citizens? The sentence of two hundred lashes as punishment for victim the "Qatif girl" rape case is a gruesome example of the perversity of Saudi justice, although, fortunately, this young woman's sentence was commuted by the king in response to worldwide condemnation.

• A fleet of vessels from the United States and other nations patrols the Arabian Gulf, in essence riding shotgun on Saudi oil loadings and protecting Saudi ports and national integrity. This enterprise costs our national treasury nearly one hundred million dollars a day. Will Saudi Arabia understand and honor its obligation to share a major part of these costs, which permit oil shipments, from which the Saudis profit shamelessly, unencumbered access to the high seas?

• Early in 2007, with the price of oil hovering around $50/bbl, Saudi Arabia (as the leader of OPEC) organized a production cut of 1.7 million bbl per day from OPEC's quotas. Since then, the price of oil has escalated by 100 percent, touching $100/bbl just two weeks ago. Such an increase in price is virtually unprecedented and is beginning to wreak havoc on world economies, especially in the poorer nations. Obviously, the production of 500,000 bbl per day that was reinstated in November is a far cry from what is needed. Why, in spite of this dramatic price escalation, has Saudi Arabia not persuaded OPEC to reinstate, at the very least, the full 1.7 million bbl?

• Our energy department is confused. It knows so little about Saudi Arabia's true production capabilities. Saudi Arabia has let it be known for many years that it holds 260 billion bbl of crude oil reserves. Yet in March of last year, the head of reservoir management at Saudi Aramco estimated the kingdom's reserves were almost three times that size, closer to 716 billion bbl, and possibly as great as a trillion bbl. Saudi Arabia has steadfastly refused to lift the veil of secrecy and share data on output and reserves, even though much of the world's economy and its economic forward planning is heavily dependent on this data. Will Saudi Arabia recognize its responsibility and provide this data henceforward?

- In the summer of 2004, during the US election campaign, the Saudis announced that they would increase oil production capacity to 11.3 million bbl per day and, if called upon to do so, could increase production to twelve million bbl per day in short order. Have the Saudis ever met this pledge? They are now pumping barely nine million bbl per day.

- In mid-2004 with oil prices reaching into the $30/bbl range, Saudi oil minister Ali al-Naimi declared himself yet again to be in favor of the cartel's then-broadcast twenty-two- to twenty-eight-dollar target range. He went on to comment, however, "the market is wishing for $35 because it's scared of [the price rising to] $50." He repeated his old maxim that the Saudis were too frightened of that price, because it might damage the world economy and propel the search for alternative energy sources (Alex Lawler and Stephen Voss, "OPEC to Decide in June on Saudi Quota Proposal [Update 8]," *Bloomberg.com*, May 23, 2004, http://www.bloomberg. com/apps/news?pid=21070001&sid=aDaCdM3VnBTA). That was then, and this is now. Oil prices are in the $90–$100/ bbl range, a staggering increase from the already high $49.90/ bbl price of just a year ago. This shocking move is without any apparent trigger other than an OPEC production constraint. The question then becomes when will the Saudis put enough oil on the market to bring it back, at the very least, to the potentially destabilizing $50/bbl level they feared not so very long ago?

A better indicator of the true quality of the relationship between King Abdullah and President Bush, between the United States and Saudi Arabia, became clear today. President Bush played further on the self-perceived close relationship and asked OPEC, which is beholden to and guided by Saudi Arabia as its most important producer and exporter by far to make more oil available to the marketplace, a request repeated a few days later by Samuel Bodman. With our economy barreling into recession, the greed of the Saudis and their front men in OPEC continued unabated. *Reuters* was able to nail it yesterday with the headline, "OPEC Dismisses US Calls For More Oil." With friends like these!

A suggestion might be that, if the administration cannot get answers to these queries to the satisfaction of Congress, they should give the Saudis a copy of *Jane's Encyclopedia of Military Weapons* and politely suggest that they go shopping elsewhere. Congress might even use the occasion to take King Abdullah at his word, when he branded the US presence in Iraq "an illegal foreign occupation" and exit Iraq altogether (Hassan M. Fattah, "Saudi King Condemns US Occupation of Iraq," *New York Times*, March 28, 2007, http://www.nytimes.com/2007/03/28/world/middleeast/29saudicnd.html).

Bush's Hypocrisy, OPEC's Arrogance, & the Oil Mess We Are Living In
March 7, 2008

Yesterday's *New York Times* had a front-page article whose title said it all: "President Fails to Budge OPEC on Production." The *Times's* Jad Mouawad reported the cartel's rebuff of the president's pleas for a production increase in its inimitably straight-faced, uncritical manner, visiting on us what might as well have been an OPEC flack's handout. It isn't OPEC's fault, you see—it's the dollar; it's the speculators; it's the troubles along the Venezuelan and Colombian border; it's mismanagement of the US economy.

The *Times* quoted that reliable, disinterested observer of oil patch machinations, Rex W. Tillerson, chairman and chief executive officer of ExxonMobil, who reassures us that "[t]he market continues to be well supplied. There has been no interruption in supplies" ("President Fails to Budge OPEC on Production," *New York Times*, March 6, 2008, http://www.nytimes.com/2008/03/06/business/worldbusiness/06oil.html?pagewanted=print). Well, feel better now? How about those with the good fortune to be pumping gas at the Americo station in the town of Gorda in coastal California, where you can get uninterrupted supplies of gasoline at $5.19 a gallon for regular and $5.39 a gallon for premium?

The *Times* informs us that we, and our dollar, are primarily to blame for the current vertiginous oil prices. Why, in the past year alone, "the dollar has lost 17 percent of its value against the euro." Naturally, no mention is made of the fact that, in January of 2007, the price of oil touched $50/bbl, thus making the increase in price since then some 110 percent—a long way from the 17 percent being trumpeted by the *New York Times* and by OPEC flacks. By the way, if you're doing your sums, a 17 percent increase compensating the fall of the dollar's value on the January 2007 price would bring prices to $58/bbl, not the $104/bbl we have today.

The *Times* goes on to applaud the Saudis for steadily producing 9.2 million bbl per day, "day in and day out" to keep the market "well supplied." No investigative journalism here to determine what the Saudis *could* produce going at full tilt (most likely well in excess of ten million bbl per day, and given what we know about a modest estimation of their reserves at more than 260 billion bbl and probably closer to seven hundred billion bbl, they could continue doing so for well over a hundred years).

As for the patent nonsense that the "mismanagement of the American economy" is to blame for high oil prices—as promulgated by Chakib Khelil, Algeria's oil minister and the 2008 OPEC president—it's a bit like saying our customer has experienced a train wreck, so we'd better charge him all the market can bear. It makes no sense at all.

As to the speculators, yes, they play a role, but why isn't there any question of who is speculating and why? To give credence to the comment from Saudi oil minister Ali al-Naimi that "[t]oday there is no link between oil [market] fundamentals and prices," as reported by Morocco's Ashraq al-Awast, boggles the mind (Matthew Robinson, "Oil Ends Down, Eases Off Record Above $106 a Barrel," *Reuters*, March 7, 2008, http://www.reuters.com/article/2008/03/07/us-markets-oil-idUSSYD3274320080307).

But wait, we have also made our contribution to this clown's mise en scène. Our star is none other than President George W. Bush. His role has been fashioned by the following lines recited earlier this week and quoted by *Reuters* (Chris Baltimore, "Bush Urges OPEC to Weigh

Pain of High Oil Prices," March 5, 2008), "My advice to OPEC—of course, they haven't listened to it—my advice to OPEC is understand the consequences of high energy prices, because I do."

What? This from a president who:

- has seen the price of oil quadruple on his watch and has done virtually nothing to counter it;

- has, during his presidency, done virtually nothing to abate demand for fossil fuels (for instance, by mandating truly meaningful mileage standards for automobiles);

- has pushed Iraq to rejoin OPEC as practically the first order of business after the removal of Saddam Hussein;

- has not in a meaningful way caused OPEC to moderate its aggressive pricing policies;

- came to the oil industry's and OPEC's rescue as the price of oil was slipping below $50/bbl by announcing a policy of doubling the strategic petroleum reserve in January 2007;

- continued to fill the strategic petroleum reserve, irrespective of price, causing the likes of Frank Verrastro of the Center for Strategic and International Studies to exclaim this past week that, if the White House was truly interested in lowering oil prices, it would stop sending crude oil into the strategic petroleum reserve ("If you're begging people to put oil on the market why in the world are you taking it off?" Verrastro asked, probably while scratching his head; Chris Baltimore, "Bush Urges OPEC to Weigh Pain of High Prices," *Reuters*, March 5, 2008, http://www.reuters.com/article/2008/03/05/us-oil-bush-idUSWAT00903520080305);

- appointed as secretary of energy a likeable but untested personage, Samuel Bodman, whose naïveté about how things work caused his energy department to respond to criticism about continuing to fill the strategic petroleum reserve, even in the face of President Bush's comments, by saying "reserve shipments have a miniscule price impact." This betrayed a total lack of understanding of how markets function, as did Bodman's simplistic comment, "Look, the price of oil is set in the trading rooms in New York and London and Tokyo and Frankfurt and all around the world.[…] Whatever it is, it is" (Chris Baltimore, "Bush Urges OPEC to Weigh Pain of High Prices," *Reuters*, March 5, 2008, http://www.reuters.com/article/2008/03/05/us-oil-bush-idUSWAT00903520080305).

No comprehension whatsoever that the United States, as by far the largest consumer of oil in the world, has the means by word and deed to influence the mentality and behavior of those trading rooms. As we learn almost every day, prices are influenced by strikes in Nigeria, border incursions in Iraq from Turkey, storms in the Gulf of Mexico, skirmishes in the Persian Gulf, Middle East political disequilibrium … even fog along the Houston ship channel. The list is almost endless. Yet here is our Department of Energy, asleep at the switch, as usual.

If President Bush means, when he claims to understand the consequences of high energy prices, that his friends in the oil industry are doing fabulously well, that the oil companies are raking it in, and that OPEC is setting up sovereign wealth funds to buy America, well, then, he hit the nail right on the head.

OPEC Must Understand Access to Our Market Can No Longer Be Taken for Granted
September 9, 2008

It is beyond time that all imports of crude oil and major downstream products (i.e., gasoline) coming into the American market should require an import license designating a specific country of origin.

OPEC meets this week to set production quotas. Venezuela and Iran are pressing for production cuts to assure prices do not slip below $100/bbl. Saudi Arabia, forever playing its usual double game, is making mollifying noises, having King Abdullah quoted by its ever pliant mouthpiece, the *New York Times*, stating that "one hundred dollars was too high" (Jad Mouawad, "As Oil Prices Fall, OPEC Faces a Balancing Act," *New York Times*, September 4, 2008). This while sending a message to the rest of the OPEC coven by sharply marking up prices for October shipments of heavy crude to Asian refiners ("Saudi Crude Price Hikes May Offer OPEC Production Hints," *Gulf Times*, September 7, 2008, http://www.gulf-times.com/site/topics/

printArticle.asp?cu_no=2&item_no=240094&version=1&template_
id=48&parent_id=28).

So here we sit, waiting for the nabobs to tell us what they will produce and what they will graciously allow us to consume. Why not? It is a poker game they have been playing with us for eight years now, and our hand has been held by the three oil industry "stooges"—Bush, Cheney, and Bodman—who are happily letting us be fleeced while their oil industry cronies cluck contentedly. Times are good for the OPEC boys. Pass them another cigar.

Well, the times, they are a-changing. Economic conditions and consumption restraint are beginning to take hold. The public has become keenly aware of the risks inherent in the unbridled consumption of fossil fuels, of its dangers economically, environmentally, and in terms of our national security. Further, the public has come to understand the voracious and shameless opportunism of the oil producers, who move the price of oil ever higher for as long as they can and for as much as they can. The oil patch has left the public with an indelible conviction of mistrust, being patently unreliable as providers of a significant but diminishingly important resource. For these reasons, alternative energy programs are being set in stone and are not about to be displaced, as they have been in the past, by the sudden erosion of crude oil prices.

In four months' time, the three stooges will have been retired, and a new relationship will emerge between oil producer and the oil consumer. Then it will be the time to play our ace in the hole. Rarely talked about or alluded to in the past eight years is the fact that, in being the world's most important consumer of fossil fuels, our market is as important to oil producers as their product is to us. As such, even as our consumption decreases, as it will in the years ahead due to increased use of alternative fuels, mass transit, natural gas, and fuel-efficient vehicles, etc., we will provide oil producers with their most important market for years to come.

That market should no longer be taken for granted by oil suppliers. It should not be available to all comers irrespective of their adversarial policies and their pricing strategies. Henceforward, all imports of foreign crude oil into the United States should require an import license designating a specific country of origin. Ideally, it would be a system put into place with import licenses freely available and with no need to impose restrictions.

But consider, for example, Venezuela's hawkish stance in pushing prices higher, combined with its confrontational and malign policies. It has invited Russia to joint naval exercises and is extending invitations to the Russians to establish military bases on Venezuelan soil. It has even permitted Hezbollah to set up a base of operations in the Americas, creating terrorist cells looking to kidnap businessmen. There is the further prospect of Hezbollah using Venezuela as a staging ground for terrorist incursion into the United States (Chris Kraul and Sebastian Rotella, "Fears of Hezbollah presence in Venezuela," *LATimes*, August 27, 2008).

Given their intentions and their dangerously contentious policies, would it not make sense, especially as our needs diminish and as other supplies become available (such as alternative fuels, natural gas, offshore, North Slope, shale, and crude from Brazil), that our government have in place a program that could stop or limit imports of oil from countries whose policies are inimical to our national interests? We would simply limit or refuse issuance of oil import licenses. Perhaps our ability to establish such a system would encourage Venezuela and others to reexamine their hostile policies. Of course, one could argue that oil is a fungible or widely interchangeable commodity, whereby substitution or exchanges with other national producers could, in some measure, neutralize the objectives of such a program. Yet if there is a serious willingness to implement a viable licensing regime, this too can be dealt with effectively.

In the meantime, rest assured that whatever decision is trotted out by OPEC this week, it will be dressed up as an exercise in OPEC's beneficence, a caring response to the needs of the world's consumers, for which our sincere appreciation should be forthcoming.

OPEC's "Noble Cause"
December 17, 2008

Remarkably, breathtakingly, and while holding us all for idiots at a level of presumption comparable to that of Bernie Madoff (with whom he shares the talent for ripping people off), OPEC's senior nabob, Saudi oil minister Ali al-Naimi, told us, "You must understand that the purpose of the $75 price [Saudi King Abdullah's target in the short-term] is for a much more noble cause. You need every producer to produce, and marginal producers cannot produce at $40 a barrel" ("OPEC Makes Largest Ever Cut to Oil Production," *The Times, London*, December 17, 2008, http://business.timesonline.co.uk/tol/business/industry_sectors/natural_resources/article5360099.ece). Yes, I kid you not. It was reported with a straight face, with no commentary or query, by the ever-acquiescent press.

Not to be outdone, the *New York Times*'s oil ballet choreographer Jad Mouawad, anticipating today's OPEC meeting, penned a poignant paean to higher oil prices that found its way to yesterday's front page. "Big Oil Projects Put in Jeopardy by Fall in Prices," ran the headline, and in its sister newspaper, the *International Herald Tribune*, the story was "Low Prices Cripple Oil-Exploration Push."

There followed a fulsome litany of projects halted and/or suspended with the wreckage being foisted on the suffering oil patch, which was a perfect setup for OPEC to announce a major cutback today that, according to Mouawad's insinuation, we should greet and cheer.

In these dour times, it's nice to find a happy ending. At the conclusion of today's meeting, OPEC announced an additional production cut of more than two million bbl per day. Then, surprise, surprise, the price of oil fell by some $3/bbl, a not inconsequential drop, breaking $40/bbl at one point and certainly dampening the Saudi oil minister's brush with nobility. Sic transit gloria!

The Nightmare Scenario: Thank You, Saudi Arabia, for Looking After Our Future
February 14, 2009

Saudi Arabia has such concern and respect for the United States and the perceptiveness of its citizenry that it feels compelled to offer us instruction and advice. It was this nation whose loquacious oil minister, Ali al-Naimi, told us back in December 2008 that it was Saudi Arabia's noble cause to see to it that the price of oil be clawed back to at least $75/bbl as soon as possible. You see, anything less would discourage investment in new production, according to our friend in Riyadh, not to speak of curtailing the purchase of yachts, palatial residences, and Ferraris and the funneling of billions upon billions into Wahhabi schools, madrassas, mosques, social centers, and charitable organizations throughout the world to teach civility and good citizenship.

This week, our new president's secretary of energy, Steven Chu, postulated that a revolution in science and technology would be required if the world is to reduce its dependence on fossil fuels and to curb emissions of carbon dioxide and other gases linked to global warming. He thereby set forth a key goal of the new administration while our friends in Saudi Arabia were instructing us otherwise.

At an oil industry conference in Houston earlier this week, Mr. Ali al-Naimi, who has been the minister of petroleum and mineral resources for Saudi Arabia since 1995, ran roughshod over our concerns about global warming and energy independence with feigned lack of self-interest. He cautioned us, according to his clearly self-serving tenets, that we were veering toward a nightmare scenario if we sought to speed up development of alternative fuels. Thank you so much, Mr. Oil Minister. This wisdom comes from the world's largest oil exporter: "[W] e must be mindful that efforts to rapidly promote alternatives could have a chilling effect on investment in the oil sector" (Jad Mouawad, "Saudi View of Alternative-Fuel 'Nightmare,'" *New York Times*, February 11, 2009). Then, of course, he gave a list of projects that have been or may be canceled. Fasten your seatbelts; this refrain will be heard over and over again from the OPEC and oil patch boys in the days, months, and years to come.

The true nightmare scenario would be if we let Saudi Arabia and the oil industry flacks sway us one iota from the course our new president has set to turn us away from fossil fuels once and for all.

Britain's New Royalty: The Oil Potentates
August 24, 2009

Where British tradition once mandated that subjects genuflect before their royals, Britain is now busy teaching itself to render proper homage by prostrating itself, nose to the ground, before its new potentates, the oil barons of Araby.

There he was, Libyan Abdel Basset Ali al-Megrahi, who was found guilty of the murderous Lockerbie air disaster, which took the lives of 270 people; he stepped off his specially chartered Libyan aircraft to a cheering crowd in Tripoli. Eichmann being received by a cheering crowd in Germany would have been the same, if not in degree then certainly in kind.

al-Megrahi's release was trumpeted by Mr. Kenneth MacAskill, Scotland's justice secretary, as an act of compassion for a man said to be diagnosed with prostate cancer and having but three months to live. It was a decision met with outrage by family members of the victims and by a general outcry of disgust throughout much of the world, ranging from President Obama to FBI director Robert Mueller, who rightly said it "makes a mockery of the grief of the families who lost their own on December 21, 1988" (Joshua Gallu, "FBI's Mueller Says al-Megrahi Release Is 'Mockery' of Justice," Bloomberg.com, August 22, 2009, http://www.bloomberg.com/apps/news?pid=newsarchive&sid=anQSA_ofd2Fw).

The British foreign secretary, David Miliband, said that the release was the decision of the Scottish justice secretary alone. Was it? Or is it the case that politicians are now prepared to go to extra lengths to maintain good relations with Libya, the richest country in North Africa and an important supplier of energy to Europe? According to Lord Trefgarne, chairman of the Libyan British Business Council ("New Questions in Lockerbie Bomber's Release," *New York Times*, August 21, 2009), Mr. al-Megrahi's release cleared the way for Britain's leading oil companies to pursue multibillion-dollar oil contracts with Libya, which had demanded Mr. al-Megrahi's return in talks with British officials and business executives.

Scandalous? Maybe. But then again, perhaps not, if this has become Britain's new norm. Kowtowing to moneyed Middle Eastern and North African oil interests may not be new, but it does assume a singular level of malice when it is dealt with in such a brazen manner, trashing tradition and principles of law in the lust for lucre or in response to outright intimidation and blackmail.

Just a year ago, the United Kingdom's highest court provided details on how the Saudis had pressured Prime Minister Tony Blair to close down a politically inflammatory bribery investigation implicating the Saudi ambassador to Washington, Prince Bandar (often referred to as

Bandar Bush, given his close ties to the Bush family), in effect buying the British government by getting Britain's Serious Fraud Office to drop a probe into the two billion-dollar commissions and multimillion-dollar transfers through the now defunct Riggs Bank in Washington. These funds were allegedly paid out to Prince Bandar as part of the British aerospace system's eighty-five billion-dollar "Yamamah" arms deal to sell British warplanes to Saudi Arabia.

The Saudis didn't simply threaten to substitute French jets for British jets if the probe wasn't brought to an end; they also threatened to cut off cooperation on critical anti-terrorism operations, in effect blackmailing the British government.

A *Newsweek* article (Michael Isikoff, "Gag Order: How Saudi Arabia's Prince Bandar Muscled Tony Blair into Silence," July 30, 2008) quoted Ali al-Ahmed, director of Washington-based think tank The Gulf Institute as saying, "Terrorism is being used to blackmail the West. You watch; it is only a matter of time before they do this in the US."

The US justice department is investigating allegations that BAE Systems has paid millions of dollars in bribes to Prince Bandar and other Saudi officials in possible violation of the Foreign Corrupt Practices Act. Yet little has been forthcoming to date. And no wonder, when Louis Freeh can retire as the head of the FBI and be retained by none other than Prince Bandar to represent him in connection with the justice department probe, while William Bradford Reynolds, the chief of the justice department's civil rights division during the Reagan administration, is representing Prince Bandar in ancillary lawsuits. It raises the question of how the government can gainfully serve and be objective in the face of such potentially conflicted relationships such as those between the need for fair and objective governance and the personal career tracks of those representing the electorate while in positions of public authority.

But getting back to Libya.... Along with the United Kingdom, Libya has been locked in a running battle with Switzerland. It seems Switzerland had the effrontery to arrest Hannibal Qaddafi (Colonel Muammar el-Qaddafi's son) for beating service staff with a belt and hanger while in a Geneva hotel. In retaliation, Libya cut off all of its oil shipments to Switzerland and withdrew five billion dollars from Swiss bank accounts, while awaiting an apology.

Libya's UK triumph was not in isolation. The *Financial Times* reported that, hours before Mr. al-Megrahi's plane landed in Tripoli, the president of Switzerland, Hans-Rudolf Merz, was in the Libyan capital apologizing publicly for Hannibal Qaddafi's arrest in Geneva. President Merz would subsequently defend his public and humiliating apology as the only way of getting exit visas from Libya for two Swiss citizens being held there.

Colonel Qaddafi, in this triumphal moment, was moved to proclaim, "And I say to my friend Brown, the prime minister of Britain; the Queen of Britain, Elizabeth; Prince Andrew, who contributed to encouraging the Scottish government to make this historic and courageous decision, despite the obstacles" (John F. Burnes, "Qaddafi Praises Britain over Lockerbie Release," *New York Times,* global edition, August 22, 2009, http://www.nytimes.com/2009/08/23/world/africa/23lockerbie.html).

May one make a suggestion? When greeting your new friend, remember, your body must be prostrate on the floor with arms flung forward and with nose and forehead touching the ground.

Good. Excellent. You've finally got it!

If the OPEC Cartel Is Being Tolerated, Why Not a Grain Export Association?
February 14, 2010

OPEC and the manipulation of the commodity markets have successfully doubled the price of oil since the outset of the Obama administration, when oil was quoted around $30/bbl in February 2009. The administration has been helpless—or unwilling, given the influence of the oil industry and Wall Street—to confront the manipulation of a market that is literally overflowing with product. Producers, importers, and traders are pushing prices up by keeping millions of bbl at sea in supertankers, because there is insufficient storage on land. This results in higher prices at enormous cost to American and world consumers, while being a major drain on our balance of payments and our economy at this precarious moment.

Given OPEC's success, given our tolerance of its activities, and given its enormous cost to our society, why should we not, in our own self-interest and in an effort to level the playing field, follow its example?

This past week, an article on Bloomberg.com ("Soybeans Rise as US Farmers Withhold Offers After Prices Slide," February 12, 2010) informs us that "[s]oybeans rose for the third straight day as US farmers, the world's biggest producers, withheld supplies after prices slumped in the previous five weeks." Encapsulated in that sentence is the very essence and fundamental operating philosophy of OPEC. Simply put, the cartel colludes to reduce the availability of oil in order to raise oil's price in the world market.

After the current financial calamity and the demise of our industrial underpinnings, such as the automobile industry, food grains, the efficiency of our farms, and our vast expanses for crop growth are fast becoming the core industry of America's future once again.

Malthusian precepts are quickly coming into focus. With food supplies increasing arithmetically and with population growing geometrically, the world population will risk food shortages. As Thomas Malthus wrote in his 1798 publication, "An Essay on the Principle of Population," "The effects of these two unequal powers must be kept equal [...] This difficulty must fall somewhere and must necessarily be felt by a large portion of mankind." Now we are nearing a tipping point, a fact masked in large measure by problems in the world economy, as detailed by Carlisle Ford Runge and Carlisle Piehl Runge in their comprehensive study "Against the Grain" in the January/February 2010 issue of *Foreign Affairs*.

We take the availability of food grains for granted, whereas oil is viewed as a rare and diminishing resource. These perceptions suggest all manner of rationalizations for prices cut completely adrift from the laws of supply and demand. Grains are viewed as a renewable resource and are traded on the open market, reflecting at least nearly accurate price determinations by market forces. Well and good, but it rests on an erroneous market concept. If the public at large excuses distortion in oil pricing, because it is a diminishing resource, then the same must apply to food grains.

Why? Because the dramatic rise in agricultural productivity, which likely has reached its limits, is anchored in the broad application of fertilizers, herbicides, insecticides, and genetically engineered seed advances. Fertilizers especially are at the core of the Green Revolution, and they are consumed in the millions upon millions of tons by farmers worldwide. Phosphates and potash are mined extensively and are at greater risk of diminishing dramatically in their availability than is oil. Without these fertilizer inputs, together with nitrates and ammonia, the ability to feed the world would be nil this very day.

This raises the further question. If the oil producers, whose output is a prerequisite of the world's economic well-being, can organize into a cartel to hype the price of their product, why shouldn't our farm sector do likewise?

Under normal circumstances, collusion between producers within the United States would run counter to our stringent, existing antitrust laws. Yet there exists a legislative anomaly called the Webb-Pomerene Act, which permits American companies to openly collude in setting export marketing policies—in essence, to set up an export cartel. It permits Webb-Pomerene associations "to pool resources, identify strategies for specific foreign markets, and benefit from economies of scale."

A Webb-Pomerene grain association could be organized through regional co-ops, grain elevator operations, and so on. The question then becomes, would the creation of a food grain export cartel be unethical, given the world's basic needs? The answer flips back to OPEC. If the world and individual nations are tolerant of OPEC's manipulations, it would be the height of hypocrisy to castigate a grain cartel.

Yet if a grain cartel is held up to a general challenge because of the essential nature of its product, then the same must apply to OPEC and all the manipulation manifest in hyping oil prices. The time for that to happen is long past due.

"If You See Something, Say Something": Oil and the Failed Times Square Bombing
May 13, 2010

"If you see something, say something" is an expression that has now gone global. Yet the very root cause of what nearly became mass murder in Times Square, what had already taken the lives of thousands of people on September 11, 2001, has been allowed to fester, studiously ignored by acquiescent American administrations, whose policies frequently border on the complicit.

The failed Times Square bombing provided prima facie evidence of Pakistani involvement in plots to conduct attacks on American soil. Pakistan's former ambassador to the United States was moved to comment, "The element of threat is definitely different from the last few months." As quoted in the *New York Times* (Jane Perlez, "U.S. Urges Action in Pakistan After Failed Bombing," May 8, 2010), an American official observed, "Last week's incident makes it more urgent" to bring stability to the tribal areas where militancy thrives and into Karachi, the biggest city, where the radical religious schools known as madrassas are popular.

It is these very madrassas that have become the source of the lethal proselytizing that has destabilized much of the world. Faisal Shahzad, the failed Times Square bomber, may not have personally attended a madrassa, but it is the madrassas in Pakistan and elsewhere, their glorification of jihad, their vilification of the West, that have, along with their moneyed sponsors, lain the groundwork for much of the world's current tensions between civilizations. Who are the sponsors? One might look to the Saudi royal family and its ardent sponsorship through its oil wealth of radical Saudi clerics who adhere to the vision and tenets of the Saudi imam Juhayman al-Otaibi, whose followers seized the Grand Mosque of Mecca in 1979.

Since that time, billions of dollars have flowed to madrassas and community centers around the world, institutions that teach a virulent hatred of Western civilization and that radicalize Afghanistan, swaths of Pakistan, and everywhere from Europe to the Philippines to Indonesia— to nearly every corner of the world, truth be told. While entire nations were being radicalized, our government was somnolent, if not complicity silent. Virtually nothing of consequence was attempted during the two Bush administrations to contain the geyser of hatred. Holding the Saudis to account would have been unthinkable in those years, with all the Saudi money sloshing around Washington into various think tanks and Washington-based private investment funds.

During the Clinton years, Saudi munificence included millions of dollars in donations to the Clinton Presidential Library. Little or nothing was done by our government to contain the propagation of teachings to thousands upon thousands of young minds being formed to hate and destroy. The issue was exacerbated by senior administration officials from the state department on up, as well as by senior military personnel, who were dazzled when received by Saudi royalty. The royals assured them, in dulcet tones, that everything possible was being done to diminish support of Saudi radical institutions and to liberalize the day-to-day lives of the Saudi population. Yet 50 percent of the Saudi population—the women—has yet to be permitted to do so much as drive. One could easily multiply examples. Has Saudi Arabia done anything to dilute its world-threatening poison? Are the occasional protestations and proclamations of willingness to cease and desist genuine? Consider the following: Just a few weeks ago (on March 28, 2010), a *Times* of London headline by Bojan Pancevski in Skopje reported that "Saudis Fund Balkan Muslims Spreading Hate of the West."

"Saudi Arabia," the piece begins, "is pouring hundreds of millions of pounds into Islamist groups in the Balkans, some of which spread hatred of the West and recruit fighters for jihad in Afghanistan.[...] Islamic fundamentalism threatens to destabilize the Balkans.[...] Strict Wahhabi and Salafi factions funded by Saudi organizations are clashing with traditionally moderate local Muslim communities." Given Saudi real-time funding and intentions in the Balkans, the matter becomes urgent. Can one assume that Pakistan and Afghanistan cannot be far behind, that perhaps they are even leading the pack?

A smoking car bomb in Times Square ... this is the real thing. Do we have a problem in Pakistan? Yes. But it seems the rotten core lies in Riyadh. There they know how to play us like a violin. We see it, but instead of saying something, we just go on singing their deadly tune.

Washington Gets Tough on China but Plays Patsy with OPEC
September 30, 2010

In the upside-down world that passes for our government, the House has just passed legislation pressing China to raise the value of its currency. According to the House of Representatives' Ways and Means Committee chairman, Sander Levin, in an interview with *CNBC*'s Carl Quintanilla (September 24, 2010, entitled "China's Mercantilist Exchange-Rate Policy Drags on US Economy"), [I]t has a major impact on American businesses and American jobs ... That's really what it's about."

That may well be true, but an important segment of American

business—including, among many others, such American industrial icons as Corning, FedEx, General Motors, and Goodyear Tire and Rubber—has voiced concerns that such legislation would poison the well of US-China commercial relations, exacerbating feelings of mistrust. In New York last Thursday in a meeting with Chinese Premier Wen Jiabao, President Obama indicated that he wants to see more action relating to the value of the yuan. Apart from that, other significant trade issues with China need to be addressed, like market access, technical data, patent protection, and copyright infringement.

While the legislation has passed in the House, it remains to be seen whether the Senate will follow suit. The irony of this situation is that, by holding down the value of the yuan, China is able to flood us with goods cheap enough for many of our unemployed and newly impoverished to afford. Over the first seven months of the year, China's trade balance with the United States has widened to $145 billion from $123 billion the year before. Significant? Yes, but hardly so when compared to the distortions visited upon us by OPEC and its allies in the oil industry.

The price of oil has escalated over the last decade by a factor of more than five; since the first months of the Obama administration, it has more than doubled and climbed over $40/bbl (from the $30/bbl to the over $70/bbl). Multiplied by the current oil consumption in the United States of some twenty million bbl per day, that comes to an increase of eight hundred million dollars a day or nearly three hundred billion dollars a year going into the rapacious pockets of OPEC and the oil industry and its interests.

Where is the outrage here? Where are our vigilant Congress, our administration, our somnolent justice department and Federal Trade Commission while the oil boys are taking us to the cleaners? At least the Chinese are delivering bargains. Where is the outrage from this White House at OPEC and its policies and that of its putative leader, Saudi Arabia, in restricting oil production to achieve artificially high prices? Where is the outrage at their supportive allies in the oil industry, who reap tremendous rewards in the wake of the OPEC cartel's manipulations?

Where is the intercession of our oversight agency, the Commodity Futures Trading Commission, led by Goldman Sachs alumnus Gary Gensler, in those highly suspect oil-trading activities on the commodity exchanges that keep prices at astronomical levels? In January, the

Commodity Futures Trading Commission announced it would vote to set position limits on energy trading on the exchanges. Since then, there has been a deafening silence. Are there laws in place prohibiting these commissioners from taking employment within the very firms and industries they oversee, or is serving on these commissions simply a pathway to a sinecure in the industries under surveillance? If the latter, how long can we tolerate it?

Bringing the price of oil down to levels that reflect a true market dynamic—say, achieving a price level in the around $30/bbl as was the case in February 2009—would save the nation hundreds of billions now being transferred to oil interests.

Would lower prices result in higher consumption? Yes. But paying oil interests to keep consumption in check borders on the insane. We need government programs restricting the usage of petroleum-based gasoline (not biofuels, electric, and so on) to current or lower levels through voucher programs or whatever program is workable, rather than facilitating the transfer of our national wealth to the oil nabobs.

Consider what those sums could do were they applied to a national infrastructure program such as high-speed rail or the improvement of our inland waterways and port facilities. We could enhance our export capabilities and create thousands upon thousands of jobs in the process. We'd even begin to give China a run for its money from our level and enhanced playing field.

PART II

Gouging Starts at the Well

A Funny Thing Happened on the Way to the Gas Pump
January 15, 2006

Gasoline prices are creeping up again, responding in large measure to tenacious oil prices that are near three-month highs—touching almost $65/bbl, which was surpassed only in September and October by market conditions influenced by hurricanes Katrina and Rita. Over the past few years, the price of crude oil has advanced almost in lockstep with the price of natural gas, and the advance in natural gas prices has served as a persuasive explanation of and rationale for the extraordinary escalation in crude prices and, in turn, the prices of gasoline and refined petroleum products.

But something strange has been happening. During the past few weeks, with unseasonably warm weather, supply balances, and so on, the price of natural gas has plunged from a peak of $15.75 per million British thermal units (BTUs) on December 13, 2005, to a close of $8.79 on January 13, 2006—a drop of some 45 percent. On the same day, oil closed near its three-month high at $63.92/bbl. If the prices of natural gas and crude oil have been so closely tied on the march to ever higher highs, why this sudden divergence in market pricing as natural gas prices erode? Could it be that one commodity is responding to market conditions and the other commodity is not, that the market price for crude oil is manipulated while that for natural gas is not?

The market for natural gas is, geographically speaking, North American; it is produced and consumed in the United States and Canada, with some Caribbean and other offshore imports of liquefied natural gas that represent but a small portion of the total. Given the players in natural gas production and distribution and given what happened with Enron, it does not lend itself to manipulation; the risk of antitrust infringement and consequent prosecution is too great.

Crude oil is another story. Crude oil, much more so than natural gas, is a global commodity that is produced in worldwide locations and priced on international exchanges on a minute-to-minute basis. OPEC controls some 40 percent of the world's oil trade, and its paramount concern is keeping oil prices high. It was reported this week that OPEC's revenues in 2005 were at record levels and were expected to reach $522 billion in 2006, an increase of 10 percent according to the US Department of Energy. "It's just been a phenomenal transfer of wealth from consuming to producing nations," said an analyst at Merrill Lynch (Carola Hoyos, "OPEC Nations 'set for record oil revenues,'" *Financial Times*, Global Economy, January 11, 2006, http://www.ft.com/cms/s/0/e35bb7ae-82d3-11da-ac1f-0000779e2340.html#axzz1GDvlxDMA).

The oil patch, its supporters in and out of government, and all those who benefit from high oil prices—be they oil companies, suppliers, financial institutions, or K Street lobbyists—will tell you that it is free market forces of supply and demand that determine oil prices. But is this so? Consider that the price of oil is set on the futures markets, which are traded on exchanges in New York, London, Dubai, Singapore, and so forth and now increasingly through electronic trading. Trading is virtually unregulated as well as opaque; that is to say, one doesn't know who is buying or selling, and trading can be done anonymously through straw men or accounts. Thus, it lends itself to manipulation—see the allegations of trading malfeasance at Refco—by those who have the interest in pushing markets higher or lower and the means to do so. The members of OPEC certainly have a keen interest in pushing markets higher, and given the flood of billions being cashed in, they have the means to do so as well.

A funny thing happened on December 12, 2004. After a slight and inappropriately timed fallback in oil prices, OPEC's president and Saudi oil minister Ali al-Naimi said, "Watch what happens tomorrow. I will tell you, [prices] will go up tomorrow" (AFP, "Naimi Expects Oil Prices to Rise," *Arab News*, December 12, 2004, http://archive.arabnews.com/?page=6&section=0&article=55949&d=12&m=12&y=2004). Indeed, with some unusual gyrations, the quoted price of oil did go up on December 13. The only way al-Naimi could have been certain that the price of oil was going to go up the next day was if either Saudi Arabia—through its national oil company, Aramco—or OPEC or its agents played with and manipulated the oil futures markets on that day. If, indeed, the oil futures markets were manipulated, it raises some very important questions. When, before and since, have the oil futures trading markets been tampered with? How blatantly have the markets been distorted? How have these manipulations affected the price of oil?

It is of urgent necessity that the trading of oil on commodity exchanges be closely scrutinized and subjected to immediate Congressional investigation and requisite action. The time to act is now.

ExxonMobil Now Huckstering Bottled Water
February 15, 2006

The world's oilmen gave us a little lecture when they met in Houston on Tuesday, February 7, 2006. They corrected a couple of our mistaken impressions.

For openers, they explained that we really need to stop getting nauseated as we watch the numbers on the gas pump spin. We've got it wrong, they said; the price of gasoline isn't all that high. In fact, it's a bargain. At a national average of $2.34 a gallon, chided ExxonMobil's senior vice president Stuart McGill, gas is a positive *steal*. Compare it to the price of bottled water, which can cost as much as $10 a gallon and won't even make your car go. There, feel better? I don't.

Consider this. If you don't want pricey bottled water, there's a much cheaper alternative flowing out of your kitchen faucet. If you want gasoline, you have to deal with the oilmen—period, end of story. Gasoline could be a lot cheaper, too, but the oil industry knows that higher prices make for higher profits. Proving the point, McGill's company just raked in thirty-six billion dollars in profit for a single year, which is more than any other company has ever made (Simon Romero and Edmund L. Andrews, "At ExxonMobil, a Record Profit But No Fanfare," *New York Times*, January 31, 2006).

Oil used to be like tap water in that it flowed freely in a market in which producers competed for customers, and the world price was less than $10/bbl. Then the OPEC cartel persuaded its rival producers and its customers in the industry as well to manipulate the market to keep prices high. OPEC has created the illusion that the world is rapidly running out of oil, even as its member nations refuse to allow anyone to verify their improbable statistics on oil reserves. They claim to be pumping as fast as they can, but their real maximum capacity is also a state secret. That lets them feed just enough oil into the market to keep the world running and the price of oil high and rising.

The truth is that there hasn't been any actual shortage of oil since OPEC boycotted the market back in 1973, but the carefully nurtured threat of a shortage keeps customers nervous and serves as an excuse for prices that can only be called outrageous. Every passing storm in the Gulf of Mexico sends the price skittering up, and somehow it never falls back quite as far as it rose.

All the conspirators were there at the Houston energy conference, from Saudi oil minister Ali al-Naimi and Fu Chengyu, chairman of China's CNOOK, Ltd., to American executives like McGill—all of whom happily connive the fiction of scarce oil. al-Naimi looked amused when someone asked him whether Saudi Arabia might raise its daily production anytime soon. "Oh," he said, I imagine, "I thought you didn't want any more of our oil. Didn't President Bush call it an addiction?"

Addiction to Middle Eastern oil is another fallacy, the oilmen assured us, as wrongheaded as the thought of getting off the stuff altogether. The notion of American self-sufficiency in energy is ridiculous, they all agreed—"simply not feasible" in any "relevant" time period, said McGill (Nelson D. Schwartz, "The Hard Truth about Oil," *Money,* CNN. com, February 9, 2006, http://money.cnn.com/2006/02/08/news/international/pluggedin_fortune/index.htm) Daniel Yergin, one of the industry's big insiders, said the idea was "at odds with reality"(Sheila McNulty, "Energy Leaders Seed to Diversify Resources," *Financial Times*, February 9, 2006, http://www.ft.com/cms/s/0/2fd4bf50-9912-11da-aa99-0000779e2340.html#axzz1GDvlxDMA).

Any attempt to wean ourselves from Middle East oil would be both dangerous and provocative to our faithful allies, they warned. "In today's global economy, there is no denying our interdependence," said al-Naimi in his address to Cambridge Energy Reseaerch Association's fourth annual global oil summit on February 7, 2006 ("A Roadmap to the Energy Future: Saudi Arabia's Perspective," http://www.saudiembassy.net/archive/2006/speeches/page60.aspx). "We no longer have the option to go it alone or to let the other guy solve the problem." Thanks. We needed that.

There's still one more tiny nagging point. US consumption of bottled water is running at 6.8 billion gallons a year, which sounds like a lot. But we use 335.7 billion gallons of gasoline a year, which is a humongous amount. Each of us drinks about twenty-five gallons of bottled water a year, which even at McGill's ten-dollar price will set you back just $250. But since most of us drink a lot more than twenty-five gallons a year, an awful lot of water is still coming from the faucet. Your car consumes roughly seven hundred gallons of gasoline a year. Wouldn't it be nice if someone made OPEC open the tap?

The Gouging Starts at the Oil Well
April 19, 2006

One of the great misconceptions distorting today's energy debate is that price gouging at the pump is a key cause of today's high gasoline prices. Now, pump gouging may indeed be a factor, but it pales in comparison with the gouging that's going on at the well, which is the real reason prices have catapulted during the past many years. It is OPEC and its oil industry cronies ratcheting up and manipulating the price of crude that lies behind the astronomical price of gas. The lack of focus on this issue is a ringing victory for the oil patch propaganda machine that has brainwashed our leaders into looking (and posing) at the point of pain rather than confronting the real problem.

For example, Senator Charles Schumer of New York, while standing in front of a gas station surrounded by the assembled press and television cameras, loudly called for an investigation into gasoline price gouging. The gas station attendant, his boss, the station's supplier, and the refinery producing the gasoline are, by implication, at fault. This on a day when crude oil prices touched new highs. I believe Senator Schumer would have better served his constituents if he had held his press conference in front of an oil well. That would send a signal that he is truly serious about finding the real culprits.

The price of crude (which accounts for more than 60 percent of the price of gasoline) has doubled in the past two years, thanks to a series of manipulated price hikes and phony production constraints orchestrated by OPEC and abetted by big oil companies and the lobbyists and politicians who serve them. These players have persuaded us and lulled our government into accepting and repeating the fiction that crude prices are out of our control and dictated by free market forces. The media has, for the most part, accepted this as gospel, without a critical or questioning eye. If only Senator Schumer and his colleagues would look at the big picture and the big players in this oncoming train wreck, instead of always focusing on the photo opportunity.

The Enron Loophole Helps OPEC Serve Up a Hefty Helping of Oil-Price Baloney
July 20, 2006

Last week, the price of oil hit an all-time high of $78.40/bbl to the pious discomfort of OPEC. In the words of Edmund Daukoru, this year's president of the oil cartel and Nigeria's Minister of State Petroleum, the world economy is hurting.

"The latest shoot-up to the mid-seventies and above is very uncomfortable," Daukoru told *Reuters* (Estelle Shirbon, "OPEC: Oil Price Spike 'Very Uncomfortable,'" *Reuters*, July 19, 2006). As for the increasingly deadly clashes in the Middle East, the oil czar commented, "It is always unfortunate if we have to address issues outside the power of OPEC." Without skipping a beat, Daukoru went on to advise that OPEC had plenty of spare production capacity.

I found Daukoru's comment about spare capacity particularly interesting, given that the oil patch whines endlessly about oil production being stretched to the limit and that high prices are its consequence. Yet, we know that inventories are generally larger than they were last year at this time, and now it seems that OPEC can add even more if it wants to.

So why are prices heading for the moon when there is oil available to draw down from storage and spare capacity to pump if the market needs it? Sure, the political turmoil is making the market anxious. But is that enough to propel prices to a new record when there is no evidence of shortages? Highly doubtable.

Something else, it seems, is happening. Not many years ago, oil and other commodities were traded on a real wet barrel basis. Producers sold to buyers at posted prices. When the market got tight, producers might extract a premium or more stringent payment, loading or discharging terms to reflect given conditions on a given day for a given trade. Conversely, if storage tanks were full, there was always a willingness to discount or to make other adjustments to move product.

Then, some years back, futures trading came along, and prices were set in trading floor shouting matches in New York, Chicago, London, and Singapore. They fluctuated in real-time, and volumes grew. Now prices are set electronically as well. Virtual barrels on the futures exchange, rather than wet barrels of actual product, came to determine the purchase and sale prices of oil and downstream products.

Last week, at the Global Forum on Energy, Economy, and Security in Aspen, Colorado, a discussion ensued about the reasons for the very high price of oil and the ever-present perception of shortages. While there, I heard James Ragland (director of the economic research group of Aramco Services Company, the Saudi government–owned Aramco Oil Company) say that Aramco had ample spare capacity but no takers. He volunteered that the big oil producer was ready to load additional cargos at any time.

Donning my old trading hat, I asked a simple question: "Why don't you lower the price?" I reminded him that, when you have too much product, traditional business theory suggests that if you cut the price a bit, you may be able to move your product more readily. The Saudi representative answered, "Why should we sell for less than the prices quoted on the futures exchange?" He went on to suggest that the refiners are making too much money as it is.

"So how much are you making on each barrel?" I cheekily responded. My follow-up question was met with an icy dismissal that Saudi profits were none of my concern. That's probably true, but I wouldn't have asked had he not brought up refining margins. It was quite clear that this issue was not open to discussion.

So there we have it, straight from the horse's mouth. The price of oil for the Saudis, the godfathers of the OPEC cabal, is based on trading of virtual barrels of oil, not on real-time product in storage or in the production chain. In pointing to the futures market as the determinant factor of price, the obvious question becomes whether the futures market is a fair reflection of market forces or whether it is a manipulated cipher behind which the Saudis and others can hide to rationalize away market price distortions, claiming that the free hand of the market is in control and that producers can do nothing but set their prices accordingly.

In July, I called into question the presumption that oil and product trading on the futures exchange is free of manipulation. I am not alone.

Senators Carl Levin and Norm Coleman, the ranking minority member and chairman, respectively, of the Senate Permanent Subcommittee on Investigations, are urging Congress to enact legislation that would close major loopholes in federal oversight of oil and gas trades. The so-called Enron loophole put limits on the ability of the Commodity Futures Trading Commission to prevent speculative trading in energy and commodity markets. It's interesting to note that, since the Enron loophole went into effect in 2000, the price of crude has risen by nearly 500 percent. Coincidence? Perhaps.

To quote Senator Levin, "Right now there is no US cop on the beat overseeing energy trades on over-the-counter, electronic exchanges or foreign exchanges [...] Enron has already taught us how energy traders can manipulate prices and walk over consumers if they think no one is looking." Senator Coleman cut to the chase, saying, "We need to explore legislative ideas to ensure that energy prices reflect the true market forces of supply and demand" (Senate Committee on Homeland Security and Governmental Affairs, "Levin-Coleman Report Finds Speculation Adding to Oil Prices: Put the Cop Back on the Beat," June 27, 2006, http://hsgac.senate.gov/public/index.cfm?FuseAction=Press. MinorityNews&ContentRecord_id=648ca6ed-b5b0-46ef-82b3-19e69163592e).

In the meantime, OPEC and the oil patch are munching on their baloney sandwiches, which are salted with crocodile tears, as they lug their loot to the bank.

The Urgent Need for Congressional Oversight of Oil and Gas Futures Trading
December 11, 2006

The consumption of fossil fuels, given its impact on our environment, is dangerous to our civilization but perhaps no more so than the high price of oil. One of the reasons why prices have escalated exponentially over the past few years is the lack of transparency and government oversight in oil futures trading, both domestically and overseas. It is essential that the new Congress come to grips with this issue. This is not a call for lower prices to encourage greater consumption. That is another issue altogether and will be dealt with separately. Rather, this is a call to bring the price of oil within the parameters of real market forces and to cease the transfer of hundreds of billions of dollars to corrupt and dangerous regimes.

It has been my contention that the price of oil has been and is being manipulated to undreamed of heights by the oil industry and its allies, a complacent government, the policies of OPEC, the panic factor of threatened supply disruptions, and the constant refrain of the peak oil scaremongers, who have been predicting the end of oil since the first well was drilled in Pennsylvania more than a century ago.

There has been growing appreciation that, with the trading of oil and oil product futures on the commodity exchanges and the burgeoning electronic markets, a vast new terrain has opened and, with it, an opportunity to orchestrate the price of oil in a global and sparsely regulated arena.

BP, the hero of Alaska, has been in the crosshairs of the Commodity Futures Trading Commission of late as it tries to fend off charges that it has rigged prices of oil and gas futures. It's not a bad payoff for BP, should the Commodity Futures Trading Commission be on the mark. Manipulating an increase of a mere $1/bbl on the commodity exchange would add nine hundred million dollars to BP's annual bottom line. Nice work, if you can get away with it.

Last week, the *Financial Times* reported that Energy Transfer Partners, the largest intrastate gas pipeline system in the United States, is under investigation by federal regulators over physical gas purchases and gas swap trades executed on the Intercontinental Exchange in an attempt to influence the outcome of their swap trades.

But compared to OPEC, BP is only a bit player. The riches that would be achieved through the rigging of the futures market by only $1/bbl is staggering. OPEC produces near thirty million bbl per day. Multiply that by 365 days a year, and you do the math. Talk about an incentive to rig. Combine that with the torrent of dollars being showered on OPEC, and you have not only the motive but also the means.

If the manipulation is closer to ten or twenty dollars (which is my contention, that it is not so much political risk but futures trading that is imposing a twenty-dollar premium on the price of oil), you begin to understand the enormous transfer of wealth taking place and the existential risks we as a society are facing given the vast sums flowing to malign regimes and terrorist enterprises. In Iraq alone, according to the US Iraq Study Group, millions upon millions of dollars have been flowing from Saudi citizens to fund the Iraqi insurgency against the Iraqi government and the United States–led coalition (Iraq Study Group Report, released December 6, 2006, page 25). That doesn't speak of Iran's nuclear program, of the murderous civil strife in the heart of Africa, or of the instability in Indonesia, Malaysia, Chechnya, and so on. And next?

The bottom lines of the oil companies have exploded without their adding an ounce of economic value. Riding the coattails of OPEC and hiding behind prices determined on the commodity exchanges, they have been able to justify their runaway profits as market-driven to an all-too-acquiescent government and press.

Then there is OPEC. It is open about its attempts to limit supply in order to affect price. Manipulative behavior is inherent in a cartel. Why should it stop there? The pricing of oil on commodity markets gives OPEC and the industry the cover of market forces while gouging the public. In this regard, it is an invaluable public relations tool.

Up until now, the commodity markets, and especially the now-predominant electronic trading markets and over-the-counter markets, are close to opaque. Anyone buying or selling who does not want to be identified can accomplish that goal easily through agents or straw men. Does it not stand to reason that OPEC and others producers of crude oil, along with hedge funds, would be sorely tempted to rig the futures market?

If one has the means, which OPEC certainly does, the execution becomes almost easy, given the commodity trading world's focus on chart movements and the recent phenomenon of black box and gray box trading; with this "look, no hands" method, which has been adopted by innumerable hedge funds, preprogrammed and mathematically-determined trading limits automatically kick off buy and/or sell orders according to price points reached. OPEC's agents or straw men can readily identify these fault lines and trade accordingly, defending a predetermined price level in the confidence that their actions will induce the hedge funds to pile in as soon as certain chart levels are reached.

Of course, for OPEC to be successful, the market needs be ignorant of its and the oil patch's trading objectives. That's why the scrutiny of

BP's and Energy Transfer Partners' trading activities may well be the tip of the iceberg, but only if Congress seriously addresses this issue. The need for government vigilance in the realm of oil futures trading is now urgent and undeniable if the price of oil is ever to reflect true market conditions. The new Congress will be tested to determine how beholden it is to the oil industry. The industry's K Street lobbyists will fight tooth and nail to have this issue swept under the rug. We will soon know how determined Senators Levin, Coleman, and Feinstein are to go head-to-head with big oil.

Average Gas Prices Hit All-Time High: Congress Must Act Now
May 7, 2007

In a little-noticed event reported in the *Wall Street Journal* (Mary Jacoby, "Cartel Arrests in US Bolster Europe Probes," May 4, 2007) last week, the United States arrested eight non-Americans in connection with an international cartel accused of fixing prices for industrial rubber hose. Industrial hose is employed to transfer oil between tankers and storage facilities. Between 1999 and 2007, hundreds of millions of dollars' worth of hose were purchased by the defense department and an array of oil companies (including Royal Dutch Shell and ExxonMobil), leading the justice department to invoke the US's tough criminal laws against cartels.

Industrial rubber hose? What does that have to do with the price of gasoline? Very little, in the grand scheme of things. But, wait, what about the justice department and those criminal laws against cartels and all the oil flowing through that industrial rubber hose? Now, perhaps, we're on to something.

The rubber hose cartel may well be effective, but no offense to that industry, it's Mickey Mouse compared to the granddaddy of all cartels, OPEC. What have our justice department, our oil industry ambassadorial headquarters (the Department of Energy), or our Federal Trade Commission done about that cartel? The answer is zip, nothing. In a style reminiscent of that American hero, Alfred E. Neuman, they offer nothing but a communal "What, me worry?" shrug at the OPEC loophole of sovereign immunity, which means that since the OPEC banditry is undertaken by state-owned companies, our antitrust laws can't be applied. So don't worry, be happy. Smile at the pump. Certainly, Shell and ExxonMobil do when the gas is flowing the other way.

Well, wait, it needn't be that way. Why should OPEC be given a free pass? That question has been kicked around Congress since 1978, when the International Machinists and Aerospace Workers sued the cartel. The suit was thrown out by the courts, which in their wisdom decided that the cartel was protected against lawsuits by the foreign sovereign immunity doctrine, as though it were Saudi King Abdullah himself pumping gas at the local filling station.

Then, in 2005, a bipartisan group of senators, led by then-Senator Mike De Wine and Senator Herb Kohl introduced the No OIL Producing and Exporting Cartels Act (called the NOPEC Bill), which was designed to give the justice department and the Federal Trade Commission explicit powers to process legal action against OPEC. The Senate Judiciary Committee unanimously advanced the bill to the full Senate, while a companion bill was introduced in the House. The measure was eventually killed in House and Senate negotiations over the administration's energy bill. Why?

One may conjecture that oil patch influence played a major role. Remember, the more successful OPEC is at pushing up prices, the fatter the bottom lines of the oil companies and their friends. Certainly, this administration is going to do nothing to cause OPEC to play by market rules. Its friends in the oil industry would feel betrayed. As to the rest of the American consuming public, well, let them spend billions more for gasoline and petroleum products than they ought to.

That was then. This is now. Today, we have a new Congress with leadership that has promised us a new direction. Here is an issue totally within their competence. If they don't act, one can only conclude that the new Congress is as beholden to oil money as was the previous one.

Would it do any good to act? Probably. The mere attempt to change things would send a powerful signal of this nation's displeasure. Would the president veto such a bill with its provisions to bring OPEC into the sights of the justice department? Perhaps he would. After all, he has been practicing his veto signature with a flourish. But such a veto would be as shameful as a Congress not confronting him with that choice.

A Short Tutorial on the High Price of Oil and the Falling Dollar
October 19, 2007

As the price of oil heads toward and exceeds $90/bbl, news stories are replete with explanations tying these new highs to the deterioration in the value of the dollar. Nothing could suit the oil industry better than this red herring, which supports its well-rehearsed "Who, me?" stance. In any case, and as we have all learned, the high price of oil is a pure reflection of the marketplace … or so the oil industry and its vested allies would have us believe.

Let me run some numbers by you. On January 18 of this year, the price of crude oil was quoted on the New York Mercantile Exchange at $49.90/bbl. On January 20, in his State of the Union address, President Bush vowed to double the size of the strategic petroleum reserve from 750 million bbl to 1.5 billion bbl. Since then, there has been no holding back the price of oil. For this reason and others having to do with the oil industry's posturing and its restraint of available supply, prices continue to go through the roof in dollar and all other currency terms.

In mid-January with the price of oil shadowing $50/bbl, the value of the dollar versus the euro was 129.50 and the dollar index stood at 85.40. Today those exchange values are 143 and 77.50, respectively. In percentage terms, that comes to a touch over 10 percent in each instance. Now compare those changes to the increase in the price of oil from January to October, escalating from $49.90/bbl to over $90/bbl yesterday. This comes to an almost unprecedented jump of 80 percent in a major industrial commodity over a very short period of time. It leaves the comparable exchange rate differentials of other currencies versus the dollar in the dust.

You had better believe the oil boys will move heaven and earth if they can make the dollar the bogeyman for such a gargantuan change in oil prices, thereby keeping the spotlight away from themselves.

Energy Trading Oversight Awakens from Its Slumber with Anticipated BP Settlement
October 25, 2007

Writing as recently as in this past Sunday's *Washington Post* ("Energy Traders Avoid Scrutiny," October 21, 2007), David Cho has noted that commodity trading, known as "the Wild West of Wall Street," is currently subjected to precious little oversight, even though many of the products traded—oil, gas, uranium, and so forth—are critical to our national security.

Since 2000, when some of the biggest energy companies, including notorious, defunct Enron, got Congress to deregulate the energy trading markets, the Commodity Futures Trading Commission has been shackled by flat budgets, short staffing, outdated technology, revolving-door leadership, and an appalling lack of a clear mandate. That would be a recipe for trouble at any oversight agency. In this case, given the six-fold growth in energy trading volume and the greater complexity of the markets brought about by derivatives, electronic trading, and a widening network of international exchanges (to say nothing of the heightened impact of single-trader wunderkinder with access to enormous leverage, as in the $6.6 billion natural gas trading debacle brought about by Amaranth Advisors last year), a neutered and defanged Commodity Futures Trading Commission is an open invitation to disaster.

By divorcing oil trading from the physical product itself and from the producers who once needed to maintain cordial, trustworthy commercial relationships with their buyers and users, oil traders in the now barely regulated futures trading markets are concerned only with price. Any producer with the wherewithal to trade in futures contracts (at $90/ bbl, show me a producer who doesn't have the necessary resources) can readily manipulate prices higher, without fear of being caught, since the identities of both buyer and seller are often unknown and unknowable under the current structure.

The potential for mischief by those with a vested interest in ever-higher oil and energy prices has been exacerbated exponentially by the emergence of Sovereign Wealth Funds (SWFs). These funds control some $2.2 trillion dollars, and that tally could jump to twelve trillion by 2012. Their operations and lack of transparency are of such growing concern that the SWF question was discussed at the European Union's Lisbon summit last week. It is no surprise that a number of OPEC members rank high, as does Russia, on the list of the largest SWFs.

I have always contended that oil prices are being manipulated by oil interests and their allies, and now comes a sweeping validation of these contentions. According to the *Wall Street Journal* (Ann Davis, Matthew Dalton, and Guy Chazan, "BP Moves to Clean Up Troubles," October 24, 2007), the justice department is expected to seek indictments against four former BP traders, while BP itself is expected to pay $303 million to settle civil charges and avoid criminal prosecution for allegedly manipulating and cornering the US propane market in 2004. The settlement does not include a specific assurance, which BP sought, by either the Commodity Futures Trading Commission or the justice department that they will not take future action against BP related to a long-standing investigation of the company's crude oil trading.

Given the Commodity Futures Trading Commission's meager and stripped-down capabilities, a question is raised. What else has been overlooked? By my estimation, a great deal. The key to this ongoing imbroglio is, as Senator Levin has put it, whether to "put a cop back on the beat [...] to stop excessive speculation and trading abuses" (Senate Committee on Homeland Security and Governmental Affairs, "Levin-Coleman Report Finds Speculation Adding to Oil Prices: Put the Cop Back on the Beat," June 27, 2006, http://hsgac.senate.gov/public/index. cfm?FuseAction=Press.MinorityNews&ContentRecord_id=648ca6ed-b5b0-46ef-82b3-19e69163592e). He has led the fight in the Senate for more market oversight and transparency to curb any such illegal activity. His bill would require largely unregulated exchanges like London's Intercontinental Exchange, which figured prominently in the Amaranth collapse, to register with the Commodity Futures Trading Commission and set trading limits on investors. Several of Senator Levin's colleagues, and even some oil industry figures, now agree that more regulation is urgently needed. Naysayers claim that it's impossible to enact meaningful rules in fast-changing energy markets. An aide to Senator Levin has responded that traders "hesitate when somebody's watching. And when nobody's watching, traders will go wild" (David Cho, "Energy Traders Avoid Scrutiny as Commodities Market Grows, Oversight Is Slight," *Washington Post*, October 21, 2007).

We've all seen that wildness in oil prices, which have skyrocketed more than 80 percent this year alone from $49.90/bbl in mid-January to more than $90/bbl recently. With triple-digit oil prices looming just on the horizon, we can ill afford any more complacency or half-hearted measures. Our economy and our national security are fundamentally tied to these issues. The Commodity Futures Trading Commission must be given the necessary resources and clear marching orders by Congress to do its job—now!

The Trade That Brought Us Oil Prices of $100/bbl Teaches Us to Be Afraid, to Be Very Afraid
January 7, 2008

On January 2, a single trade on the New York Mercantile Exchange pushed the price of oil to the psychologically freighted $100/bbl. That trade made headlines on the front pages of newspapers all over the world. The trade itself was for a single futures contract of one thousand bbl of crude. The price quotation on the exchange prior to the fateful hundred-dollar trade was $99.53, so when that one contract at $100/bbl crossed the ticker, it jumped the market price of crude everywhere by nearly one half percent, 47¢/bbl, to be exact. At that moment, that was the price on which all crude oil transactions were based. The next trade on the exchange would have incurred a loss of six hundred dollars to the trader who executed it; that trader was understood to be one Richard Arens. Thus Mr. Arens, by being the first trader to close a $100/bbl trade on the New York Mercantile Exchange, purchased a slice of immortality at a cost of but six hundred dollars.

But consider the following. By making that trade at some fifty cents above the going market, Mr. Arens, with an investment of $6,750 (the margin required by the exchange for an oil futures contract), was able to move the market dramatically by himself. At that moment and for as long as the one hundred-dollar marker was on the trading board, all oil transactions in the United States and on markets throughout the world (given their close interrelationship) reflected that forty-seven-cent jump. With some eighty-five million bbl of oil being produced and shipped each day, that one trade alone increased the value of oil by more than forty million dollars at that moment. All that based on one trade, requiring only $6,750 as a margin deposit—an incredible and frighte   we have been shown the clearest, most   of the risks inherent in basing the global   of the commodity trading floor.

On these postings, I have repeatedly attempted to alert the field that the trade in oil futures on world commodity exchanges (electronic, New York, London, Singapore, and so forth) is not a straightforward, unencumbered market. It is influenced by oil patch agendas and riddled with special interests who push oil prices up as high as will be tolerated or, as in this case, past a historic breakthrough. My arguments have been met with considerable skepticism by the press (which says the market sets the price) and with outright hostility by those who have a vested interest in high oil prices. Yet here is incontrovertible evidence of the susceptibility o   ets to manipulation. Mr. Arens, with jus   enting a thousand bbl of oil, was able to

Saudi Arabia, Kuwait, the United Arab Emirates, and Russia all have SWFs (Sovereign Wealth Funds). Saudi Arabia alone has nine hundred billion dollars to invest, to trade, or to go dancing with. We don't know how these funds are spent or invested, because their activities and goals are completely opaque. The exception is when a Citigroup or Merrill Lynch goes knocking at their door.

Oil is the core of these countries' economies, and the higher the price of oil, the fatter those SFWs grow. It is the price of oil on the commodity exchanges that determines the price at which the physical product is bought and sold. Is it then unreasonable to assume, given the market's susceptibility to direction, that a portion of that ocean of money in the hands of the world's most important oil producers is being used to trade prices toward the highest levels the world's oil-consuming economies can either bear or tolerate? If a single trader with only $6750 can move the market, how can you expect those with billions at their disposal not to do the same?

Be afraid. Be very afraid.

Questions Energy Secretary Samuel Bodman Must Ask at This Weekend's Summit in Saudi Arabia
June 20, 2008

The grand pooh-bahs of the oil world, both producers and consumers, will be meeting this weekend; they have been summoned to Jeddah, Saudi Arabia, by King Abdullah and Saudi Arabia's oil minister Ali al-Naimi. The question is why prices are at levels that nobody seems to be able to explain—levels that seriously, negatively affect the world economy, especially the economies of developing nations? Our energy secretary, Samuel Bodman, needs to take things one step further in getting answers to questions not usually asked or discussed. Might I suggest a few?

- Regarding the price of oil, the current OPEC president Chakib Khelil has asserted, "the central issue [...] is speculation" ("Oil: Tight Supply + High Demand = Higher Prices," *USAToday*, June 20, 2008. http://www.usatoday.com/money/industries/energy/2008-06-19-one-forty-oil_N.htm). His position has been echoed by other OPEC members and many in high positions in the consumer class, as well as oil executives, politicians, and pundits. Simultaneously, the oil-exporting nations have accumulated vast reservoirs of wealth of into the hundreds of billions. Despite requests for transparency by governments and global financial institutions, the operations of the SWFs remain opaque. The sums they represent are so enormous that they are an undeniable invitation to mischief.

- Given the importance of oil and oil markets to the well-being of the countries in question, what assurances does the oil-consuming class have that this wealth is not being used by the SWFs to game the oil futures market, supporting virtual barrels (oil futures markets) to control and maximize the price of wet barrels (the bbl being loaded onto oil tankers and into storage facilities around the world). Certainly in terms of funds available, the capability is there, and given the opaque nature of the commodity exchanges around the world, it could be— is being?—used for that purpose, unless hard questions are asked. Therefore, can we have assurances from the oil-producing nations that their SWFs are not being used, directly or indirectly, to manipulate oil prices on commodity exchanges around the world?

- You here in Saudi Arabia are the custodians of the largest reserves of crude oil in the world, which is both fortuitous and fraught with responsibility. Yet they have not shared with us a reliable assessment of their reserves and production capabilities in spite of entreaties from governments around the world, the International Energy Agency, and the G-8. When will they be forthcoming with that information, so those responsible for forward economic planning worldwide will have hard numbers to go by?

- As an example of the confusion prevailing on this issue, they have generally let it be understood that their current reserves are approximately 261 billion bbl. Yet on December 27, 2004, Saudi oil minister Ali al-Naimi said, in a statement issued after opening new oil fields in eastern Saudi Arabia, that the 261 billion bbl still waiting to be pumped might actually turn out to be 461 billion bbl—"There are big chances to increase the kingdom's producible reserves by 200 billion barrels [...] this will come either through new discoveries or through increasing production from known deposits" (Raymond J. Learsy, *Over a Barrel: Breaking the Middle East Oil Cartel*, Nashville, TN: Nelson Current, 2005).

- In a front-page article more recently ("Oil Innovations Pump New Life into Old Wells," March 5, 2007), the *New York Times* quoted Nansen G. Saleri, the head of reservoir management at state-owned Saudi Aramco, who said that new seismic tools (which give geologists a better view of oil fields), real-time imaging software, and the ability to drill horizontal wells could all help boost global reserves. Mr. Saleri said that Saudi Arabia's total reserves were almost three times higher than the kingdom's officially published figure of 260 billion bbl or about a quarter of the world's proven total. He estimated the kingdom's resources, including both oil already produced and less certain reserves, at 716 billion bbl. Thanks to more sophisticated technology, Mr.

Saleri said he wouldn't be surprised if reserves in Saudi Arabia eventually reached one trillion bbl. Your comments would be welcome.

- Over the past month, Ali al-Naimi proclaimed that all future expansion of production capacity would be foreclosed after the announced expansion of Saudi oil production to 12.5 million bbl per day. Given the apparently huge reserves on hand and the world's growing need for oil, is this not a grossly irresponsible, self-serving, and arrogant policy? Again, your comments would be welcome.

- By contrast, Saudi Aramco prepared a long-term plan in 1970, calling for the kingdom to increase its production capacity to twenty million bbl per day by 1990, with a clear vision of the growing demand for oil to come. Is a copy of this farsighted planning document still available?

- It is generally understood that Saudi Arabia sits atop eighty important reservoirs of oil, of which only eleven are being tapped with one additional reservoir coming online in days. illusion of shortage? Your comments would be instructive.

- In early 2007 with price of oil near $50/bbl, OPEC cut its production quota by 1.7 million bbl per day under the leadership of Saudi Arabia. Since that time, the price of oil has escalated by some 160 percent to roughly $135/bbl; for those keeping track, the dollar has given up some 25 percent during that period. Yet OPEC has reinstated production of only eight hundred thousand bbl of that cutback, with next month's two hundred thousand-bbl increase bringing the total to one million bbl. Clearly, the cutback has been devastating to oil consumers worldwide, yet OPEC has refused to bring production levels to what they were before. What about the massive price increase, which now borders on gouging and is creating an economic and social crisis in countries throughout the world, especially developing ones? What are we to make of this lack of concern for OPEC's customer base?

- While traveling through your fair city, I noticed that the price of gas was 0.60 riyals per liter or 60.6¢US per gallon. If the price of crude constitutes some 60 percent of the price of gasoline, then on the basis of 60 riyals per liter, the crude cost basis is about $15/bbl. Compare this with the $130/bbl that the rest of the world is paying. Elsewhere, whole industries are being driven out of business. There are strike actions in France and Spain and riots in India and far beyond. How can OPEC reconcile these differences with the assertion that it is acting in a commercially responsible manner?

- In late March of 2007, King Abdullah proclaimed that US presence in Iraq was an illegal occupation. Couched in that statement was a seeming invitation for us to leave Iraq. Does that mean that, if we follow the king's advice and up and leave, Saudi Arabia's oil policies will become more pliant, more in keeping with those of a responsible supplier, aware of the impact that its policies can have on the well-being not only of the United States but also of economies and consumers around the world?

Mr. Bodman, just this once, please earn your spurs.

Oil Prices in Steep Decline: Be Afraid, Be Very Afraid!
November 1, 2008

Here we go again. Oil prices are tumbling in the steepest four-day decline in history.

The sense of relief throughout the land is palpable. For now, the fact that we are still at levels that are more than 160 percent above prices of only a year and a half ago—prices unheard of before—seems lost in the ebullient moment. Silenced, too, is the inane commentary of President Bush and of stalwart Secretary of Energy Samuel Bodman, not to speak of Federal Reserve Chairman Ben Bernanke, of myriad oil company pooh-bahs, or of our former Wall Street, Treasury Secretary Henry Paulson, who understands that when his cronies on Wall Street are bleeding, it's because of the manipulation of the short sellers, but when it's you and me paying through the nose at the pump, it's all about supply and demand.

Our regulatory commission, the Commodity Futures Trading

Commission, has become more casino huckster than vigilant overseer by forever whitewashing the commodity exchanges, proclaiming, "[they] have no evidence of oil manipulation" or "speculation is driving the prices" (Tom Doggett, "CFTC Says No Evidence of Oil Manipulation, Hoarding," *Reuters*, June 10, 2008, http://uk.reuters.com/article/2008/07/10/businessproind-congress-cftc-dc-idUKN1036879720080711), as if an eighteen-dollar plunge in four trading days had everything to do with supply and demand—thereby shamelessly providing this administration, especially our energy secretary, with talking points to rationalize inaction.

But something far more sinister is afoot in the steep descent in oil prices. Our national sense of outrage at the egregious actions of the oil industry, of oil producers, is at risk of being mollified. Just when we'd become deadly serious about alternative fuels, suddenly, magically, the price of oil retreats, and we go back to the gluttonous consumption habits that have been such a major factor in the dilemma in which we find ourselves. Just think of the post-Carter years, when administration after administration did nothing of consequence to mitigate our binging on fossil fuels. Even the one policy initiative set in place (the national fifty-five mile-per-hour speed limit) was laid to rest.

In those years and before September 11, 2001, we were not nearly as conscious of the deep downside of our fossil fuel addiction. Issues of global warming and environmental destruction were hardly on people's minds. The economic and social consequences (such as the erosion of the value of the dollar) of the transfer of billions upon billions of dollars of our national wealth to the oil producers and oil-producing countries were not an issue much in focus. Nor were we as aware then as we have been since September 11, 2001, of how this transfer of wealth risks not only our economy but also our national security.

Will the price of oil continue to recede? I don't know by how much, when, or even *if* it will. Certainly a fair return on the production cost of installed capacity could and should reflect a price of less than $50/bbl. At that level, the Saudis, as one example, would still be making some thirty-three times their production costs per bbl of crude oil sold.

But that is not altogether the point. We have learned something of deep importance from this run-up in crude oil prices. Unlike the neighborhood grocery store selling our families a container of milk at what might be a fair, albeit recently higher, price, the oil producers are voracious and shameless in their drive to gouge each and every one of us here and across the world. The higher they can push the price of their fossil fuel poison, the more they will. They are dangerously unreliable, and we can no longer permit ourselves and our economies to be held hostage to their excess of greed, spite, and arrogance.

Just consider the metaphorical and humiliating poke in the eye that our president received when he went to Saudi Arabia in May 2008 to ask King Abdullah to significantly increase the production and availability of oil on world markets. After all, like him or loathe him, he is still our president. This was with oil relentlessly clambering to levels in excess of $130/bbl, which have never seen before. Humiliating our president was not enough. Shortly thereafter, the Saudis called their OPEC brethren and major consumers to a hastily organized producer/consumer summit in Jeddah. Such luminaries as the United Kingdom's Prime Minister Gordon Brown and US Secretary of Energy Samuel Bodman dropped everything to be in attendance. One could say that the summit was inspired and themed by King Abdullah's ruminations and profound ponderings (i.e., "We are very concerned for consumers in all countries" ("Oil Summit Calls for Supply Boost" BBCNews.com, June 22, 2008, http://news.bbc.co.uk/go/pr/fr/-/2/hi/business/7467653.stm) given the miasma descending on the world's economies.

What was the result of this professed concern? The summit came and went, and other than listening to lectures and background commentary by the Saudis and OPEC President Chakis Khelil on their versions of markets and economics, the only thing that was achieved was a realization that the Saudi-led OPEC was not even going to reinstate the full 1.7 million bbl per day in production that was cut in late 2006 and early 2007; less than half of which will have been reconstituted by the end of this month. This in spite of the fact that the price of oil has skyrocketed. With no meaningful effort on the part of the oil producers to abate the runaway price of oil, the price continued to shoot up from about $130/bbl to more than $147/bbl in the fortnight after the much-publicized meeting. So much for the concern of kings and the oil producer economic babble.

What to do? There are many possible solutions—from keeping prices at current or higher levels ("the cure is not cheaper crack") as espoused by Thomas L. Friedman on July 20, 2008 in his current column in the *New York Times*, "9/11 and 4/11," to reining in demand through a voucher program calling for an absolute national ceiling on fossil fuel consumption. Each has its pros and cons. Friedman's could be viewed as regressive, while the voucher program smacks of rationing, which is anathema to many (though from cursory personal observation, I am amazed by how many people would be willing to sign on were the system fair). The important thing is that we must begin to have national leadership and a serious national debate on this issue, which is of existential importance to the future of the United States. We cannot let lower oil prices in any way deter us from the initiatives undertaken to get this oil monkey off our back once and for all.

The Oil Patch Vaudeville Act
March 30, 2009

The beat goes on. It was so nice and quiet on the oil front for a little while. Had the price of oil held at $147/bbl, we would have been regaled endlessly with all the most sensible reasons why it should go even higher. Prognostications came from far and wide and were trumpeted loudly for all to hear. Next stop would be $200/bbl (Goldman Sachs) (Louise Story, "An Oracle of Oil Predicts $200-a-Barrel Crude," *New York Times*, May 21, 2008) and onward to $250/bbl (as Alexei Miller, chief executive officer of Gazprom, estimated on June 10, 2008; Carola Hoyos and Javier Blas, "Gazprom Predicts Oil Will Reach $250," *Financial Times*, June 10, 2008), but what about $500/bbl (Matt Simmons, the Old Faithful of oil price insanity, with apologies to T. Boone Pickens; Brian O'Keefe, "Here Comes $500 Oil," *Fortune*, Sept 22, 2008, http://money.cnn. com/2008/09/15/news/economy/500dollaroil_okeefe.fortune/index. htm)? But then, watching the price fall from the undreamed of heights of $147/bbl to the dowdy mid-fifties and below seemed to make the oil guys and gals tongue-tied in disbelief. Not for long. This past week, they came out with guns blazing.

First to answer the call of duty was Jad Mouawad of the *New York Times*, a scribe who must be one of the oil patch's favorite cheerleaders and who, during the entire oil price bubble, never met an increase he didn't like, couldn't support, or wouldn't do double somersaults to rationalize away. In an article this week ("Rising Fear of a Future Oil Shock," March 27, 2009), he tried to light a fire under our collective angst. He quoted extensively from a report by the Cambridge Energy Research Associates, an oil consulting firm with deep and close ties to the industry. With their findings splashed over the pages of the *Times* by Mouawad, we were thus initiated into the new oil patch gospel.

It goes like this:

When oil was veering toward $147/bbl, we were advised by Mouawad and the oil industry flacks not only that the price of oil was a reflection of true market dynamics but also to watch out above. "We are going ever higher" was the general theme. You see, peak oil theory was fed to us by the bbl by oil industry public relations departments, like the American Petroleum Institute and various friendly scribes in the media. The gospel then was that we were running out of oil. It was in the spirit of Samuel Kier, hawking his rock oil patent medicine back in 1855 when crude oil was still bubbling up in Pennsylvania. "Hurry, before this wonderful product is depleted from nature's laboratory" was the tagline then—and it still is at $147/bbl.

Then—*poof!*—the price of oil decreases more than 60 percent, falling from heights never before imagined. Guess what? Now we are told, "There's plenty of oil out there, but we poor folks in the oil patch just need to get higher prices to justify going after it."

As if on cue, the *Wall Street Journal* piles on with its own take on the same issue (Guy Chazan, "Falling Oil Supply Risks a Price Rise," March 27, 2009). It presents the usual high drama about the prospect of a surge in crude prices, because "falling oil prices have squeezed oil companies' finances and forced many to cut capital spending and postpone projects." Then it goes on to quote the Cambridge Energy Research Associates (CERA) chairman, who said, "A price collapse of this magnitude really registers on the Richter scale, and its impact on levels of future investment will be felt for years."

But wait, "price collapse of this magnitude"? Really? Consider that, in March of 1999 ten years ago, the spot price for crude as determined by the Energy Information Administration was less than $13/bbl (US Energy Information Administration website (http://www.eia.doe.gov/dnav/pet/hist/LeafHandler.ashx?n=PET&s=WTOTWORLD&f=W). Thus, the current level of $52/bbl reflects an increase of 300 percent.

What else in your day-to-day experience has gone up that steeply in the past decade? Think about it.

The *Wall Street Journal* reported that CERA hedged its dire predictions in part, citing their uncertainty of the rate at which oil demand will recover. If it doesn't begin to rebound next year, as many predict, CERA says the oil market could face a "large surplus of production capacity for the next several years" ("Low Oil Prices Putting Supply Growth at Risk," CERA press release, March 27, 2009, http://www.cera.com/aspx/cda/public1/news/pressReleases/pressReleaseDetails.aspx?CID=10189). Certainly the most positive comment comes at the end: "Government policies to counter climate change and increase energy efficiency could also drive down the West's appetite for oil." It is encouraging that the new administration is saying and, one hopes, doing all that can be done to achieve that end. With its success, the price of oil will also be driven down, as will the oil industry's hegemony over our lives.

The administration has its hands full, but given the rapacity of the oil industry and its willful dependence on the OPEC cartel, it may be time to consider the Norway Oil Trust solution for the development of oil and gas on public lands. Simply put, in Norway, the nation's wealth of oil and gas resources is developed and distributed under the overall management of a national oil trust (i.e., Petoro and Statoil). The systems works, and all Norwegians are its beneficiaries.

The Price of Oil Has Doubled on Obama's Watch: The Time for Action Is Now
June 11, 2009

The price of oil has leapt by more than 100 percent since February from a shade under $33/bbl to over $71/bbl at yesterday's close on the New York Mercantile Exchange. The sudden and sharp escalation in prices represents a looming danger to a very fragile economic recovery. Adding insult to injury, the price is being driven by investor sentiment rather than by fundamentals (see the *Wall Street Journal*, "Some See Replay of 2008 in Crude Oil's Recent Surge," June 8, 2009). This combined with tabulated oil stocks being 19 percent higher than a year ago, according to the US Energy Information Agency, and not taking into account the scores of millions of bbl of oil and oil products in storage, floating at anchor in supertankers from Rotterdam to the Mediterranean to the Eastern Seaboard and beyond.

Combine this with the inane remark of Nobou Tanaka, the executive director of the International Energy Agency, who after whitewashing OPEC's manipulations and complementing them for keeping their output steady was quoted saying "Our message to OPEC is they made a sound decision." OPEC, all the while, has been making it clear that its current intended price target is between $75/bbl and $80/bbl. No mention from Mr. Tanaka that Saudi Arabia alone has shut down 4.5 million bbl/day of production capacity, and the rest of OPEC has shut down some millions more.

A price escalation of this magnitude for a commodity so fundamental to our economy is untenable. You can be sure that, if OPEC's members get away with achieving their goal of $75–$80/bbl, $100/bbl will be their next target after a short hiatus. It is imperative that the administration take action now. Otherwise, our government and our economy will be steamrollered by oil interests, both here and abroad.

First, where is our Department of Energy? What steps are being taken to alert the public to the dangers the economy will face from these speculation-driven prices? Where is the bully pulpit confronting oil interests and OPEC? Mr. Steven Chu is a fine gentleman, academic, and Nobel Laureate, but is he up to the barefisted rough-and-tumble of the oil patch? His focus on alternative energy is and should be a high priority, but here we are dealing with the beginnings of a real-time crisis demanding real-time solutions. Who are the people around him? Much of the Department of Energy and the Department of the Interior was staffed under the Bush administration by oil patch cronies. What kind of advice is Chu getting and from whom?

Second, psychology and speculation go hand in hand. The Department of Energy has it within its powers to change the temper of the marketplace. It can forcefully signal its dissatisfaction with the current ratcheting up of prices simply by stopping all purchases for the strategic petroleum reserve until prices come down significantly. Oil storage throughout the world is filled to bursting, and adding more oil to the strategic petroleum reserve is only helping to prop up the price of oil. Stopping purchases would send a powerful message to the market, to the market makers, and even to OPEC that this government is not sitting idly by while oil interests bleed us dry.

Third, in order to go the extra mile in deeming the steep current price of oil a strategic threat to our economy, we should release measured quantities of the strategic petroleum reserve back into the market at intervals that would upset the one-way direction of oil prices. If speculators knew that they had releases from the strategic petroleum reserve to worry about, they wouldn't be so quick to play what has lately been a risk-free winning hand.

Fourth, it is imperative for the Department of Energy and the new management team of the Commodities Futures Trading Commission to liaise closely to determine the nature of oil speculation on the commodity exchanges. Who is doing the trading, under what auspices, and to what end?

Fifth, given the oil exchanges' level of distortion and their manifest potential for manipulation, one might go so far as to close them down altogether. This may seem like a draconian measure, but remember that oil was traded some years ago on a wet barrel, contract, and spot market basis. Yes, there were spikes and valleys, but at least one knew where all the bodies were buried. The march to the price of $147/bbl last summer was a clarion call to recognize that the current pricing mechanism is deeply flawed. Perhaps it needs to be done away with.

BP's Smoking Gun and the Manipulation of Oil Prices
June 30, 2010

In an eye-opening front-page article (Nelson D. Schwartz, "BP Loses Trading-Floor Swagger in Energy Markets," June 27, 2010), the *New York Times* gives smoking-gun evidence of the manipulation of oil and oil product prices through trading on the commodity exchanges. It brings into focus the question of what benefit is derived from these exchanges as currently constituted other than providing a speculation platform and con game for insiders and an instrument for oil producers to hype the price of their commodity. At the heart of the article and as a shining example of miscreant trading behavior is our good friend, BP.

As the *Times* informs us, "BP, whose reputation for taking risks in the oil fields is matched only by its daring in the energy markets," has remained committed to aggressive trading that has brought in as much as a fifth of the company's profits or some two to three billion dollars per year, which was big money, before the cost of the massive destruction in the gulf. Given its size, its ability to make enormous bets, its massive financial resources permitting it to hold onto positions almost indefinitely, its vast infrastructure, and its standing as one of the largest producers of oil in the world, it was able to take on huge positions with little risk and hold onto them until they paid off.

Now this raises a question. Using the commodity exchanges as a pricing tool, would BP or any other major producer (say, Shell, or the national oil companies of OPEC or its agents) trade on the exchanges to pressure prices lower? That is the crux of the issue. Permit me to quote a statement that Leon Hess, the founder of Hess Oil and that erstwhile sage and eminently successful general of the oil wars, made before the Senate Committee on Government Affairs some twenty years back. His words are as true now as they were then, when they were incorporating all the trading exchanges that have blossomed around the world. He said, "I'm an old man, but I'd bet my life that if the Merc [New York Mercantile Exchange] were not in operation there'd be ample oil all around the world at reasonable price" (Mark Potts, "Price Rise Blamed on Speculation; Oil Company Chief Calls Market Distorted," *Washington Post*, November 2, 1990).

That brings us back to BP. Would BP trade on the exchanges to bring down the price of the company's basic profit-generating commodities? Given BP's huge interest and investment in production resources, that's highly unlikely. One can fairly assume that BP would trade in a manner that would be supportive of the overall objectives of BP, which is to sell its oil and downstream products, including gasoline and propane, at the highest price possible. When it does, it occasionally gets caught trying to manipulate the market.

In 2005, BP agreed with the New York Mercantile Exchange to pay a substantial settlement to resolve allegations of improper oil trading activities; BP offered assurances to clean up its trading activities in the future. The settlement cited so-called wash trades—the simultaneous swaps of the same amount of a commodity for the same price. The technique is used to improperly boost trading volumes or revenue and, most significantly, to influence market pricing. Clearly, the constraints on BP's activities on the New York Mercantile Exchange would have little or no impact on their ongoing trading on the London, Singapore, Hong Kong, or other world exchanges. Nor did it stop them from subsequently trying to corner the propane market. That woke up our otherwise somnambulant Commodity Futures Trading Commission to seek indictments against BP that resulted in a fine of $303 million to settle civil charges and thereby avoid criminal prosecution for allegedly manipulating and cornering the US propane market.

Ironically, given a recent appearance before a Senate committee in which he showed himself to be a wanting expert on gulf oil spills and much else, Tony Hayward, who would have deep inside knowledge as the chief executive officer of BP, proclaimed earlier this year that the "drop in the dollar is a major factor behind oil prices breaking through $75/bbl" (Patrick Allen, "BP CEO: Dollar's Fall Is Major Factor in Oil's Rise," CNBC.com, October 20, 2009, http://www.cnbc.com/id/33394782/BP_CEO_Dollar_s_Fall_Is_Major_Factor_in_Oil's_Rise). There, now you have heard it from an expert without an agenda and without any interest in putting forward self-serving explanations for every jump in the price of oil.

Clearly, the commodity exchanges are susceptible to manipulation. Without a doubt, they have been—and in all likelihood continue to be—manipulated. Consider that more than 137 billion bbl of oil were traded on the New York Mercantile Exchange last year alone. That is not counting all the other exchanges throughout the world. Yet the world consumes barely thirty billion bbl of oil annually. We also have BP evidently in the game to maximize profits, and the higher it can push prices through its trading on the exchanges, the better for its bottom line. How many other producers worldwide are playing the same game? How many Wall Street or London or Singapore bank oil trading desks with no interest in consuming or producing oil but with wide access to banking resources and to oil company trading intelligence are going along for the profitable ride?

Who pays the bill? Yes, you guessed it—you do. You pay it not only at vast economic cost but also at grave risk to our national security.

Thanks for the lesson, BP!

PART III

The Usual Suspects:
The Middle East, Russia, and Beyond

The Head of the Snake: Iraq's Unspoken Risk
January 8, 2006

On January 5, 2006, 130 Shiites were brutally and senselessly slaughtered in a series of Sunni-executed car and suicide bombings throughout Iraq. The intensity and viciousness portended Iraq's further descent into a sectarian civil war and placed the formation of a cohesive central government at risk. The bloodletting continued unabated with no evident or announced purpose other than to remove American forces from Iraqi soil while pushing Iraqi society into a miasma of chaos and slaughter.

Concurrent with the continuing disintegration of Iraq, the price of oil has skyrocketed by more than 100 percent in the past eighteen months alone to vertiginous levels, exceeding $60/bbl. The price appears poised to go higher under existing market conditions. At this level of pricing, Saudi Arabia pockets some billion dollars every two days from its sale of oil and oil products. This enormous flood of money into the coffers of Iraq's neighbors, Saudi Arabia and Kuwait, raises the question of whether there is a relationship between their bonanza and Iraq's misery.

Behind Saudi Arabia, Iraq has the largest oil reserves in the Middle East, despite the fact that only 10 percent of its landmass has been prospected for oil. Its potential as a producer and exporter is enormous—second only to Saudi Arabia's and perhaps, in time, with stability and calm, it could be second to none. Given its known reserves and with extensive investment in its oil infrastructure, Iraq's exports could reach six million bbl per day in a few years' time. It was reported on Friday that Iraq's exports totaled 1.1 million bbl per day last month ("Iraq Oil Exports Hit Post-War Low," *BBC News*, January 2, 2006, http://news.bbc.co.uk/go/pr/fr/-/2/hi/business/4574954.stm), which is the lowest level since the official end of the conflict in 2003. For Saudi Arabia, which is trying to maximize its profits from oil, the prospect of absorbing the full magnitude of Iraq's supply capability into the marketplace is frightening. In all likelihood, it would ring the death knell for today's elevated global oil prices (which are 600 percent higher than the price of oil half a dozen years ago).

For Saudi Arabia, as the OPEC cartel's most important member, it is imperative that a lid be kept on Iraq's oil production so that prices can be controlled. Adding to Saudi concerns is the fact that Saudi Arabia's largest oil reserves lie under its Eastern Province, the one sector of Saudi Arabia with a significant Shiite majority. Given Iraq's huge oil potential and the prospect of a Shiite-majority government that could offer solidarity to the downtrodden Shiite population of the Eastern Province, the stakes in Iraq have become critical for Saudi Arabia's ruling class.

It has been reported that Saudis account for the vast majority of the foreign suicide bombers in Iraq (and, of course, fifteen of the September 11, 2001, hijackers were Saudis). The flow of suicide bombers continues unabated, and many are the product of, or are abetted by, the perverse zealotry of Wahhabi schools and imams to which Saudi Arabia has directed billions of dollars in support over the years.

Of particular interest, though not widely reported at the time, Prime Minister Ibrahim al-Jaafari of Iraq made it clear during his interview with Wolf Blitzer on *CNN* (June 26, 2005, http://edition.cnn.com/TRANSCRIPTS/0506/26/le.01.html) that foreign insurgents, weapons, and funding were entering Iraq via not only the Syrian border but also the Saudi Arabian one. Since that interview, the bloodletting has continued unabated. This week alone, more than two hundred Iraqi civilians were murdered, and more than twenty American servicemen lost their lives.

With the stakes so high and given the players at hand, we are faced with a grim prospect. In Iraq, we are confronted by a clandestinely supported insurgency with access to limitless oil money and an endless stream of terrorists acting to thrust the country into debilitating chaos, thereby keeping Iraq's oil production low and world oil prices high.

Is this conjecture? Yes. Yet, if it is validated, what end strategy is available to us? Saudi Arabia has twenty-six million people, an 814-kilometer frontier with Iraq, limitless billions of dollars available to fund the insurgency should it choose to do so, and mosques spewing hatred and enlisting daily "martyrs" against our limited expeditionary force, our daily losses, our growing budget constraints. From this perspective, our mission seems increasingly overwhelming and probably untenable unless, at long last, we decide to identify and cut off the head of the snake.

Chicken Little in the Oil Patch Again: Iranian Poker
January 18, 2006

The nuclear standoff with Iran and the violence in Nigeria presented the oil patch yet again with a golden opportunity to ratchet prices up to levels approaching those induced by Hurricane Katrina. On Monday and Tuesday, the price of crude spiked up by $2.34/bbl. The *New York Times*, always happy to support the oil patch and OPEC mantra of impending shortage and disaster causing higher prices, pontificated in its editorial entitled "Energy Impasse" the day before (January 15, 2006, http://www.nytimes.com/2006/01/15/opinion/15sun1.html) that "Today's global market is so tight, there is little spare capacity left … There's no shock absorber left.[…] That leaves us with zero options when it comes to leverage against these oil producers."

What the *Times* and the press generally failed to tell us follows. Iran produces some four million bbl per day; 2.6 million are exported. The Nigerian production loss is approximately two hundred thousand bbl per day. That's a shutdown that, in all likelihood, will be short-lived. Assuming the worst-case scenario—that Iran stops all exports for a year and that Nigerian production is similarly affected—the loss of supply to the world market would be a billion bbl.

At this very moment, according to the International Energy Agency, stock levels held by International Energy Agency members alone are at 4.1 billion bbl. Of these, 1.4 billion are held in strategic government reserves; the balance is held commercially. The United States alone holds seven hundred million in its strategic petroleum reserve, whereas our commercial reserves approach 318 million bbl, some thirty million bbl more than a year ago.

Given the reserves at hand, one only wishes that Iran would embargo its oil exports. Its economy, which is almost wholly dependent on oil revenue, would likely collapse within the year; the current Iranian government would go with it. The United States does not import Iranian oil, but because oil is a fungible commodity and thereby readily interchangeable with oil from any other country, Iranians are counting on their oil card to bluff and browbeat oil-consuming nations into acquiescing to their nuclear and other national policy goals.

What a coup it would be if we, together with the International Energy Agency, had the gumption to say to Iran, "Make our day. Stop exports, and we will release our strategic stockpiles to the market as they are needed, including to those markets most directly affected by your supply cut—China and India." Just a declaration of intent to that effect by Secretary of Energy Samuel Bodman would probably cause oil prices to drop by $10/bbl almost overnight. Even more importantly, by calling Iran's bluff, we would force it to fold its hand with all the strategic and political implications that would entail.

Iraq's Oil Production at Post-Invasion Lows—Cui Bono?
April 2, 2006

Last month, Iraq's oil production touched a post-invasion low of 1.1 million bbl. Back in 2003, US officials confidently promised that much of the cost of rebuilding Iraq would be paid for by ramping up production in Iraq's oil fields and that the prewar output of 2.5 million bbl could be increased dramatically with the repair of the aging infrastructure and the expansion of production capability. A doubling of prewar levels to five million bbl was well within the capabilities of Iraq's hitherto untapped reserves. If all that had happened, the added supply of oil from Iraq would have brought another boon to the world economy, easing the purported bottlenecks in oil production that have pushed prices into the stratosphere.

Instead, since this time in 2003, world crude oil prices have more than doubled, increasing by a staggering $30/bbl or more, which when multiplied by a daily world consumption in excess of eighty million bbl represents history's most massive transfer of wealth to the oil patch—an exorbitant tax on the world economy and on each and every one of us, sheikhs and oil barons excepted. Tragically, the reality has evolved differently, both for the Iraqis and for the allied expeditionary forces. Every effort to upgrade Iraq's oil industry has been met with sabotage by the insurgency. Wells and pipelines are blown up; new equipment is stolen or destroyed; entire oil fields are idled for days at a time while repairs are made. At a recent London oil conference, it was reported that plans to rehabilitate the industry have been scrapped; allied forces have given up any thought of the production of five million bbl per day. Actual daily production has declined every year since the invasion to

1.7 million bbl per day in 2005 and to last month's basement low of just 1.1 million bbl per day.

In the shadows, the insurgents are clearly and murderously effective. Who are they?

To answer that, we start with another, more lawyerly question: Cui bono? Who stands to benefit if Iraq doesn't produce as much oil as it could? One obvious culprit is right across the border in Saudi Arabia. The Saudis have pumped more than nine million bbl per day of oil in recent months, and at $60/bbl and up, that means a gusher of money—more than one billion dollars every two days. But if the price is to be kept that high, supply must be tightly controlled. As the designated swing producer of OPEC, it is Saudi Arabia's duty to cut production enough to offset any increase in world supply and thus keep the price up. If Iraq were producing another three million bbl per day, the Saudis would have to sacrifice income of fully $180 million every day. Do you think they would they like that?

This is a circumstantial explanation, of course, and it doesn't prove that the Saudis are sabotaging Iraqi wells and pipelines. But they do have a motive that also involves Iraq's Shia majority and its potential for conflict with Saudi Arabia's Sunni theocracy.

Perhaps influenced by our executive branch's close, personal, and many-layered ties to the Saudi leadership, our leaders keep assuring us that the Saudis are our loyal friends and staunch allies. Why, then, do their state-supported Sunni Wahhabi mosques spew hatred of America? Why is it Saudi volunteers who have become the vast majority of the foreign suicide bombers in Iraq?

In pondering the Iraqi quagmire, we must confront the likelihood that the insurgency, should this hypothesis be valid, is being fueled by limitless billions of dollars in oil money to prolong Iraq's chaos and destabilization and further raise the global price of oil. If that turns out to be the case, we will never achieve our mission in Iraq until we deal with these realities and begin to make objective and parochially unencumbered policy decisions, no matter how difficult that may be.

Iran's Ahmadinejad Lectures Us about Oil
April 29, 2006

As the price of oil soared toward its all-time record of $75/bbl the other day, Mahmoud Ahmadinejad, Iran's hard-line president, read us a little lecture. He said that oil was still priced below its true value. That is a statement of such breathtaking arrogance and greed that it's almost comical, but I, for one, can't laugh very hard through clenched teeth. What was flat-out ludicrous was Ahmadinejad's proof that oil is too cheap. The sure sign, he said, is that refined oil products "are sold at prices dozens of times higher" ("Iranian Leader Says Oil Hasn't Reached True Value," MSNBC.MSN.com, April 19, 2006, http://www.msnbc. msn.com/id/12390227/ns/business-oil_and_energy/) than what the OPEC producers get for their crude oil.

They must teach a strange kind of economics in Iran. As Ahmadinejad knows perfectly well, any basic commodity costs a fraction of the price of the products made from it. Consider a bushel of wheat; as I write, you can buy a bushel to be delivered in May for $3.58. But that bushel can produce more than seventy loaves of bread, each priced at two dollars or more. That means the wheat in each loaf cost only five cents—one-fortieth or less of the final price. But remember that the wheat must be stored and shipped; milled into flour; mixed with yeast, water, and other ingredients; baked; wrapped; shipped again; stacked on shelves in the supermarket; and rung up by a store clerk before you can eat it. To be sure, there's a small profit to be made at every step of the operation, but no one is profiteering on wheat, flour, or bread. They are sold in free markets, where prices reflect true costs and competition for buyers. That's another key difference between oil and wheat.

The true cost of wheat starts with the seed a farmer buys. It includes a large input of mineral fertilizers—phosphates, potash, and nitrogen-based nutrients (which are all, by the way, just as finite a resource as petroleum). The cost of wheat also includes the value of the land it grows on, tractor fuel, depreciation, irrigation, insurance, taxes, and the like, not to mention the farmer's labor. Factoring in all that, there isn't room for a lot of profit in a $3.58 bushel of wheat.

In sharp contrast, oil in Saudi Arabia costs, by OPEC's own admission (Ali Al-Naimi, "Saudi Oil Policy: Stability With Strength" speech before Houston Forum, Houston, TX Oct 20, 1999 www.

saudiembassy.net/1999news), just $1.50/bbl to find and pump (and probably less). Add in the cost of pipelines, processing, and shipping, and it would still be comfortably profitable at $5/bbl when delivered in Rotterdam or Houston or Mumbai. But oil producers manipulate the market to keep prices high. Now, at more than $70/bbl, oil is wildly, extortionately, obscenely profitable for the OPEC sheikhs and their oil patch cheerleaders (think ExxonMobil or Lee Raymond). It is almost as profitable for those cronies whose costs of production are higher—the producers of oil from the North Sea, the North Slope of Alaska, the wastes of Siberia, and the deepwater wells of the Gulf of Mexico. Even in the Canadian tar sands, where oil companies are investing billions to steam oil from the hard black earth, the cost of production is just $20/bbl (Wikipedia, "Athabasca oil sands," http://en.wikipedia.org/wiki/Athabasca_oil_sands), which leaves a profit of 275 percent at today's price.

If producers of wheat and other food crops could collude on prices as successfully, the world economy would probably collapse, and famine would rage around the planet. Perhaps the farmers would be happy—at least for a while. Ahmadinejad is happy, too, but he thinks he can be happier still by raking in even more dollars for his oil, and the oil patch is happy to cheer him on. Why are we happy to let them get away with it?

Iran Threatens Use of Oil Weapon.
Let It. It's Time to Call Its Bluff
June 4, 2006

In a scathing attack on the United States, Iran's supreme leader, Ayatollah Ali Khamenei, said this Sunday that if the United States makes a wrong move, energy flows in the region would be endangered. Presuming there is some semblance of sanity left in the Iranian regime, this would signal Iran's threat to cease or diminish its oil exports to world markets. Interfering with energy flows by attacking the region's shipping lanes or production and oil-loading facilities would be a *casus belli* that would certainly result in the termination of the Iranian regime as currently constituted.

Khamenei spoke from a podium emblazoned with his predecessor

Ayatollah Khomeini's words, "America cannot do a damn thing," and then went on to cite his perception of US failures in Iraq, Afghanistan, and Palestine. This from the spiritual and de facto head of a regime that is considered by our government to be the number one state sponsor of terrorism. Ironically, Iran's actions in fulfilling that threat would give us an opportunity to do a damn thing and to do it without firing a shot, using an asset already in place—the strategic petroleum reserve.

Iran produces 3.85 million bbl of oil every day. Of this, approximately 2.5 million bbl are exported on the world market. The profits generated represent that nation's primary revenue source. Without oil revenue, Iran would most likely sink into economic chaos, and it is doubtful that its government could survive even a year.

That 2.5 million bbl per day comes to slightly more than nine hundred million bbl per year. The International Energy Agency reports that its members (i.e., the United States, Europe, Japan, Korea, and so on) have some 4.1 billion bbl of strategic and commercial reserves on hand. The United States alone has seven hundred million bbl in its strategic petroleum reserve and more than three hundred million bbl in commercial reserves as oil, not counting downstream inventories of gasoline, diesel, heating oil, and so on. Consider the impact were the United States and the International Energy Agency to announce that any willful curtailment of oil shipments by Iran would be met immediately by an equal release to the market from existing reserves.

In addition, they might announce that these reserves would be made available to Iran's traditional customers, whether or not they are members of the International Energy Agency. The oil being made available would be at market prices and equivalent in quantity to the Iranian cutoff. Were such a substitution of supply put into place, Iran's absence as supplier, even for a year or significantly longer, would be felt only marginally by the world marketplace. But it would certainly be felt by Iran, and it would, in all likelihood, result in the regime's demise. Just broadcasting the intent to act in this vein would likely becalm the markets overnight.

Would the administration consider such steps? Perhaps. But it would be subjected to enormous pressure from the oil patch. A clear signal of willingness to use the strategic petroleum reserves and to cooperate with the International Energy Agency would result in an abatement of panic and speculation in the markets. As we have learned over the past years, less panic equals lower oil prices, and lower oil prices result in lower earnings for oil companies big and small.

The oil patch would argue that the strategic petroleum reserve is to be used only in extreme emergencies, as though Iran cutting off oil supplies were not exactly that. Further, they would argue that interfering with the market price mechanism presents greater dangers than the geopolitical consequences of not taking action. Sadly, the administration is so wedded to the oil interests that it may well let Khamenei and company walk all over us until the need arises to put more of our armed forces on the front line to straighten things out. I sincerely hope I'm wrong.

Iran and Russia Learn to Dance the Natural Gas Contango
February 12, 2007

(Note: "Contango" is a trading term for a situation in which the future price of a commodity is quoted higher than the price for current delivery.)

What's worse than one bully? A whole mafia of them. If Iran's supreme leader Ayatollah Ali Khamenei has his way, the world's largest natural gas producers (Russia, Iran, Qatar, Saudi Arabia) might try to form such a mafia to manipulate markets and push gas prices higher and higher, just as the OPEC cartel has so successfully and destructively done with oil prices.

Thanks to the tag team provocations of President Mahmoud Ahmadinejad and the Ayatollah, Iran has built a nasty reputation as a troublemaker. Now comes word from the *Wall Street Journal* of the Ayatollah's efforts to enlist support for a gas cartel from another of the world's confirmed bullies, Russian President Vladimir Putin. Those who have not yet had a chance to "look deeply into his eyes" and doubt this aspect of his character may want to consult Mikhail Khodorkovsky. Alas, I don't have his telephone number; you might check the telephone book for Chita, Siberia.

As you will recall, Putin cemented his iron-fisted reputation early last year when he allowed state-controlled Gazprom to turn off the gas to neighboring Ukraine during a pricing dispute. Unfortunately, the wintertime confrontation also set teeth to chattering further down the pipeline in Europe, which buys 25 percent of its natural gas from Russia. For those who may have convinced themselves that Europe's gas shortages were unintentional byproducts of someone else's contract dispute and not likely to be repeated, Putin shot an arrow through their trusting little hearts when he hinted that European gas consumers might suffer again were the United States to intervene in a subsequent spat between the Kremlin and Georgia.

Given the cast of characters, it's hardly surprising that Khamenei's overture and Putin's reported response that "a gas OPEC is an interesting idea" (Neil Buckley, "Putin Considers Creation of 'Gas OPEC,'" *Financial Times*, February 2, 2007, http://www.ft.com/cms/s/0/f4e756a4-b261-11db-a79f-0000779e2340.html#axzz1GmCoRFdi) have caused energy traders and nervous consumers to speculate on the potential for turmoil. Russia and Iran together control almost half of the world's known gas reserves, and Putin has been currying favor with other big producers. Last year, for instance, he signed agreements with Algeria, and he is scheduled to visit Qatar.

Qatari oil minister Hamad al-Attiya is on record stating that forming a gas cartel to control prices would be difficult to do, because most gas supply deals are locked-in for long periods and thus are not susceptible to short-term production manipulation. Michael J. Economides, editor-in-chief of *Energy Tribune*, however, voiced a contrary opinion last March in the online edition of *Foreign Policy* magazine ("The Coming Natural Gas Cartel," March 28, 2006). Economides, who contends that fast-growing global demand for clean-burning natural gas is changing the landscape, says producers "are certain to organize a natural gas cartel, similar to OPEC." The United States is particularly vulnerable because, historically, we have relied on domestic sources that are dwindling given the current constraints on offshore drilling. Importing liquefied natural gas from abroad will be our only other option, which thereby gives major producers the upper hand, says Economides.

But perhaps the most worrisome comment came from Jonathan Stern, director of gas research at Britain's Oxford Institute for Energy Studies. Speaking of an attempt six years ago to set up a gas exporters organization, Stern complacently remarked to *Wall Street Journal* reporters ("Russia and Iran Discuss a Cartel for Natural Gas," February 2, 2007) that the group hasn't "gotten it together to even meet" since 2005, "much less coordinate anything." That said, Stern allowed that he was unexcited by the latest talk concerning Russia and Iran.

Anyone who knows the history of OPEC knows that the cartel was a disorganized, squabbling bunch of oil producers that grew in fits and starts until the day it finally coalesced. Since then, OPEC has robbed consumers of some seven trillion dollars. Meanwhile, President Bush mentions our addiction to fossil fuels year after year (six and counting) in his State of the Union address but almost nothing convincing has been done to break that addiction, constrain our consumption, or develop alternative sources of energy in a meaningful way. As we teeter on the brink of environmental disaster, we learn that yet another group of fossil fuel producers is making plans to pick our pockets. If we are stupid enough to sit by and let them get richer as we despoil the only planet we have, we will deserve everything we get.

It Was Always about the Oil, Stupid
September 18, 2007

Finally, someone in a position of influence in Washington, D.C., someone who can't be accused of playing partisan politics, has spoken the truth about George W. Bush's invasion of Iraq: It was primarily about the oil.

Alan Greenspan, the former Federal Reserve chairman who attained rock star status during his tenure in Washington, declares in his new memoir, *The Age of Turbulence: Adventures in a New World* (London: Penguin, 2007) that "the Iraq War is largely about oil." Calling his admission a "politically inconvenient fact," the maestro, as his fans pronounced him during his star turn in our nation's capital, has struck a rather dissonant chord for the Bush administration, which has insisted—and will vehemently continue to insist—that oil had nothing to do with our disastrously divisive and tragic invasion of Iraq.

We all know the changing and changeable list of White House–proclaimed motives for our decision to start a war, ranging from Saddam Hussein's alleged store of weapons of mass destruction to America's duty to bring freedom and democracy to Iraq to the need to deal a decisive blow to Islamic terrorists. We also know that we are now bogged down in a civil war with no apparent end. But I do not intend to discuss herein whether this war is right or wrong. Rather, I would like to describe some evidence that points to the truth of Greenspan's assertion. The administration has begun to hit back, with Secretary of Defense Robert Gates challenging Greenspan's version of events during an appearance on ABC's *This Week* (which aired September 16, 2007), and we can expect that the self-serving pronouncements will flow freely. So it's important to recall the facts.

To begin with, after toppling Saddam Hussein, the United States passed up a golden opportunity to break Iraq's ties with OPEC, thereby removing its vast reserves of crude oil from the cartel's manipulative grip. Instead, the Bush administration hastened to reinstate the connection, claiming that America had no business intervening in Iraq's dealings with the malevolent cartel.

Of course, we had no such qualms about intervening in every other aspect of Iraqi life, randomly arresting and imprisoning thousands of Iraqi men, dissolving the Iraqi army, purging the country's institutions of the only people who knew how things worked, and virtually guaranteeing that an anti-United States insurgency would emerge despite, or perhaps because of, the amateurish ministrations of Paul Bremer, head of the Coalition Provisional Authority.

But when it came to oil, we pretended to be hands-off. In reality, however, we first enlisted oil professional Philip J. Carroll, formerly of Shell, to advise the Iraqi oil ministry. Then, after Rob McKee, a former ConocoPhillips executive with ties to Halliburton, entered the picture, it was full steam ahead on building a strong national oil company that would be dependent on big oil consultants and destined to rejoin the OPEC band of extortionists. As Greg Palast wrote in *Harper's* ("OPEC on the March: Why Iraq still sells its oil à la cartel," April 1, 2005), any objections from the Iraqi governing council were summarily dismissed, while Vice President Dick Cheney openly advocated an OPEC-friendly policy for Iraq.

For the oil boys, it was merely business as usual, the American consumer and the world economy be damned. Oil has climbed from $28/bbl in September of 2003 to more than $80/bbl in September of 2007. This increase in oil price alone is costing the American consumer an additional four hundred billion dollars a year. The consumer is only peripherally on the mind of an administration beholden to big oil and big oil prices, even if that means war, with all its costs in blood and treasure.

Boycott Iran's Oil Immediately
June 21, 2009

What we are witnessing on television and over the airwaves is an abomination and an outrage to all fair-minded people. The sight of the street beatings of innocents, of the shooting of demonstrators, of the silent march of millions in Iran exposes the emptiness and extremism of the governing mullahs. How events will unfold is as yet unknown, but the world is watching and absorbing the tweets and blog commentaries now making the use of brute force against the demonstrators a matter of record.

There is no doubt that the current Iranian government holds two trump cards. The first is guns and a trained and disciplined coterie of government enforcers to turn on the dissidents. The second, of course, is the huge cash flow coming from the nation's sales of oil. As Thomas L. Friedman pointed out in today's *New York Times* op-ed "Bullets and Barrels," the mullahs have been using their oil income to "buy off huge swaths of the population with [...] subsidized food and gasoline. It's also used its crude to erect a vast military force—namely the revolutionary guard and the Basij militia—to keep itself in power."

Well, there is something that could be done immediately to show the world's solidarity with the courage of the demonstrators and to show disgust with the behavior of the Iranian government. We, the world, could simply stop buying Iranian oil. Though the United States does not currently import Iranian crude, the fungibility of oil is such that our government's support for such a boycott would carry a great deal of weight. The cutoff of Iranian oil shipments through a boycott is feasible, given the structure of today's oil market. Inventories throughout the world are filled to overflowing, and supertankers are loaded with hundreds of millions of bbl of oil, lying at anchor at sea, waiting for customers or for storage on shore.

Then there is the production capability of other sources. Saudi

Arabia alone has 4.5 million bbl of daily crude production and shipping capability shut in and readily accessible. This 4.5 million-bbl-per-day production now sitting idle is more than twice the level of Iran's daily exports of some 2.1 million bbl per day.

Without an income from oil, Iran's dictatorship would be increasingly vulnerable. It is long past time for the world to draw the line on the political and ethical perversions of those who control the oil supply. It would be a significant step in breaking oil's grip on our future and an enormous gesture of support to Iran's brave people. Let the boycott begin as the world's answer to the murder of Neda Agha-Soltan.

Oil Nabobs Slouching Toward Iran:
Time for a People's Boycott
May 23, 2010

On March 15, the tanker *Front Page* left the port of Fujairah in the United Arab Emirates, reportedly to drop anchor at another port in the United Arab Emirates. Then it was scheduled to sail on to Saudi Arabia. This is according to the *Wall Street Journal's* front-page article of May 20, 2010, entitled "Oil Trade with Iran Thrives, Discreetly."

Tracking information, however, revealed a different course. The *Front Page* made an unreported stop along the coast of Iran to load a cargo of Iranian oil. Illegal? No. Impolitic? Very much so, given the acute political tensions and the draconian oppression the Iranian government imposes upon its people—hardly the kind of company one would like to be seen keeping. Who was the charterer of the *Front Page*? None other than Royal Dutch Shell, the same company currently in the process of petitioning Alaska and the US government to drill exploratory wells in the Arctic's Beaufort and Chukchi Seas this summer. The Department of the Interior is presently reviewing Shell's application for a permit to drill. Given the BP gulf oil disaster, there is widespread concern and push back in Congress to hold back any and all permits until causes of the disaster are known. Given the evident duplicity of those with whom they are dealing, this is clearly not a bad idea.

The rest of us should know that the next time we tank up at a Shell station, we might well be helping the mullahs of Iran. But Shell is not alone in doing a "brisk business buying Iranian oil" (Steve Stecklow,

Spencer Swartz and Margaret Coker, "Oil Trade with Iran Thrives, Discreetly," the *Wall Street Journal*, May 20, 2010). Yes, you guessed it; here, too, BP stands tall. Along with BP, there is Total SA, the French oil giant. Being a dutiful yet circumspect customer of the mullahs, a Total SA–chartered tanker recently turned off its tracking transponder throughout its sail into Iranian waters and its loading of oil at an Iranian port of call. In case you may not have known, this is the same Total SA, parent of Total Petrochemicals USA, Inc., that has production facilities in Louisiana and Texas that produce a range of base chemicals, including polyethylene and polystyrenes.

The *Journal* goes on to report that none of current sanction proposals in the United Nations or the United States would target Iran's export oil business, which happens to generate nearly half of the Iranian government's revenue. The reason for this is concern that an embargo would cause a spike in the price of oil and severely affect the economies of such major importers of Iranian oil as Japan, India, and China. One needs to question whether this is anything more than the rationale trotted out by the oil companies themselves and delivered by their well-heeled lobbyists to our gullible bureaucrats. These are the very oil companies and oil interests who find it convenient, not to mention highly profitable, to trade in Iranian oil!

Consider the following. Today, the world is awash in oil. Oil storage is bulging at the seams from Cushing, Oklahoma, to Rotterdam, to Singapore. Iran currently exports some two million bbl per day, a quantity that would scarcely be missed given the supplies currently available. Then there is Saudi Arabia, which is capable of producing more than twelve million bbl per day, but it's currently pumping just eight million; the four million-bbl difference is twice Iran's exports. The Saudis could easily, and probably happily, make up for any Iranian shortfall without moving the price of oil a nickel. Should the Saudis not be cooperative, should they seek to exploit the situation to their own advantage, they need only be reminded that, if the Iranians should come knocking someday with pistols in hand and should the Saudis lift the hotline to call Washington, no one will be home to answer.

It stands to reason that embargoing Iranian oil through governmental or business initiatives could be a highly effective way of dealing with the renegade Iranian regime and with minimal impact on the price of oil, if done thoughtfully. This combined with a policy of shaming those who continue to do business with Iranian agencies, either directly or indirectly, would be an effective adjunct to such an embargo policy.

Finally, if governments don't act, we as consumers can take much into our own hands by boycotting those products that may well have been produced from Iranian oil. Given the sourcing policies of oil companies such as Shell, BP, and Total SA, one should be cognizant of the fact that he may be supporting Iran by doing business with Iran. If the international oil companies and our government do not take the initiative of boycotting Iranian oil in order to bring down a murderous regime, then we must exercise our individual initiative, in solidarity with the oppressed people of Iran. It is past time for each of us to commit to a people's boycott of any product produced in whole or in part from Iranian oil, be it gasoline, heating oil, fuel oil, base chemicals, and so on. It is the least we can do, given the depredations suffered by the Iranian people.

Chavez Foolishly Threatens Oil Cutoff
July 28, 2010

The United States is the largest oil consumer in the world. The United States consumes some nineteen million bbl per day, while China remains a distant second at around 9.2 million bbl per day. Yet the American public has become keenly aware of the growing risks inherent in the unbridled consumption of fossil fuels—economically, environmentally, and in terms of our national security. Further, our public has come to understand the voracious and shameless opportunism of the oil producers in moving the price of oil ever higher for as long as they can and for as much profit as they can grab.

Among the leading miscreant producer nations is Hugo Chavez's Venezuela, not only in terms of being a rapacious oil supplier but also in terms of confrontational and malicious policies toward the United States—to say nothing of the increasing subjugation of Venezuelans. Now Chavez threatens us with the absurd boast that Venezuela "would suspend oil shipments to the United States even if we have to eat stones here," (Frank Jack Daniel, "Chavez threatens US oil cut in Colombia dispute," *Reuters*, July 26, 2010) should hostilities break out between

Venezuela and Colombia. This should awaken us to the trump card we have never taken to the oil gaming table, probably because our oil industry and lobbied interests prevent us from using it.

That trump card—the reality that we are the world's largest oil consumer and will be for years to come—bestows on us an importance in the realm of buyer/seller equal to and exceeding the ability of any individual nation to supply us its oil. Therefore, would it not make sense—especially as our needs diminish and as other sources become available from alternative fuels and natural gas—to limit imports from nations that espouse policies inimical to our interests?

Such limitation could readily be accomplished by subjecting all imports of oil to import permits according to country of origin. By simply limiting or refusing import permits to those nations whose policies run belligerently counter to our interests, we would finally—as far as oil matters go—be instituting the normal relationship between buyer and seller in which the buyer calls the tune or, at the very least, can play his hand. These import permits need not be draconian nor a hindrance to the free flow of goods. But when a Hugo Chavez's bellicosity goes one step too far, we will at least have a tool of policy to make him aware that access to the American market can no longer be taken for granted.

Oil Market Manipulation Has Crude Prices Sky High
August 23, 2010

It makes no sense. Today's price of oil is $74/bbl, which shows a retreat these past days from more than $80/bbl. This price is more than 100 percent higher than the $33/bbl touched in February 2009. Land storage, meanwhile, is so filled to the brim that more than thirty million bbl are kept in floating storage at sea. As but one example, Kuwait's crude oil exports to Japan plunged by 47 percent to less than five million bbl per month. In spite of the summer driving season, inventories of gasoline in the United States are rising. Supplies of oil at Cushing, Oklahoma, the delivery point for the New York Mercantile Exchange futures contract, are less than 1 percent below the all-time high that was reached in May of this year. According to a Department of Energy report, inventories in a fifteen-state region that includes Illinois rose to 97.7 million bbl earlier this month, which is the highest it's been since the department started recording data in 1980. The price of crude, taken together with the country's jobless rate of 9.6 percent, makes no sense at all. Clearly, the price of oil has lost all ballast with respect to the dynamic of supply and demand.

I have written extensively about the machinations of OPEC, the speculative excess on the commodity exchanges, the manipulated oil trading by the oil producers, and myriad other factors responsible for making oil prices—and the prices we pay for downstream products like gasoline, heating oil, and diesel—an outrageous and indefensible tax on the public weal. Please, I am talking about the price of oil, the price of these products, and the transfer of billions upon billions of dollars to oil interests. The issue of oil and fossil fuel consumption and the impact on the environment is something else altogether and cannot be solved by making the oil producers and speculators richer.

It's interesting to note that an article in the *Wall Street Journal* (Carolyn Cui, "Stocks, Oil Moving in Lockstep" [was "Oil Gets a New Dance Partner: Stocks"], August 16, 2010, http://online.wsj.com/article/SB10 001424052748703382304575431332123881218.html) marveled at the correlation between stock prices and oil prices. Yet, as we dig a little deeper into the article, a much more significant fact is touched upon. The author writes, "Oil and stocks are joined up by actual money flows as more fund managers start to trade in both markets. Many of them are so-called 'algorithmic traders,' who trade based on technical signals instead of fundamentals."

The article goes on to explain that "[i]n recent years commodity exchanges have built up their technologies to allow easier access for computer-based traders, which have become a dominant force in some markets." Wayne Penello, the founder of Risked Revenue Energy Associates, was quoted as saying that traders "tend to do the same things at the same time not because of the fundamentals, rather because there's so much money under management that they have become the markets." According to Walter Zimmermann, chief technical analyst at United-ICAP who was quoted in the article, "Whatever is producing this phenomenon is growing in force, not waning in force."

For those who doubt that the oil market can be or is being manipulated, note that only last week, the Commodity Futures Trading

Commission reached a twelve million-dollar settlement with ConAgra Trade Group, which the Commodity Futures Trading Commission accused of purposely executing a trade for an oil futures contract at a non–bona fide price. In January 2008, ConAgra instructed a floor trader on the New York Mercantile Exchange to close a spot market futures contract at $100/bbl, thereby giving him the bragging rights of being the first to break the $100/bbl barrier. The basis of the Commodity Futures Trading Commission's action was that the trade was an infraction of the exchange rule that "prohibits transactions that cause a price to be reported that is not a true and bona fide price" (Edward Wyatt, "Ex-ConAgra Unit Settles with U.S. Over Artificial Oil Trade," *New York Times*, August 16, 2010, http://www.nytimes.com/2010/08/17/business/17ftc.html). Scott D. O'Malia, one of the Commodity Futures Trading Commission commissioners, made it known that he would have preferred the commission to vote to pursue a case for attempted manipulation rather than the lesser charge.

Well, there it is. If ConAgra Trade Group was hit with a twelve million-dollar fine because it caused a non–bona fide price level to be reported, then a strong argument must be made that those algorithmic traders—those responding to technical signals rather than to fundamentals or trading simply because there is so much money under management that they become the market and override the fundamentals—are breaching the guidelines set forth by the Commodity Futures Trading Commission and replicating in form and spirit the non–bona fide price level that resulted from ConAgra's trade, except in far greater measure.

Of course, the situation of distorted trading on the commodity exchanges could be contained in large measure if Congress stepped in to restrict participation of computer-based traders. But don't hold your breath. The oil boys would harness their K Street lobbying teams, who are the best that oil money can buy, and combine forces with the Wall Street speculators in order to squelch any effort to bring some rationality, some sanity, some semblance of fair play back to the oil-trading pits.

The oil interests have the money to do it, and we have a Congress whose election campaigns yearn for the money they can provide and are thus happy do their bidding. As consumers, we in turn have no alternative but to pay, pay, pay; the oil interests and the speculators gorge themselves on billions in undeserved margins and profits, while great swaths of our population are suffering massive economic turmoil.

Yet our administration continues to snooze away on this issue that is central to the nation's economic well-being.

Saudi Arabia Takes a Leadership Role in Confronting Iran
December 8, 2010

Perhaps it was only a dream, perhaps it was a WikiLeaks moment, but whatever the case, I hasten to pass along this news I stumbled upon.

> We here in Saudi Arabia are fully cognizant of the existential danger that Iran and its nuclear program now present to the kingdom and to the peace and well-being of the gulf region. We know that a conflagration would be cataclysmic not only to Saudi Arabia and its neighboring states but also to the world at large.
>
> Saudi Arabia also understands that beseeching the United States to "cut off the head of the snake," meaning the government of Iran, is unbecoming to its dignity and standing in the world. This is especially true in that a US naval task force, at a cost of some one hundred million dollars per day to American taxpayers, is already patrolling what we here identify as the Arabian Gulf and the Straits of Hormuz. This task force is present to keep shipping lanes open and, as is understood, to act as protector of the Saudi coastline and as guarantor of Saudi Arabia itself against any Iranian aggression.
>
> Saudi Arabia further understands that it must assume responsibility for its own lax attitude toward the funding of terrorist groups by Saudi financial institutions, extremist organizations, wayward citizens, and other entities.
>
> Given its worldwide influence, the moment has come for Saudi Arabia to take up the mantle of leadership in dealing with the issue of an irredentist Iran, which is moving the region toward a crisis.
>
> Saudi Arabia has also come to understand that the

blessing of its vast oil reserves not only gives it a path to vast riches but also vests it with major responsibilities. Henceforward, it will exercise these responsibilities in a manner worthy of its standing and traditions to bring honor and peace to a troubled region and to win the respect of the family of nations.

It is well understood that Iran's oppression of its people and its nuclear ambitions are financed almost exclusively by its production and export of oil. Income from oil is almost the sole source of revenue for its illegitimate regime. Without oil revenues, this government would falter, and the flow of vast amounts of Iran's wealth to its nuclear development and missile program would come to a halt.

Saudi Arabia understands the world's fear that the disruption of Iran's oil shipments would cause the price of oil to increase dramatically, thereby setting back an already tenuous economic recovery.

With the cooperation of the world's oil consumers, Saudi Arabia has it within its purview to end the malign regime in Iran without a shot being fired. It can do so without interrupting the free flow of oil either, ensuring that the world's economies are not affected in any way by oil scarcity or higher costs—matters of grave concern in any scenario of confrontation with Iran.

Saudi Arabia, with the assistance of consuming nations and responsible governments worldwide, will call for a total boycott on purchases of Iranian crude. It can and will make available the consequent shortfall by increasing its own production to levels replacing normal Iranian oil exports (or more) to guarantee price stability. No warships need be engaged. The world will simply stop buying Iranian oil, which can be replaced by Saudi Arabia alone or in coordination with other gulf producers such as Kuwait, the United Arab Emirates, and Bahrain—nations equally vulnerable to a bellicose Iran.

Iran exports some two million bbl of oil per day.

Saudi Arabia's oil production capacity is 12.5 million bbl per day. Currently, and for the past few years, Saudi production has been but 8.5 million bbl per day, leaving an excess production capability of four million bbl per day. That is twice Iran's export loadings.

Saudi Arabia would keep this policy in place until the current Iranian regime is dissolved and the Iranian people are free to choose its successor.

Although the above has been garnered from this writer's imagination, if sometime in the near or distant future, you should read this or something similar, remember, you read it here first.

SECTION II

Enemies Domestic

Part VI

Policymakers and Big Oil

versus the Rest of Us

Bravo, BP! Those Record Earnings Really Help. Alaska and the Nation Thank You!
August 9, 2006

Last quarter, BP's earnings stood at $7.3 billion—another record. Its earnings continue at stupendous levels, but a lot of good that has done for the care and maintenance of its Alaska pipeline infrastructure. The level of mismanagement, purposeful or otherwise, has Representative John Dingell calling for Congressional hearings and expressing his outrage. He said, "It's appalling that BP let this critical pipeline deteriorate to the point that a major shutdown was necessary."

MSNBC reported that allegations about BP's maintenance practices have been so persistent that a criminal investigation is underway into whether BP has deliberately shortchanged maintenance and falsified records to cover it up for years. Furthermore, current BP employees claim they've been told to falsify records and to cut back on chemical applications that are ordinarily put into the system to retard rust and corrosion. A federal official confirmed that many of these workers have also talked to the FBI.

In announcing the shutdown, BP acknowledged that a key maintenance procedure to check for sludge, otherwise known as "pigging," had not been performed for more than a decade. In an interview with *NBC News*, Thomas J. Barrett, a federal official with the Department of Transportation's Office of Pipeline Safety, stated bluntly, "What disappointed me was their failure to maintain these lines to an accepted industry level of care" (Aram Roston, Lisa Myers, and the NBC Investigative Unit, "Was the BP Pipeline Problem Preventable?," msnbc. msn.com, August 9, 2006, http://www.msnbc.msn.com/id/14251436/ ns/nightly_news-nbc_news_investigates/). So much for oil company profits and the use to which they are put to husband the nation's natural resources. One must begin to ask whether the nation is being taken advantage of by the oil industry and the deeply vested interests, whose avarice is now veering far afield of the nation's trust and well-being.

I have one last point, if the above isn't enough. While grievously shortchanging pipeline maintenance (not to speak of the Texas City Refinery disaster the year before), BP found $8.5 billion—I repeat, $8.5

billion—to buy back 725 million of its shares during the first half of 2006 alone and to raise its dividend by 11 percent.

Nice work if you can get it. Thanks, BP.

The Department of the Interior Plays Patsy to the Oil and Gas Industries
November 3, 2006

The Department of the Interior's inspector general, Earl Devaney, recently accused top officials in his agency of fostering a culture of managerial irresponsibility that tolerates conflicts of interest. "Short of crime, anything goes at the Department of the Interior," ran Devaney's *j'accuse* ("Fixing Interior," *New York Times*, December 16, 2008, http://www.nytimes.com/2008/12/17/opinion/17wed1.html).

Representative George Miller was moved to comment, "If things keep going like this, we're going to need two sets of handcuffs—one for the oil companies and one for the bureaucrats" (Edmund Andrews, "Interior Official Says She Will Not Try to Recoup Lease Money," *New York Times*, September 22, 2006). That was after the Department of the Interior's announcement, in mid-September, that it would not try to recover the billion-plus dollars lost as a result of flawed oil and gas leases it signed in the late 1990s. According to the Government Accountability Office, the investigative arm of Congress, losses of more than twenty billion dollars could accumulate over the next decades.

One would think, given its performance in crafting the flawed leases, the department would be doubly vigilant and aggressive in pursuing malfeasance in the oil patch. Yet if anyone still doubts that the fix is in at the Department of the Interior, just read Edmund Andrews's damning story entitled "US Drops Bid Over Royalties from Chevron" in the October 31, 2006, *New York Times*.

Petitioning under the Freedom of Information Act—apparently the only way to get to the truth—Andrews learned that "[t]he interior department has dropped claims that the Chevron Corporation systematically underpaid the government for natural gas produced in the Gulf of Mexico, a decision that could allow energy companies to avoid paying hundreds of millions of dollars in royalties.[...] The decision also sets a precedent that could make it easier for oil and gas companies to lower the value of what they pump each year from federal property and thus their payments to the government."

After charging that Chevron's accountants had been systematically stiffing the US government for payments owed on gas taken from the Gulf of Mexico, the Department of the Interior asked the energy giant for a six million-dollar back payment in royalties. But now it has stepped away from even that modest effort, claiming that it's useless to fight Chevron, because a department appeals board previously shot down another similar case. This reasoning looks like an industry-friendly stretch, because state governments and private landowners were successful in winning seventy million dollars more in royalties from Chevron in what was an essentially analogous situation. Why did the federal government cave in so easily?

The energy lobby has spent hundreds of millions of dollars to curry favor with the administration and members of Congress, which have subsequently allowed the companies to gain oil and gas drilling rights on federal lands for a pittance and pushed through very generous depletion allowances (the allowance available to account for the reduction of resources as a product is pumped or mined and sold), favorable tax incentives, and royalty-relief giveaways (that translates to allowing the royalty payments for the extraction of resources to be reduced or waived altogether). Meanwhile, the Department of the Interior has made things worse by letting the companies get away without proper audits.

Foot-dragging by the administration has only compounded the calamity. According to the piece in the *Times*, "[A]dministration officials knew that dozens of companies had incorrectly claimed exemptions from royalties since 2003, but they waited until December 2005 to send letters demanding about $500 million in repayments." Given the Department of the Interior's management style, many more billions in royalty payments could be lost to the US treasury.

Robert T. Dorman, a lawyer for private citizens who are suing Chevron, stated that "[t]he government is giving up without a fight," and he's right. This crony-infested agency, whose seemingly willful incompetence and managerial irresponsibility have already been documented by government investigators, is an outrage. And it's outrageous that our government lets the US Department of the Interior continue a campaign to grease the way for the gas and oil companies as they rape our resources. After all, the money being lost is money owed on the natural resources on public lands, which does not belong to the oil companies but is part of *our* national patrimony.

The Department of Energy's Craven Obeisance to the Oil and Gas Gougers
November 14, 2006

According to *Reuters*, the Bush administration has little complaint with the production cuts OPEC plans in its attempts to support oil prices that now hover around $60/bbl. Quite incredibly, Secretary of Energy Samuel Bodman was quoted as saying, "I can't tell you that I'm dissatisfied with where it all is, but we'll see" ("US Energy Sec Says Not Dissatisfied with OPEC Cuts," *Reuters*, November 13, 2006, http://uk.reuters.com/article/2006/11/13/energy-usa-opec-idUKWAT00656420061113).

For our own Department of Energy to provide public cover to any attempt by OPEC (price gougers par excellence) to manipulate oil prices is patently outrageous. It is tantamount to providing moral blessing and political support to monopoly behavior that would be showered with indictments were these American corporations that were acting in a similarly collusive fashion. Only an administration that is bought and run by oil interests would permit itself such an egregious position that is so blatantly against the common good and the nation's economic interest (though, through the resulting inflated oil prices, highly profitable for the oil industry). Expressions of outrage at the oil cartel's attempt to artificially raise prices would have been the appropriate response, which would have exactly reflected the national weal.

According to the International Energy Agency, the cuts are especially ill-timed "because demand will increase as the heating season nears" (Stephen Voss and Maher Chmayteli, "OPEC Agrees to Cut Production to Stem Oil-Price Slide (Update 7)," Bloomberg.com, October 20, 2006, http://www.bloomberg.com/apps/news?pid=newsarchive&sid=ahDA_MZkxovY&refer=home). Compare Bodman's reaction to the pointed response of the agency's executive director, Claude Mandil, to the announced OPEC cuts and the threat by Saudi oil minister Ali al-Naimi for further cuts in December. Mandil said, "I think this cut comes at the worst time possible. I don't like the idea of OPEC trying to defend prices of $60 a barrel. That is not helpful to consumer nations and poorer countries"(Stephen Voss and Maher Chmayteli, "OPEC Agrees to Cut Production to Stem Oil-Price Slide (Update 7)," Bloomberg.com, October 20, 2006, http://www.bloomberg.com/apps/news?pid=newsarchive&sid=ahDA_MZkxovY&refer=home).

It's long past time that we, as a nation, took our government back from the oil and gas interests.

An Energy Agenda for a New Age and Newly Energized Congress
November 17, 2006

Before last week's midterm election, Speaker-to-be Nancy Pelosi and her colleagues spoke about reducing oil industry subsidies and rescinding the tax cuts that Congress bestowed on energy companies last year. That's all well and good, but now, with the significant changes in the House and Senate, an opportunity has presented itself to do much more. Given the election results, Congress has a public mandate to fashion a comprehensive, long-term policy that corrects our most glaring sins and deficiencies—to name only a few: rigged prices, federal subservience to the industry, weak support for alternative fuels, and minimal support for conservation—and to put us on track to achieving true energy independence. The time for paying lip service to this issue has passed.

What steps might we take as a nation? Here are some I would like to propose to guide our thinking as citizens on these important issues, to help shape dialogue in Washington, and to point us toward a rational energy future. I suggest that we:

- create a National Oil Trust to oversee our still-undeveloped and hugely significant energy resources;

- clamp down on oil industry royalty and depreciation practices, which shortchange the American taxpayer, fatten oil company profits, and deprive the nation of a clear and significant revenue stream that could be dedicated to programs aimed at reducing our dependence on fossil fuels;

- make efforts to bring the price of oil down, starting with greater transparency and oversight in energy trading markets to prevent price manipulation (Remember, high oil prices transfer enormous wealth to malign regimes, fund international terrorism and insurgencies around the world, and place our nation at grave geopolitical risk);

- make the oil industry's monetary contributions and lobbying initiatives, which are designed to influence government energy policy, transparent;

- restructure the Department of the Interior to eliminate deep-seated oil industry favoritism;

- ensure that the Department of Energy ends its acquiescence to OPEC manipulation and begins to take a more cogent and proactive policy when OPEC and other suppliers insist on playing monopoly games and colluding to cut supplies to drive up their prices and profits;

- revoke the sovereign immunity of OPEC suppliers, thus opening them to antitrust charges;

- mount a full-scale drive to achieve energy independence by backing the full gamut of alternative fuel sources, including conservation initiatives, citizen-initiated lifestyle changes, and tax support for hybrid vehicles; and

- consider introducing consumer vouchers for gasoline, diesel, and other oil-related products, which would reduce their usage by establishing a national cap on their consumption. With a voucher program in place, we would have the added benefit of having a system extant to quickly and fairly allocate energy resources were a major oil shock ever to occur.

Time for a National Oil and Gas Trust
November 20, 2006

The new Democratic leaders in Congress may need a few days to get their governing legs, but they might ideally reach across the aisle and join hands with the Republicans to stop, once and for all, our government's ongoing and abject relinquishing of power to the oil industry. The new

Congress could strike a powerful first blow by spearheading a bipartisan effort to set up a national oil trust.

A national oil trust would be empowered to develop and manage, with pointed environmental sensitivity, the enormous, still-untapped energy reserves located on our public lands and underneath the oceans just off our continental shelf. The Western oil shale reserves are the largest in the world; it is time for them to be developed so that we might wean ourselves away from dependency on oil imports from unstable and exploitative suppliers.

The trust could be modeled on Norway's petroleum directorate, the stated objective of which is to contribute and create the greatest public value for Norwegian society from Norway's oil and gas deposits. The Norwegian government also created a national oil company, Statoil, whose primary function is the marketing and distribution of the Norwegian state's direct interest in each production operation.

The Norwegian state owns a 70-percent share interest in Statoil. The viability of this arrangement is best attested by the fact that the twenty largest shareholders of the remaining 30 percent include such decidedly unsocialist entities as J.P. Morgan Chase, Mellon Bank, Citigroup Global Markets, State Street Bank and Trust, and Fidelity Funds Europe. Profits from oil and gas operations accrue to the Norwegian government's pension fund and are invested in conservative bonds and stocks.

Were we to work out a similar arrangement, out trust could and should be mandated to direct its revenues from these investments toward developing alternative energy sources and expanding mass transportation, thereby becoming a cornerstone of a long-term program toward breaking our environmentally deleterious addiction to fossil fuels.

Why set up a trust? So that we can stop the giveaway to the oil and gas companies and start developing our national patrimony for the good of all Americans. The energy companies currently pay pitifully small royalties to the federal government for the privilege of extracting and profiting enormously from resources that rightfully belong to the public. Who provides those enormous profits? We consumers do when we are forced to buy back our oil and gas in the form of refined products like gasoline, heating oil, and diesel fuel—all priced at extortionist, monopoly-derived prices (read, OPEC). These prices bear no rational relationship to the companies' costs of production. In other words, the American public is getting fleeced at both ends of the pump.

Congress should also restructure the Department of the Interior to ensure that oil industry interests don't continue to blatantly trump those of the nation as a whole. Right now, between the up-front royalty rollbacks, depletion allowances on oil and gas already pumped, tax depreciation credits, and shockingly weak oversight, the energy producers are profiteering with the approval of an oil-lobby-addled government at our expense. The energy industry must pay its fair share in monies that could be better used to help liberate us from our addiction through myriad alternative energy programs. A national oil trust would go a long way to remedy these distortions. Given the new Congressional slate, the time for action is now.

"House Votes to Void Oil Company Tax Breaks. Humbug. We Have Former Interior Secretary Gale Norton on Our Side."
January 19, 2007

The title reflects the tune Shell is probably whistling while skipping down the halls of Congress to make sure that the Senate dilutes the House measure to void oil company tax breaks until it is meaningless. This administration has excelled at making appointments that could be characterized as "the less competent you are, the higher your position or award," and in that vein, Gale Norton has hit a home run.

As President Bush's appointed Secretary of the Interior, Gale Norton served from January 2001 to March 2006. In an administration in which the buck has generally stopped nowhere, her tenure was highlighted by the Department of the Interior's inspector general, Earl Devaney, commenting that "[s]hort of crime, anything goes at the Department of the Interior" ("Fixing Interior," *New York Times*, December 16, 2008, http://www.nytimes.com/2008/12/17/opinion/17wed1.html). This from the man whose mandate it is to provide independent oversight in order to assure integrity and accountability effectiveness and efficiency within the program's operations and management of the Department of the Interior.

But not to worry. The oil patch can handle it. Who does the House think it is, anyway? The nation has a higher calling, and Shell is riding to the rescue of all its brethren in the oil game. Because of Shell's beneficence, Gale Norton is back. She has been hired by Shell to serve as general counsel for Shell's unconventional resources division (i.e., the branch focusing on emerging technologies for oil shale and heavy oil). That's all well and good, but it would be interesting to see her telephone log in the weeks to come. How many calls will she make to the Department of the Interior, and how many calls and visits will she make to the Hill?

It raises the whole issue of public sector employees being hired by industries with whom they have had a fiduciary relationship. It is a problem that has been rampant in the Congressional past to the grave detriment of the nation's interests and to the great benefit of the well-oiled and well-connected special interests. Will this new Congress really change anything, or will it just be all talk and no substance? What do you want to bet?

Twenty Billion Dollars Later, Halliburton Moves Its Headquarters to Dubai
March 12, 2007

Business must be slowing down in Iraq. After booking more than twenty billion dollars in revenues from its work in Iraq—some on no-bid contracts—and now under Congressional scrutiny for both the quality of its work and its billing practices, Halliburton is moving its headquarters from Houston to Dubai. The company, together with its KBR unit, has been the Pentagon's largest contractor in Iraq.

The move is being met with outrage on Capitol Hill. Senator Patrick Leahy, chairman of the judiciary committee, voiced his anger, saying, "This is an insult to the US soldiers and taxpayers who paid the tab for their no-bid contracts and endured their overcharges for all these years" (Sonya Crawford, "Halliburton Moves Its Headquarters Abroad: Critics Pounce on News of War Contractor's Planned Move from Houston to

Dubai," *ABC News*, March 11, 2007, http://abcnews.go.com/WNT/Business/story?id=2942429&page=1).

Halliburton's chief executive, David Lesar, told reporters, "At this point in time, we clearly see there are greater opportunities in the eastern hemisphere than the western hemisphere" ("Halliburton to Move Headquarters to Middle East Hub of Dubai," *Reuters*, posted on FoxNews.com, March 12, 2007, http://www.foxnews.com/story/0,2933,258274,00.html). Halliburton did say it would maintain its legal registration in the United States. You see, that's not altogether unimportant if you want to continue doing business with the Pentagon.

To where, exactly, are Mr. Lesar and his band of brothers moving? Let me quote from an article on *BBC News* ("A Pakistani Laments Dubai," December 21, 2006) by one Masud Alam, a reporter from BBC's Urdu service. He said:

Dubai has always wanted to be something different from what it is. It has metamorphosed from a tiny fishing village to a modern city, then a shopper's paradise, a playground for the rich, a tourist's haven, and a lot more in just over half a century.[...] The city's skyline is made up of cranes.

He goes on to say:

> One aspect that hasn't changed in all these years is Dubai's fixation on 'quality expatriates'—a euphemism for white Europeans, or the rich and famous, or in particular the rich and famous white Europeans [...] I used to work for a newspaper here that paid different salaries to employees of different qualifications and work experience based on their ethnic origin. Whites topped the list, followed by Arabs, Indians and Pakistanis, the Filipinos, the Bangladeshis [...] This bias seems to be institutionalized now.
>
> The Asians, who make up the entire labour force that builds these fancy structures, are still the worst-paid workers, forced to live in out-of-town labor camps away from their loved ones for years at a stretch because they

cannot afford to travel back home or bring their families to live in Dubai.

A recent newspaper survey found that the labourers' pay and benefit packages have not been revised in more than a decade, whereas the cost of living has doubled or tripled in sectors like housing, healthcare, and utilities.

A company's values come from its leadership and its traditions. Maybe we should simply bid good riddance to Halliburton, but somebody on Capitol Hill should look into their continuing registration as a United States company.

Oil and the Eclipse of the American Century
April 16, 2007

Some one hundred years ago, Teddy Roosevelt was president of a robust and self-confident nation whose growing stature on the world stage permitted him, with great wisdom, to solemnly intone, "Speak softly and carry a big stick." A century later, those words have sadly been reduced to "Fractured syntax spoken loudly while wielding a broken stick."

Roosevelt understood the danger of overweening economic power. Heralded as the trustbuster, he did not hesitate to take on the powerful and the vested interests. He understood that constituencies, such as the railroads and the burgeoning oil industry, needed competition to unleash their full potential to service America's growing economy or, as with the railroads, some government oversight to keep their operations in line with the nation's interests. Thus, he argued for an interstate commerce commission with teeth to bring the excesses of the railroads to heel. He enlisted the Sherman Antitrust Act to break up the Standard Oil Company.

In 1904, an action was brought against Standard Oil, which was then controlling 91 percent of the nation's oil production and 85 percent of crude oil sales. Roosevelt understood that Standard Oil, as then constituted, would never of its own accord let the oil industry grow and nurture the nation's rapidly evolving needs without extracting monopoly profits, in essence a tax on the nation as a whole. Seven years later, the Supreme Court upheld earlier court rulings, and the great Standard Oil was broken up into thirty-four separate entities. With the government's victory, the oil industry embraced competition, and the nation prospered.

Today, by contrast, we have an administration wedded to the oil industry and a Congress prepared to do its bidding. We have a Department of the Interior that is, for all intents and purposes, an adjunct to the oil patch and a Department of Energy whose policies are supportive of ever-higher oil prices to the oil industry's benefit and the consuming public's detriment. The Department of Energy has never evinced the slightest willingness to confront the manipulation of oil prices, though it has helped higher prices along by filling to excess what has become that monster oil patch boondoggle, the strategic petroleum reserve.

One of the great anomalies of the oil industry today that is helping to distort the price of crude oil and that of gasoline, heating oil, fuel oil, and diesel is the vertical integration of the oil industry, whereby the oil companies are both producers and consumers of the industry's core raw material: crude oil. This fact has distorted the dynamics of crude oil trading and given carte blanche to OPEC to drive prices of both crude and gasoline, as well as the full gamut of downstream products, ever higher.

As President Bush, the former oilman, correctly informed us recently, "a lot of the price of gasoline depends on crude oil" ("President Bush Makes Remarks on the Emergency Supplemental," Office of the Press Secretary, April 3, 2007, http://georgewbush-whitehouse.archives. gov/news/releases/2007/04/print/20070403.html). We have a series of gargantuan and virtually unfettered integrated oil companies (Shell, BP, Occidental, Chevron, and so on) that both produce and trade oil while simultaneously being their own biggest consumers of oil, be it in their refineries or in their marketing outlets at the gas pump, the propane tank, or the home oil distributor.

The integrated oil companies have no incentive to bring down the price of crude. That's where the money is in billions upon billions. Simultaneously they have successfully diverted our focus to the nickels, dimes, and quarters at the gas pump or on our monthly heating oil bills, keeping us oblivious to the Beltway robbery going on down the road.

The rigging of the price of crude, helped along by the oil industry's vertical integration, has spun off undreamed of profits, making the oil companies as powerful and as ominous as the old Standard Oil. Today's oil industry enhances its clout by spending millions to buy influence in Washington through the brawn of its K Street lobbyists and with its generous contributions to key political action committees. Its influence is so pernicious that it not only gets a free pass in much of what it does domestically, irrespective of its impact on the nation's citizenry, but it also receives extensive government handouts in the form of tax credits, royalty abatements, and generous depletion credits through the Energy Policy Act of 2005, the Deep Water Royalty Relief Act of 1995, and the Federal Gas and Oil Royalty Management Act of 1982.

Most ominously, its influence has been instrumental in creating a national policy of irresponsible energy consumption that is leading the nation into foreign entanglements that have dramatically eclipsed America's stature and influence around the world, not to speak of the frightful volumes of blood and treasure expended. All this while the oil industry continues to prosper unashamedly.

Teddy Roosevelt fought for competitive markets. Now our government covers for manipulated markets because they're where the money and influence are. Take ExxonMobil; being the largest company, it is the one that most readily comes into focus, but it is by no means the only one. Its annual sales are $337 billion, from which they reported the largest after-tax profits ever for an American company at $39.5 billion (and an EBITDA well in excess of seventy billion dollars). ExxonMobil highlights that its profit margin, therefore, is a normal 10.4 percent of sales, and the company walks away smiling, firm in the belief that we have been duped once more.

Now this number does not deal with cash flow. It gives us no immediate sense of possible accelerated expenses, the method of inventory write-downs, or offsetting depletion allowances. Nor do we have an immediate sense of the enormous salaries being paid (to get a good sense of oil industry excess, consider that Occidental Petroleum paid its chief executive officer, Ray Irani, four hundred million dollars last year); nor of the additional golden parachutes comparable to the four hundred million dollars doled out to ExxonMobil's retiring chief executive officer, Lee Raymond; nor of the millions going to

Washington's K Street operatives; nor of the monies being poured into organizations, such as the Competitive Enterprise Institute, the Heartland Institute, and the International Policy Network, among others, devoted to questioning the science of global warming; nor the set-aside for the Valdez oil spill. All of these figures would give us a truer picture of what ExxonMobil's cash bonanza is being used for and what the company is doing to reduce—yes, reduce, not increase—its bottom line.

Crude is unquestionably the mainstay of its balance sheet. Consider that ExxonMobil reported in their 2007 summary annual report a production of more than six million bbl per day, which is the sum made up of 2.6 million bbl of crude products and 4.2 million bbl per day of oil equivalent, by converting gas production at six million cubic feet equals one thousand bbl. At today's price for crude, that translates to more than $130 billion a year on crude oil alone. The cost to produce this crude is certainly no more than $20/bbl. By far most of ExxonMobil's production was brought onstream more than a decade ago, when crude was selling in the low twenties or less and production and wells would in large measure have been capped were their production costs higher than the then-going market. The investment in many of these wells has long since been amortized. Using twenty dollars as an average cost basis (it is probably significantly less) and sales at sixty dollars would mean a gross profit on each bbl of forty dollars. ExxonMobil's fuel refining, lubricants, and petrochemical operation become bells and whistles when compared to crude oil's profit quotient. They do, however, serve as an effective cover, diverting our attention from the astronomical earnings generated by their in-house crude oil production.

Here's the rub, which Teddy Roosevelt would have understood: crude oil and its derived products are a patently manipulated market. Most of the end users—the integrated oil companies—have absolutely no incentive to push down the price of crude oil. Their brethren in OPEC blithely cut production whenever it suits them to ratchet up prices, and the integrated oil companies are their biggest cheerleaders. Together, they have successfully duped us into believing their spin that high crude oil prices are all about the invisible hand of market forces. It may indeed be the invisible hand, but it is the invisible hand of market manipulation.

There are, for example, the massive trading desks of the integrated oil companies doing what they can to support the pricing interests of their production divisions. BP, for one, made a substantial settlement with the New York Mercantile Exchange to resolve allegations of improper oil trading activities. Last year, the Commodity Futures Trading Commission outlined what it said was a scheme by BP to manipulate the price of propane to cause higher prices for residential and commercial consumers. Then, of course, there is the well-documented case of Enron's manipulation of the California gas market.

There seems to be nascent willingness in Washington to examine this issue. Senator Norm Coleman has said, "We need to explore legislative ideas to ensure that energy prices reflect the true market forces of supply and demand, and Senator Carl Levin said, "Right now, there is no cop on the beat overseeing energy trades on over-the-counter, electronic exchanges or foreign exchanges [...] Enron has already taught us how energy traders can manipulate prices and walk over consumers if they think no one is looking" (Senate Committee on Homeland Security and Governmental Affairs, "Levin-Coleman Report Finds Speculation Adding to Oil Prices: Put the Cop Back on the Beat," June 27, 2006, http://hsgac.senate.gov/public/index.cfm?FuseAction=Press. MinorityNews&ContentRecord_id=648ca6ed-b5b0-46ef-82b3-19e69163592e). It's sad to say that no one *is* looking in a systematic way, as yet. Teddy Roosevelt, we need you back.

What this industry also needs is a good dose of competition, in which refiners are no longer tied to oil producers, in which oil producers have to compete with one another to become suppliers to independent refineries. As currently constituted, the oil market presents a clear and present danger to the nation's welfare. The orchestrated high price of oil facilitates the transfer of billions to rogue or unstable regimes that would support those who wish us harm or who would harm us themselves, for that matter. The billions pouring into the oil companies enhance their ongoing influence in the halls of government.

As Teddy Roosevelt dealt with Standard Oil and the railroads, we need our own government to take action now to create real competition in the oil patch by breaking up the integrated oil companies. We need a government that borrows Teddy Roosevelt's bully pulpit to impart individual responsibility on the issue of global warming while we, in turn, keep pressure on Congress to rein in the nation's consumption of fossil fuels, irrespective of price and especially if their price should plunge.

Don't expect much from this administration. The newly elected Congress needs to do much more. To date, we have had little more than lip service. And remember, Teddy Roosevelt was a Republican.

Oil: A Defining Moment for Our Political Class and the Press
July 9, 2007

On Friday, I attended a seminar entitled "Where Have All the Leaders Gone?" with panelists William George and Sidney Harman and moderator David Gergen at the Aspen Ideas Festival. The subject was leadership and the qualities that make a leader, as discussed by a dauntingly brilliant group of panelists. The interchange focused on the shortcomings of our political class and came to the ominously pointed conclusion that "leadership has got to become more than the ability to raise money to become reelected."

That very morning, an article appeared in the *Wall Street Journal* with the headline "Why Bid to Allow Lawsuits against OPEC May Fly," thus presenting an issue of policy and a test of leadership that could not be more clearly drawn.

Not generally understood and barely reported on outside the pages of the *Journal*, the issue of challenging OPEC is a core test of our political class. The ability of OPEC to operate freely outside the law, hiding behind our sovereign immunity shield, has made it possible for the cartel to fix pricing in the oil market in such a manner that the oil companies and oil interests have benefited in the billions, if not in the trillions, at our expense over the past years without themselves risking being accused of collusionary practices. This gusher of money has given the oil interests enormous wherewithal to influence policy. The oil patch wants no interference with the status quo and will marshal all its ammunition to defeat this bill.

But perhaps a new day is dawning. In defiance of the oil lobby, Congress and the House of Representatives have overwhelmingly voted (70 votes to 23 in the Senate and 345 votes to 72 in the House) for the NOPEC bill, so dubbed because it would allow the international oil cartel OPEC to be sued under US antitrust law as are other cartels and antitrust violators. This was an act of refreshing and courageous leadership by our Congress.

But wait. The oil industry will not be counted out. The industry and its allies in the OPEC cartel have a powerful friend in our (one begins to wonder if it still is "our") administration. That, of course, is the President. The White House Office of Management and Budget has let it be known that it would advise the president to veto the bill, because litigating against OPEC could trigger a variety of serious legal, political, and economic headaches. You can bet the farm that the White House will come up with a full agenda of arcanely documented reasons (enthusiastically supplied by the K Street oil lobby crowd) to veto the bill. One might call it the "Iraq decision syndrome."

If one would judge the merits of the NOPEC bill by its detractors, one need look no further than the vocal opposition of the American Petroleum Institute, the trade association of the industry that has overseen a near 400 percent rise in the price of crude oil in the last seven years, happily cheering exploding prices all the way. There are, of course, the warnings by those parties interested in NOPEC's defeat who are cautioning us that, if sued, OPEC might reduce or cut supplies to the United States. Let them. They need us as customers as badly as we have counted on them as suppliers. For too long, it has been a one-way street. We do their bidding while they play us for fools. When the United Arab Emirates's oil minister, Mohamed bin Dhaen al-Hamli, not-so-subtly threatens, "[I]f the United States wants to sue [OPEC] member countries, it's extremely dangerous" (Ben Lando, "OPEC: NOPEC Bill Will Hurt U.S.," UPI.com, June 28, 2007, http://www.upi.com/Science_News/Resource-Wars/2007/06/28/OPEC-NOPEC-bill-will-hurt-US/UPI-29251183080388/), he should be promptly reminded that the American taxpayer is paying nearly one hundred million dollars per day to keep a naval fleet in the Persian Gulf (I know, some would prefer it be called the Arabian Gulf) to protect his coastline and the coastlines of other OPEC producers.

An important point in response to implied threats is that oil is a fungible commodity, meaning that supplies not delivered here will be delivered elsewhere, thereby freeing up other sources for shipment here.

This would also unmask the manipulative ambitions and fundamental unreliability of the OPEC suppliers, giving us further impetus to lead our economy toward a non–fossil fuel future.

One needs to keep in mind the profound importance of this issue. Bringing OPEC to reasonableness is a beginning step toward energy self-reliance. We must show that we are no longer afraid of the cartel's threats and that we will work assiduously toward minimizing our dependence on carbon-based fuels. We must make them understand that the time is not far away when they will need us as customers more than we need them as our supplier. For example, new drilling techniques for shale gas have changed a significantly dwindling supply of gas to a vast surplus over the last five years. The enormous expansion of nuclear facilities as in India and China, along with the conversion of transportation vehicles to electric power, will bring about major changes to fossil fuel consumption in the years ahead.

It is important that the press focus on this story, telling us about those in Congress who supported the NOPEC bill and shining a bright light on those opposed to it. Here we have Congress courageously working against vested interests. They should be fêted for their initiative in the nation's interest and their willingness to stand up against the oil lobby. Many would begin to have a renewed appreciation and respect for their work. It is the press's responsibility to make us aware that here, on this issue, we have an example of a Congress that has at last gone beyond the dead-end of a leadership limited to raising money to become reelected.

As for the president's threatened veto, let it be. It will further delineate his judgment and demonstrate who he is and what he stands for. Of course, there will be Prince Bandar cheering in the wings.

The US Department of Energy Pumps for Hugo Chavez
August 15, 2007

Hugo Chavez wants oil prices of $100/bbl. "I've always said prices were headed straight to $100 per barrel. We should prepare ourselves for these prices of one hundred dollars," said Chavez in a televised address this past Saturday on Venezuelan television to an assembled coterie of Caribbean leaders in Caracas. He said it before flying off to

London to preach the virtues of Venezuela's "Bolivarian Revolution" of resource nationalization to sympathetic members of parliament, trade unionists, and activists (Reuters, "Oil for $100/Barrel, Says Chavez," *The Economic Times*, August 13, 2007, http://economictimes. indiatimes.com/news/international-business/oil-for-100/barrel-says-chavez/articleshow/2276470.cms). According to *Reuters*, Chavez was welcomed to London by Mayor Ken Livingstone, who described the Bush administration as a gangster regime. His words for Chavez had a different ring; he said, "We salute you, Mr. President. Londoners stand with you, not with the oil companies and the oligarchs" (Gideon Long, "Chavez Warns against US Attack on Iran," *The Boston Globe*, May 15, 2006, http://www.boston.com/news/world/europe/articles/2006/05/15/ chvez_warns_against_us_attack_on_iran/).

No so fast, Mayor Livingstone. Those oil companies and oligarchs stick together. The price of oil is thicker than either blood or water. That $100/bbl is music to the oil patch's ears. If Hugo can bring it to pass for them, they'll love him for it, and Ken Livingstone can rant and rave about oil companies and oligarchs all he wants. Just bring on that C-note.

Leading the cheers and frantically waving pom-poms will be none other than our own subsidiary of the American Petroleum Institute, the US Department of Energy. Though it was created to look after the nation's energy interests, it has stooped to rationalizing oil price extortion and championing a manipulated market that has cost American and international consumers literally trillions over the years. In the past decade, the Department of Energy has witnessed an 800 percent increase in the price of oil and has scarcely signaled displeasure. Quite to the contrary, it has willfully reinforced the fiction that we are dealing with a free and unfettered market. It sees and hears no evil. It takes OPEC pronouncements as gospel and goes on to validate the fiction of OPEC's purported good intentions.

In the first days of August 2007 with oil prices reaching new contract all-time highs just short of $79/bbl, there was neither hue nor cry from the very department of our government charged with maintaining a sane balance of the oil and energy markets. Where were the pronouncements of outrage that the cartel and the oil industry had pushed prices to inexcusable levels? But we needn't have held our breath. In case you have lost sight of current realities, this is more the "oil industry" Department of Energy than it is the "US" Department of Energy. Samuel Bodman, our secretary of energy, stirred himself to lambaste OPEC in no uncertain terms, saying, "I'm concerned that we probably are going to need more oil, and I'm hopeful that the OPEC ministers […] will agree to that.[…] [C]urrent supply is a little short of what we'd like it to be." There! Take that, you OPEC bullies.

But what was he really saying? Let me conjecture:

Dear Ministers of OPEC, you have programmed and purposefully cut back shipments of oil by 1.7 million bbl per day so far this year. You have thereby been extraordinarily successful in raising prices by more than 50 percent in six months from $50/bbl in January to more than $75/bbl by the end of July. Please understand I am embarrassed to bring this up, knowing you have our, and certainly the oil industry's, best interests at heart. For appearances, I have to say something.

Not, of course, that a 50 percent increase in the price of such a core commodity as oil over a short six-month period is outrageous, but simply, as I have been quoted, that 'current supply is a little short of what we would like it to be.' Sort of like saying the price has gotten a bit high too fast, so let's slow it down a touch. Now, please understand, I'm not saying the price is too high, but I have all these gas consumers that I must deal with who feel they are paying through the nose at the end of the hose. Ha! Get it? Nose, hose? Oh well."

It should become clear to all, given this ludicrous Mutt and Jeff routine, that it was preordained for Chavez to push for and to expect to achieve prices of $100/bbl.

To show that he really means business, Secretary of Energy Bodman spoke to reporters via telephone from New Orleans on Wednesday, August 8, 2007, stating, "I expect I will be talking with oil ministers" before the next OPEC meeting on September 11("Bodman to Push OPEC for More Oil," *Reuters*, August 8, 2007, http://www.reuters. com/article/2007/08/08/us-bodman-opec-idUSN0833196320070808). When asked specifically whether that meant also speaking to Saudi Arabia's oil minister, he replied, and I quote verbatim, "It depends on what everybody's schedule is." There we have it. We're in good hands with our Department of Energy.

Oil Trading: The Commodity Futures Trading Commission Brings "Duh!" to a New Level
August 21, 2008

Today, the *Washington Post* published a remarkable article by David Cho entitled "A Few Speculators Dominate [the] Vast Market for Oil Trading." The piece reported that "regulators had long classified the Swiss Company Vitol as a trader that primarily helped industrial firms that needed oil to run their business."

But then, when our valiant oversight heroes, the Commodity Futures Trading Commission, examined Vitol's books last month, they found, *mirabile dictu*, that Vitol was more of a speculator holding oil contracts as a profit-making investment rather than as a means of lining up the actual delivery of fuel. Duh. Mr. Cho's article went on to point out that, at one point this July, the firm held 11 percent of all the oil contracts on the regulated New York Mercantile Exchange alone (http://www.washingtonpost.com/wp-dyn/content/article/2008/08/20/AR2008082003898.html). The Commodity Futures Trading Commission has now determined that a massive amount of trading activity was concentrated with a handful of speculators and that currently 81 percent of the oil contracts on the New York Mercantile Exchange—I repeat, 81 percent—are held by financial firms speculating for their clients or for their own accounts. That is for the New York Mercantile Exchange alone and doesn't count London, Dubai, Singapore, Tokyo, and so on.

Vitol itself held contracts equal to 57.7 million bbl of oil or three times the amount of oil consumed each day in the United States. How many square miles of storage would have been required had Vitol taken delivery of this vast quantity?

What is extraordinary in the unfolding of this story is that it took so long for the Commodity Futures Trading Commission to access this data and reach its conclusions. It betrays a total lack of professional competence and oversight failings of monumental proportions. It reveals that our agency does not have on its staff professionals who are sufficiently versed in what they are meant to be monitoring. How else could they have been lulled into the belief that Vitol did business in oil, simply supplying industrial firms? How could they have been oblivious to Vitol's reputation in the field as a massive trader in speculative oil futures contracts? It's irrefutable evidence of a totally dysfunctional agency.

Adding insult to injury, a spokesman for the Commodity Futures Trading Commission pontificated balefully, in light of its recent findings, "To date, the [Commodity Futures Trading Commission] has found that supply and demand fundamentals offer the best explanation for the systematic rise in oil prices" (David Cho, "A Few Speculators Dominate Vast Market for Oil Trading," *Washington Post*, August 21, 2008, http://www.washingtonpost.com/wp-dyn/content/article/2008/08/20/AR2008082003898_pf.html). Thus, in one stroke, the Commodity Futures Trading Commission whitewashed the actions of the commodity exchanges themselves and brought joy to oil producers who want us to believe nothing less. It is well beyond time to close down the Commodity Futures Trading Commission for good.

Our Lob(otomized)bied Congress's Energy Bill Excludes Our Most Efficient, Cleanest, Newly Plentiful Energy Source: Natural Gas
June 28, 2009

Here is another shameful example of our government's deep dysfunction. It's bad enough that Wall Street was bailed out, dragging down the economic standing of the nation along with trillions of its citizens' dollars and still worse that we now find Wall Street blithely going back to fat bonuses and fatter salaries. We have enough to worry about with home foreclosures continuing almost unabated and retirees being forced to go back to work because their nest eggs have been devastated. On top of all that, we find our Congress genuflecting to special interests even when trying to do well.

On Friday, the House passed legislation in the form of a 1,200-page bill addressing the very real and urgent matter of global warming. Here was an effort, albeit difficult to navigate, to deal with an issue with profound long-term consequences. It was focused on transforming the way the nation produces and uses energy to curb the heat-trapping gases linked to climate change. At its core, cap and trade is a system meant to limit the emission of carbon dioxide gases rapidly building up in the atmosphere at unacceptably dangerous levels given a shelf life of up to one thousand years or, in terms of the human experience, an eternity.

The legislation would affect a broad spectrum of industries and professions, including electric power generation, manufacturing, agriculture, construction, and architectural design. Yes, there would be clear winners for those new or underutilized technologies that can become contributors to the new carbon restricted economy; wind, solar, and geothermal power would receive a big boost. The bill mandates that 20 percent of the nation's electricity come from such sources by 2020.

Here the focus is to support carbon-free initiatives and to step away from fossil fuels where possible. Coal- and oil-derived products (i.e., gasoline, diesel, and heating oil) are in the line of fire, and the coal industry is deeply concerned that consumption will diminish drastically. Coal is, of course, loaded with carbon. The bill provides concessions for clean coal projects, which is an important plus for the coal industry and for coal-producing states. It's a classic example of entrenched interests protecting entrenched infrastructure.

Yet the bill has a glaring omission. It contains no programmatic inclusion of and practically no reference to natural gas. Given the fact that natural gas, though a fossil fuel, is vastly more efficient and cleaner burning than coal- or petroleum-based products, this omission can be explained only by the malign power of vested industrial and political interests. Doubly so, in that the natural gas reserves within the United States alone have exploded with new drilling technology over the last half-dozen years. In Louisiana, the Haynesville Shale Basin is now considered to hold a store of BTUs equivalent to that of the North Slope. The huge Marcellus Basin, encompassing much of Pennsylvania and New York State, holds as much and possibly much more. Our gas reserves have expanded by a factor of nearly five, and that may be just the beginning.

To point out the obvious, these new reserves are all onshore and within the continental United States. These reserves lie beneath a massive nationwide distribution network of 2.5 million miles of pipeline. This is to say nothing of the clear benefits to our balance of payments and security interests.

The Department of Energy today is a very different organization than it was under the Bush administration. Its focus is the well-being of its fellow citizens and not the parochial interests of the oil industry and the energy field. It is staffed with individuals of scientific competence who are determined to deal with issues of global warming in a decidedly proactive way. Yet the Department of Energy is not Congress. It is a department that understands what needs to be done and understands that science is telling us that we must move aggressively. Its pragmatism is best summarized by its working credo: Are changes cost-effective, materially significant, and timely? That should be the energy bill's watchword as well. Without a clear provision and mandate for natural gas, the American Clean Energy and Security Act will be a failed bill; if not, it will certainly be something far less than it might have been.

Thank You, ExxonMobil Chief Executive Officer Rex Tillerson, for Educating Us on Oil Prices
November 13, 2009

The oil patch mumbo jumbo continues unabated. Today, Rex Tillerson, the chief executive officer of the nation's largest oil company, ExxonMobil, took a minute or two to instruct us about the reasons for the current price of oil. This is the same personage who, in 2007, informed us, his customers, about ethanol by calling it "moonshine" (Clifford Krauss and Jad Mouawad, "Exxon Chief Cautions against Rapid Action to Cut Carbon Emmissions," *New York Times*, February 14, 2007, http://www.nytimes.com/2007/02/14/business/14exxon.html). This time around, according to Tillerson, "Inventory levels are at historic high levels—especially in the [United States]" (Jennifer Dauble, "CNBC Exclusive: CNBC Transcript: CNBC'S Martin Soong Sits Down with Rex Tillerson, ExxonMobil Chariman and CEO, Today Friday, November 13th," press release on November 13, 2009, http://classic.cnbc.com/id/33911816). He goes on to provide us with his particular self-serving oil patch rationalization for high oil prices.

You see, it is not the machinations of OPEC, of which ExxonMobil and its peers are the primary beneficiaries, nor the speculation of oil traders and bank-holding companies nor the possibility that the producers, with their enormous cash reserves, might be gaming the price of oil on the exchanges. No, in the spirit of that great American philosopher, Alfred E. Neuman, Mr. Tillerson has come up with a causation that is outside the perceived responsibility of the oil industry. What, him worry? You see, in Tillerson's estimation, the trouble rests mostly with the currency effect of a weak dollar.

According to Tillerson, some twenty to twenty-five dollars of the cost per bbl is due to the erosion of the dollar. Really? Since February of this year, the price of oil has increased some 250 percent from $33/bbl to $80/bbl just a few days ago. The value of the dollar has eroded only some 15 percent in the same period. A relationship between the price of oil and the erosion of the dollar on a percentage basis should bring the price of oil to approximately $38/bbl, not the nearly $80/bbl we are transferring to ExxonMobil and its comrades-in-arms.

Far be it for the industry to play it straight, to simply state that the price as currently constituted has nothing to do with market dynamics of supply and demand. Something far more sinister is afoot, and it is long past due that our oversight agencies such as the Commodity Futures Trading Commission take a very serious look at how our commodity exchanges are contributing to these distortions.

But then again, within the confines of the oil industry's Grimm's fairy tale narrative, Mr. Tillerson's imaginative turns of phrase are always welcome.

The Commodity Futures Trading Commission and Department of Energy Snore Away While the Oil Patch Makes Hay
November 18, 2009

Late last week, the Energy Information Service advised that oil stocks surged by 1.762 million bbl—far more than expected—while the US refinery processing rate sank to 79.7 percent—the lowest level in more than two decades. Yet on Monday, the price of oil jumped by $2.50/bbl. What is going on? We don't really know for sure, apart from the fact that it has nothing whatsoever to do with the so-called free market.

Of course, the usual suspects (dollar flight, seeking safety in physical assets, speculation, peak oil theories, political concerns, contango spreads, rebounding economic activity, China, India, and on and on) are being marched out by talking heads and by those searching to rationalize the inexplicable, or more tellingly, by those within or allied to the industry who are seeking to deflect any serious examination of prices and their causes. None of these explanations, individually or in combination, justifies the enormous distortion in price for a market that is filled to the brim with product, both on land and at sea, with very large crude carrier tankers at anchor waiting for weeks and months on end to discharge their cargo.

All these in spite of the declarations broadcast earlier this year by agencies such as the Commodity Futures Trading Commission that a series of restrictions on energy trading would be set forth. As far I can tell, we are still waiting. All this activity in the oil market occurs in tandem with the Commodity Futures Trading Commission's determination that the major cause of oil price distortion was speculation. The Commodity Futures Trading Commission was not merely responding to an outraged public; it also chose to broadcast its views concurrent to the pronouncements by the heads of state of Great Britain and France, who jointly called for "transparency and supervision of the oil futures market in order to reduce damaging speculation" (Gordon Brown and Nicolas Sarkozy, "We Must Address Oil-Market Volatility: Erratic Price Movements in Such an Important Commodity Are Cause for Alarm," *Wall Street Journal,* Opinion Europe, July 8, 2009, http://online.wsj.com/article/SB124699813615707481.html). Commodity Futures Trading Commission hearings were held late in July, and Senator Bernie Sanders of Vermont presented an extraordinarily cogent testimony on the issue. Predictably, it was given very little attention by the press and successfully buried by those whose interests weren't served.

With less fanfare, our friends at OPEC simply assured us that pricing in the range of $40, $50, and even $60/bbl was not in the oil-consuming world's interest, that we would be better served by higher prices. Thus taking our interests to heart, Saudi Arabia and King Abdullah felt that prices in the range of $75 to $80/bbl would be more appropriate. Now here we are, some months later, with prices at these levels even though the world is as awash in oil as it ever has been. What is going on? It is the Commodity Futures Trading Commission's job to find out and not to be simply placated by the oil patch shibboleths referred to above. It just makes no sense.

Are OPEC and Saudi Arabia using their enormous cash holdings to game the futures markets on which the price of oil is based? Why did Saudi Arabia suddenly and only recently drop the widely used West Texas Intermediate oil contract as the benchmark for pricing its oil, substituting a new London-based Argus index? Explanations offered talk about disparity in pricing and were quickly applauded by the International Energy Agency, wearing its new mantle as oil industry apologist. But could it be that, with the potential for a more vigilant Commodity Futures Trading Commission, the West Texas Intermediate contract, which is primarily traded on the New York Mercantile Exchange, becomes more difficult to influence?

Perhaps the Department of Energy could climb down from its professorial aerie of alternative energy issues for a few moments and get its hands dirty by dealing with the everyday concerns of American consumers and their economy.

So far, the Commodity Futures Trading Commission has talked the talk while the oil patch players, from the major producers on down, have walked the walk and stepped on all of us. Who is looking after our interests while our government agencies do a little high-step grandstanding to the cheers of the Wall Street crowd?

The Oil Spill as America's Wake-Up Call: We Need an American Energy TVA
June 6, 2010

The gulf oil spill is a stunning wake-up call that brings into question our relationship to oil. It has become abundantly clear that how oil is consumed and brought to market must change fundamentally. To stop drilling offshore or elsewhere in our nation is, alas, not a realistic solution. Thus, the way extraction is done—and who does it—has to be profoundly reassessed. As long as we are dependent on foreign oil to conduct our economy, all our own resources must be put into play but subject to a very new set of rules.

I have written about the Norwegian petroleum directorate, which can and should serve as a prime example of what must now be done. I have also cited the Tennessee Valley Authority as an example of successful American governmental entrepreneurship. The Tennessee

Valley Authority has had a brilliant record of achievement in electric power generation, river navigation, flood control, reforestation, and erosion control.

Now is the moment, given our tragic wake-up call, to go one major step further to create an American energy version of TVA. It's time to put the responsibility of accessing our fossil fuel resources, both oil and gas, under an American agency and to introduce policies aimed at reducing our energy consumption and making us energy self-reliant by extracting our own resources safely in accordance with our most profound environmental concerns and our best expertise.

Clearly, we can no longer depend on the bottom line–driven oil industry to access our national fossil fuel resources. What is needed is an American-inspired central organization of the best, brightest, most dedicated minds in the oil industry and world-class environmental scientists and engineers who will all work together to access those resources safely. Those resources include our vast and newly discovered reservoirs of shale gas on land, our significant and largely untapped resources of shale oil in the American Northwest, and of course our oil reserves on land throughout the country and offshore on the continental shelf.

With such a mandate, we have the responsibility to research and develop environmentally friendly and less polluting alternatives to fossil fuel that range from highly efficient electric car propulsion to biofuels where appropriate—not exclusively, but in focused competition with and assistance to the private sector.

Among the responsibilities of the American energy version of TVA should be the introduction of national policies that limit our consumption of fossil fuels to levels that are environmentally tenable and that would help us move to fossil fuel self-sufficiency (and eventually off of fossil fuels altogether). This could include a national quota on gasoline consumption that would be distributed equitably through a system of—to suggest but one possibility—gas purchase permits, which consumers throughout the land could use in the form of magnetic debit cards. Does that sound complicated? We had an analogous program during World War II. We won that war. Back then, we didn't have the technology of magnetic debit cards.

Needless to say, the oil industry will fight any such changes in policy with all the resources at its disposal, and those resources are huge. Only a truly committed and engaged public can stare them down. Is it not time?

Food: The American Midwest on the Cusp of an Economic Renaissance
November 7, 2010

"The Midwest has lost a manufacturing empire but hasn't yet found another role," wrote the *New York Times*'s incisive columnist David Brooks in the "Midwest at Dusk" column on November 4, 2010. Brooks's Midwest is a vast American expanse that stretches from central New York and Pennsylvania to Ohio, Indiana, and Wisconsin and down to Arkansas. Here, Brooks proposes, is the place where the trajectory of American politics is being determined. "If America can figure out how to build a decent future for the working-class people in this region," he said, "then the U.S. will remain a predominant power. If it can't, it won't."

Here, as perhaps nowhere else in this nation, something is stirring that has the potential to become a game-changer, a uniquely American game-changer. This past summer, an event took place that has begun to alter the equilibrium of economic trends and influence. In July, the Russian government responded to a disastrous drought by embargoing the export of wheat and unilaterally breaking sales commitments to national buyers throughout the world. The price of wheat and other products, such as corn and soybeans, exploded as reserve stocks of grain were drawn down worldwide.

Yet the thrust of what took place has scarcely been touched upon. The world, with its steeply growing population and rapidly changing dietary habits (especially in the emerging economies), is on the precipice of food shortage. It is generally understood that, with expanding populations, world calorie production will have to double by 2050, but no one knows quite how to achieve that; the major impact of the green revolution (intense application of fertilizers, herbicides, and improved seeds) has already reached the point of dangerously diminishing returns.

In this coming crisis, America—and the American Midwest—will play a crucial role. It will become the most important provider of food grains to the world, building on an already primary but barely heralded position of leadership. The United States is now the largest grower and exporter of corn, which is vital as feed to the food chain, and the largest exporter of wheat. After Brazil, it is the second largest exporter of soybeans. As supplies of foodstuffs get tighter, this position of preeminence will become more and more significant.

Now is the moment for a government with vision to prepare the breadbasket of America to renew itself and lay the groundwork for the destiny that will be thrust upon it. We need to improve the infrastructure servicing this sector instead of producing more overbuilt highways. We should refurbish and extend our inland waterways system, over which most of our grain is transported. We should improve our port facilities, as well as refurbish and add to our grain storage capabilities both inland and at ports of export loading. We should initiate a policy that extends to farmers and agribusiness the kind of government financial support we stood ready to give to Wall Street, the finance industry, and the automobile industry.

The Midwest is blessed with vast expanses of fertile land and great human talent as nowhere else in the world and a waterway system that permits crop production to reach global markets. Now is the time to extend to our agricultural sector, through proper policies going well beyond the current assistance programs from the US Department of Agriculture, the means to ready itself for the opportunities and responsibilities on the horizon. The Midwest has the potential to become the Saudi Arabia of food in importance, and food is a commodity that will surpass oil in economic, social, and political significance. If appropriate policies are initiated now, our Midwest will become the most indispensable real estate in the world, and it will belong to an economic sector that cannot be outsourced.

PART V

OPEC, the Environment, and Peak Oil:
All the News the *Times* Gets Wrong

Friedman's "The New Red, White and Blue" Is a Foggy Green
January 6, 2006

In his op-ed "The New Red, White, and Blue" in today's *New York Times*, Thomas L. Friedman lashed out at our energy dependency and emphasized our need to make ourselves environmentally green. His reasons were all sound, and his argumentation persuasive. He cited the danger of high oil prices and the need for a more effective and courageous energy policy at home. Yet Friedman overlooked a vitally important issue, as is too often the case. Namely, he overlooked the crucial distinctions, from a policy standpoint, between crude oil and gasoline.

Crude oil is a commodity that is not only critical to our economic well-being but also, in today's world, deeply wedded to issues of our national security. At Friedman's cited $60/bbl of oil (at press time, it was actually 5 percent higher than that figure), the daily transfer of wealth to the OPEC cartel, whose eleven member nations produce some 40 percent of the world's oil, approaches two billion dollars a day. That money goes to often corrupt and/or malign regimes, some of which spend large amounts of their oil income to finance schools, mosques, and ostensibly charitable institutions that promote the virulently anti-Western Wahhabi strain of Islam while also financing Iran's manifest ambition to acquire nuclear weaponry.

Gasoline presents a different set of policy concerns. Too often, environmental groups cheer high oil prices on the grounds that they play the largest role in determining the cost of gasoline. High oil prices result in high gasoline prices, which results in diminished consumption of gasoline and a purportedly cleaner environment. The policy issues that relate to gasoline are inherently at variance with those of crude oil. The price and availability of gasoline present economic and environmental concerns, while those of crude oil present economic issues as well as, more urgently, those of national security. This is an important distinction not often delineated in national policy, nor is it in Friedman's Op-ed.

Mr. Friedman should have made it clear that the time has come to push back the price of crude oil using all the tools (economic, political, etc.) in our possession and, wherever possible, in joint cooperation with other nations equally affected. As a nation, we should determine the correct price of gasoline based on our economic, environmental, and national security goals; that price should not be set by a marketplace dominated by cartels.

The Energy Wimps at the *New York Times*
January 12, 2006

Waxing indignant in a recent op-ed entitled "The New Red, White and Blue" (*New York Times*, January 6, 2006), Thomas Friedman castigated President Bush and Vice President Dick Cheney, calling them energy wimps for not focusing on greater energy efficiency and conservation. That's fair enough, but Mr. Friedman need not go so far afield to become righteously exorcised. His own paper of record would give him plenty to say about wimpiness when it comes to covering the oil patch and especially when it comes to covering the role of oil's most manipulative players, namely the OPEC cartel and its putative leader, Saudi Arabia.

The *New York Times*'s coverage of the march of oil prices from $20/bbl to over $60/bbl today has read like a textbook compiled from public relations handouts from OPEC and Saudi Aramco. In articles appearing in the *Times* in August and September of 2004 (one of which was entitled, ironically, "Oil above $46 and Far above OPEC's Ceiling"), Jad Mouawad, the *Times*'s chief energy correspondent, flatly stated "OPEC alone is not responsible for high prices." He went on to blame the familiar litany of problems—war, strikes, political upheavals, and hurricanes in places as varied as Iraq, Nigeria, Venezuela, Norway, Russia, and the Gulf of Mexico. That OPEC has so assiduously worked to create the myth of scarcity and the climate of fear that linked all of these supposedly unconnected events was not, of course, part of the story.

Then, a year later, with the price of oil escalating to over $62/bbl, Mouawad writes, "Saudi Arabia has proved time and again that it is indispensable to the stability of oil markets" (Jad Mouawad, "Why America Is More Dependent Than Ever on Saudi Arabia," *New York Times*, August 6, 2005, http://www.nytimes.com/2005/08/06/business/worldbusiness/06saudi.html). That "stability" was publicly and forcefully scorned barely a month later when Gordon Brown, Britain's Chancellor of the Exchequer (Andrew Marr, "Brown Blames Fuel Costs on OPEC," BBC News.com, Sept 11, 2005, http://news.bbc.co.uk/2/hi/business/4234788.stm), publicly blamed OPEC for the doubling of crude oil prices over the previous eighteen months. On September 12, 2005, he advised that he had spoken to the Saudi Arabian finance minister and would be speaking to OPEC members in the days ahead. He called for OPEC to increase supplies and to relieve pressure on prices.

Rarely had someone of such stature spoken so openly about OPEC and Saudi manipulation. Would that our own government might take it as inspiration. To their shame, this brave and edifying declaration was not reported in the news or business pages of the *Times*. Submissions to the op-ed page pointing to this oversight and to its importance to the public's understanding of OPEC's manipulation of the oil market—of which the public is victim and for which the public pays the price—were rejected.

Only last month, the Saudis were complimented in the Times, with "Saudi Arabia wants to be seen as a responsible actor on the global energy scene and a reliable supplier to its customers" (Jad Mouawad, "The Hand Turning the Spigot; Saudis Aim for Precision, Not Surplus, in Meeting Global Oil Needs," *New York Times*, December 6, 3006, http://query.nytimes.com/gst/fullpage.html?res=9E01E6D91331F935A 35751C1A9639C8B63&pagewanted=2). This compliment came with the price of oil approaching $65/bbl. Thank you, Saudi Arabia, and thank you to the *Times*.

Tom Friedman Spells Out "OPEC"
February 9, 2006

The *New York Times*'s coverage of the upward trend in oil prices (from the roughly $20/bbl in 2001 to roughly $60/bbl today) has bordered on the irresponsible. Every rationale has been trotted out—from strained production capacity to increased consumption in China and India—all the while applauding Saudi and OPEC efforts to keep the oil markets stable. Last summer, with prices whizzing past $60/bbl, the *Times*'s Jad Mouawad advised us on August 6, 2005 ("Why

America Is More Dependent Than Ever on Saudi Arabia" http://www.nytimes.com/2005/08/06/business/worldbusiness/06saudi.html?pagewanted=print) that Saudi Arabia is "indispensable to the stability of oil markets." Though there is some truth lurking in this cosmeticized reporting, almost never has the real cause of high prices been traced back to the elephant in the room, namely OPEC.

What a relief, then, to read Friedman's response on February 8, 2006, to Mr. Cheney's provocative claim that "[t]he [oil] marketplace does work out there" ("No More Mr. Tough Guy," *New York Times*, February 8, 2006, http://query.nytimes.com/gst/fullpage.html?res=9D04E1DE143EF93BA35751C0A9609C8B63) incorporates the late-dawning insight that "The global market is anything but free. It's controlled by the world's largest cartel—OPEC—which sets output, and thereby prices, according to the needs of some of the worst regimes in the world. By doing nothing, we are letting their needs determine the price and their treasuries reap the profits."

It's fine to impugn Dick Cheney if that is one's inclination. That's part of his job description. But where was the *New York Times*—and the rest of the media, for that matter—while OPEC was making us dance to its tune over many years? The softball reporting has been inexcusable. In fact, it's been part of the pattern of deception that lulls us into believing the oil patch and OPEC public relations line that we are well-served by egregiously high prices because they're an effective tool for allocating a scarce resource. The media have never questioned the veracity of that contention in a meaningful way. The media has, however, steered us to accept the fiction that the enormous transfer of wealth to renegade regimes and oil patch bottom lines is the normal evolution of a free market.

Think about it. With OPEC's production of nearly thirty million bbl a day multiplied by an increase of $30/bbl in price—the price had escalated from $30/bbl to over $60/bbl that year—the daily increase in wealth transferred to OPEC cartel producers was one billion dollars a day. This is without counting the massive increase in profits to oil companies and producers outside of OPEC, including Russia, Mexico, Canada, Norway, and others.

As previously stated, Brown's candid and brave condemnation (OPEC and the Saudis do not take kindly to criticism) was not reported by the national media, despite having been issued from a figure of such prominence and credibility. Who are the media protecting? Or do they just live on oil patch, K Street, and OPEC press handouts?

Oil Is Not Scarce: The Industry Continues to Play Us for Fools
May 24, 2006

Oil industry executives have launched an especially vigorous public relations campaign to try to polish the image of an industry that Senator John McCain recently likened to that of a satanic cult (Kate Phillips and Julie Bosman, "Sympathy as Hard to Find as Oil," *New York Times*, May 3, 2006). The usual excuses and apologies are being trotted out to explain away high prices—"We're still recovering from Katrina"; "A new hurricane season is upon us"; "Iran presents a threat"; "Nigeria cutoffs are having an impact on supply"; "We're prisoners of global events"; "Prices reflect the market"; "Capacity is strained"; and on and on.

Most ominously, the industry argues in *sotto voce*, as though delivering bad news to a concerned family member, that the world is running out of oil and that shortages are imminent. Industry spokesmen also imply, without saying so directly, that mile-long lines could form at your local filling station any day now. That is why, they try to make us understand, the market is so jittery with oil prices jumping every time a pipeline leaks. The only trouble is that it isn't true. Oil, and permit me to give this special emphasis, *is not scarce*. That is one of the most important facts in our world, and yet hardly anyone you meet believes it. Most people have been bamboozled by oil industry flacks, by compliant analysts (read, Daniel Yergin et al), by peak oil spinmeisters, by a snoozing press, and by the heavy artillery brought to bear by OPEC, which works overtime and spends big to make us believe in the myth of scarcity. That keeps prices high and oilmen rich while the rest of us pay and pay and pay.

Even according to the industry's own figures, which are surely understated given the restrictive Securities and Exchange Commission reporting constraints, proven reserves of oil around the world were pegged at 1.2 trillion bbl in 2004. That's a humongous supply. And that figure doesn't include even vaster deposits of oil that will come to the market as improving technology makes it cheaper to extract. But before we go there, consider that, in 1970, OPEC purportedly had 412 billion bbl in reserves. In the subsequent thirty years, OPEC nations claim to have pumped 307 billion bbl. They now claim to have some 820 billion bbl in reserves. In a world in which pumping billions out of the ground seems to increase the billions still remaining, we are left to wonder where the real truth lies. To point to another anomaly, commercial stocks of crude oil are some 10 percent higher today than they were a year ago, yet the price of crude is some 40 percent higher than it was then.

Some other sources must be counted.

Canada's tar sands are immense. The conservative estimate of oil saturating the province of Alberta is 175 billion bbl. Producers have been working for years to lower the cost of strip-mining the deposits, grinding it up, separating the tar-like bitumen from the sand, and refining it into synthetic crude oil. These days, all of that can be done for about $20/bbl, which provides nifty profits at today's market price, which hovers around $70/bbl. Sure enough, Chevron Corporation has just announced that it will spend well over one billion dollars for a vast new project to produce more than one hundred thousand bbl per day from the oil sands.

Offshore drilling can now be done in waters as deep as two miles with the oil deposits five to six miles below the ocean floor. Thanks to innovative drills, new information technology, and sophisticated undersea robots, oilmen now have access to an estimated three hundred billion barrels of previously untappable oil.

Sensor technology, seismic surveying, and specialized software promise to open up another 150 billion bbl of reserves. The pod, a supercomputer-powered exploration system designed by a software subsidiary of Halliburton, creates astonishingly detailed 3-D seismic models that are viewed on an IMAX-style, forty-five-foot screen and take most of the guesswork out of drilling for oil.

Old oil fields still hold hundreds of billions of bbl that were thought to be unrecoverable in the early days. Wells that have been abandoned as depleted may contain as much as 70 percent of the oil originally there. Advanced recovery techniques range from the obvious—pumping in water or carbon dioxide to increase pressure in the well—to the exotic.

These days, wells can be filled with bioengineered microbes that release oil stuck in microscopic cavities.

But the big new source will be oil shale; vast quantities of sedimentary rock in the Bakken Formation located in North Dakota contain an awesome 2.6 trillion bbl of oil. In the past, efforts to get it out have foundered on technological problems. Now, new methods are being developed: drilling holes into the shale, heating the rock to seven hundred degrees to cook out the oil, and pumping it to the surface. In reasonably short order, high-quality crude will likely be extracted from shale for roughly $30/bbl.

In all, researchers at the US Geological Survey estimate that these new sources could add as much as four trillion bbl to proven reserves, giving us a more than ample cushion to develop alternative fuels and technologies at today's rate of consumption.

Oil isn't scarce. Honesty is scarce. Transparency is scarce. OPEC nations won't tell us the extent of their reserves other than to leave us with the orchestrated impression that things are worse today then they were yesterday; Russia won't tell us about its reserves, as this information is a state secret. Bold, penetrating reportage is scarce. We urgently need an invigorated and vigilant press, ready to read between the lines of the oil patch press handouts.

This is not an argument for greater consumption. Everything needs be done to wean us from our addiction to fossil fuels, no matter what the level of supply. What we also need is to end this con game that has enriched the pusher beyond his wildest dreams and to the point that we are now expected to say thank you every time we get a fix. It is time to call his bluff, to do all we can to push down the price of crude oil, and to make ourselves energy self-reliant.

We must wake up and respond to the actual facts, not the ones that the oil patch, their paid lobbyists on K Street, and an overly compliant government want us to believe. Market forces have been corrupted to the point where, for example, we are transferring more than $70/bbl to oil producers for a commodity that costs them less than $1.50/bbl to produce (as in the majority of OPEC production costs). This issue is too important to our future to continue accepting the pusher's rap as gospel.

The *New York Times*'s Smug Smog on China's Pollution
June 11, 2006

On the front page of today's *New York Times* and continuing for two full pages of section one, we are given a purportedly in-depth study of "[o]ne of China's lesser known exports, a dangerous brew of soot, toxic chemicals, and climate changing gases from the smoke stacks of coal-burning power plants" (Keith Bradsher and David Barboza, "China's Burning of Coal Casts a Global Cloud," July 11, 2006). The article is remarkable for either its incompetence or its intellectual dishonesty. To talk about China's present and future pollution without mentioning its plans for nuclear energy development is analogous to writing about the Kentucky Derby without mentioning horses.

The only reference to nuclear power in the article is this cryptic sentence: "Long construction times for nuclear power plants make them a poor solution to addressing blackouts and other power shortages now." That's it—finito. There is no mention of the central role that nuclear power will play in China's future, in China's attempts to wean itself off of coal, and more generally, fossil fuel dependence. No mention of the plants currently under construction in China or the nearly forty scheduled to be built by 2020. No mention of the role nuclear energy will play in China's efforts to contain and reduce sulfur dioxide emissions and global warming gases. No mention of China's efforts to generate nuclear energy efficiently, thereby reducing its imports of oil and liquefied natural gas.

Just an oversight? Perhaps. Yet is it possible that nuclear energy isn't part of the *Times*'s agenda? Could the *Times* be worried that mentioning it to us, the great unwashed, might stir unwelcome interest in the issue (i.e., get us thinking, "If they can do it, why not us?"). We haven't built a nuclear power plant since the 1970s. Were that the case, the *Times* is editorializing on its news pages by telling us only what they want us to hear.

Massive Oil Find in Gulf of Mexico Brings Gloom to Peak Oil Pranksters
September 8, 2006

I hate to say "I told you so," but the news of a major, new oil discovery by Chevron and two partners in the Gulf of Mexico confirms what I've been saying for years: Oil is not scarce. Big oil's price manipulators only want us to think it is. Early estimates are that the Lower Tertiary, where Chevron's new Jack-2 well sits, could yield anywhere between three and fifteen billion bbl of oil, making it the biggest domestic find since Alaska's Prudhoe Bay.

The Chevron group's discovery also raises the odds that ExxonMobil, Shell, Anadarko Petroleum, and others will hit pay dirt with their drilling in the area, too. Indeed, just a few days ago, BP announced that it had found more than eight hundred feet of oil-laden rock in its nearby discovery well. In the words of Oppenheimer analyst Fadel Gheit, the Chevron group "may be the first ones to hit the jackpot, but if the current thinking is correct, this is only a beginning" (James M. Klatell, "Huge Oil Reserve Found in the Gulf," CBSNews.com, September 5, 2006, (http://www.cbsnews.com/stories/2006/09/05/business/main1969353.shtml). If the other drillers are successful and the upper end of the production estimate is reached, US reserves would expand by 50 percent.

True to form, the oil industry cheerleaders are right there instructing us that all those profits the major oil companies have been earning are being well spent with our best interests at heart. The *New York Sun* tells us, in a gushing editorial, that one hundred million dollars has been spent digging the well and that one billion dollars may have to be spent "constructing a rig to extract the oil for market" ("Back to the Well," September 6, 2006, http://www.nysun.com/editorials/back-to-the-well/39182/). Before you start passing around a hat to help out Chevron et al, please consider that the minimum estimated yield is three billion bbl. That comes to thirty-three cents a bbl to get the oil to market, and the current price is more than $65/bbl. Yes, other costs are involved, but none of great enough significance to materially affect the Niagara Falls of profits that will be pouring in. All the more so if the reserve is at the high end of the three to fifteen billion-bbl range.

The find comes as a crushing blow to the peak oil pundits who have spent years conditioning us to believe in the impending exhaustion of crude oil production and reserves. In doing this, the pundits have been shamelessly cheered on by big oil, small oil, and middle oil as they gouge us to ever greater degrees.

It didn't take long for the chief peak oil prankster, Matt Simmons, author of the scare-mongering *Twilight in the Desert*, to deliver his verbal cold water treatment, saying, "[I]n the last fifteen years, there have so many great projects that started out and then petered out [...] there's been a lot more bitter disappointments than phenomenal surprises" (BBCNews.com, September 6, 2006, http://news.bbc.co.uk/go/pr/fr/-/2/hi/americas/5318776.stm). Simmons's book speculates that, in spite of Saudi protestations, Saudi oil output is at or near its peak. In keeping with its Halloween overtones, Simmons's acumen was celebrated by *Reuters* last October for predicting that the price of oil might well reach $190/bbl by the end of winter, if we should encounter the aberration of cold weather.

Simmons, Steve Andrews (cofounder of the Association for the Study of Peak Oil and Gas USA), Dr. Colin Campbell (founder of the Association for the Study of Peak Oil and Gas International), M. King Hubbert (creator of the Hubbert peak theory), and other peak oil prankster cohorts are always working overtime to make us believe that gaining reasonable access to oil is a profound, inherently insoluble problem. They do their utmost to make us lose focus on the importance of the fact that we've just located a huge new supply of high-quality, low-sulfur oil only 175 miles off the coast of Louisiana, which is welcome news not only because of its proximity but also because so many other global suppliers are either unreliable, politically unstable, confrontational, or all of the above in varying degrees.

Furthermore, this find, according to Chevron, confirms that oil deposits in older rock formations—the Lower Tertiary is thirty-five million years old—are both technologically and economically feasible. As I've pointed out before, proven reserves of oil even before this latest find stand at 1.2 trillion bbl. That's a lot of oil, and that figure is surely on the low side, given that some of the world's major oil producers—Saudi Arabia, its OPEC brethren, and Russia, to name just a few—have never divulged their true reserves in spite of many calls for greater transparency. Russia's underground supply of black gold has always been a state secret, and the Saudis haven't updated their figures in more than three decades even though exploration and production technology have vastly improved in that time. The new technology has made it possible to get more oil out of scores of oil fields around the world.

Then, too, there are trillions of bbl of oil to be recovered from sedimentary rock in the Western United States as well as from the Canadian tar sands.

The *New York Times* Shamelessly Shills For OPEC
September 12, 2006

Yesterday, on the anniversary of the September 11, 2001, terrorist attacks, the business section of the *New York Times* extolled the members of OPEC. Was this poor taste or simply ignorance? It's almost as if the folks at the *Times* are oblivious to oil's malign influence upon global sociopolitical affairs—for instance, its role in financing international terrorism.

Allow me to quote from Jad Mouawad's article ("At OPEC, Some Worry as Oil Prices Start Falling," *New York Times,* September 11, 2006), which comments extensively on OPEC's concerns and objectives in light of a convening of its ministers. We are given the following insight: "Members of [OPEC] account for 40 percent of the world's oil exports, and they have been pumping at maximum capacity over the last year in an effort to drive down prices." That's really quite a remarkable perception. This in the face of OPEC's actions over the years, which have led to the inexorable rise in crude oil prices as OPEC has cut production quotas again and again, punching up prices to more than $70/bbl as of just a few days ago.

The piece goes on to wrap OPEC's manipulation of production and price in the usual oil patch pabulum. It never refers to OPEC's willful actions. Instead, it rounds up the usual suspects: prospective Iran sanctions; conflict in Iraq and Nigeria; lower production from restrictive policies at home, in Iran, and in Venezuela; growth of consumption in China; production dislocations in Alaska and the Gulf of Mexico; political tensions in the Middle East; hurricane activity in the gulf. The OPEC public relations office could not have scripted this article better. The litany of reasons *other* than OPEC's actions for the tripling in prices during the last four years was worthy of enshrinement in the "Who, Me?" Hall of Fame. Then the *Times* trots out the ultimate rationalization to make us all understand what a bargain we are getting from OPEC, big oil, and the oil patch in general. You see, according to the *Times*, "[W]hen adjusted for inflation, prices have yet to reach records from the 1970s, which translates to more than $90 a barrel in today's prices."

What the *Times* conveniently omits is that, were the same parameters applied to gold, which is a bellwether for inflation, the closing price for gold would be not six hundred dollars today (2008) but closer to $1700 per ounce. Gold, after all, was selling at more than eight hundred dollars per ounce at the time base and inflation base of the *Times*'s calculation for the inflation-adjusted price of oil—so much for the *Times*'s insights and valiant attempt to celebrate OPEC and its oil patch brethren.

The *Times*'s reporting on this issue is manifestly irresponsible. It must be understood that the high price of oil presents a clear and present danger to our national security for reasons often enumerated by Senator Dick Lugar, The Council on Foreign Relations, and The Heritage Foundation, among many others. Those who become OPEC's and big oil's apologists and help to rationalize the skyward manipulation of prices do the nation a grave disservice. What is sorely lacking, certainly at the news and business desk of the *Times*, is the willingness to clearly call the whole structure of oil market pricing into question.

The nation is facing two existential dangers that are related but not the same. The price we are paying for oil is fueling and enabling the belligerence of those who hate us. It is the paymaster of terror. We must do all we can to get the price of oil down, down, down. Simultaneously, we must dramatically curtail our usage of fossil fuels and begin to seriously heed the warnings on greenhouse gases and global warming. It is an obligation to ourselves and to future generations. We are facing environmental disaster and confronting our ability to continue life as we know it on this planet. The need to restrain fossil fuel consumption becomes more urgent with each passing day.

Peak Oil RIP: Official Obituary on the Front Page of the *New York Times*
March 8, 2007

Now that sustained high oil prices and environmental concerns have stimulated massive efforts to develop alternative fuel sources, oil industry pooh-bahs are finally realizing that they have overstepped themselves. For decades, they have frightened us into accepting ever-higher prices with their posturing fears about the imminent exhaustion of oil. Suddenly, they and their allies in the media are rushing to inform us they have been wrong—for decades. Oil is not scarce, nor are we about to run out of it.

On March 5 in a first-page, right-hand column ("Oil Innovations Pump New Life Into Old Wells"), the *New York Times*'s oil specialist Jad Mouawad followed up on the recent commentary of Cambridge Energy Research analyst Daniel Yergin and has finally come around to the argument I have been making for years (Mouawad and Yergin are, by the way, two of the oligopoly's most reliable parrots). But why this sudden shift? Mouawad unwittingly telegraphs the producers' new strategy when he opines that OPEC's "clout [will be] reinforced in coming years," because the cartel "is poised to control more than 50 percent of the oil market." The king of the thieves, Saudi Arabia, is now bandying about a number closer to 1 trillion bbl for its potential reserves. You may recall that when scarcity fear-mongering was the ploy, the Saudis owned up to having just 260 billion bbl of oil. Now, suddenly, having more oil and not less is the game plan, and that makes great good sense if the goal is to run alternative energy developers off the playing field. Mouawad, who is always ready to repeat the oil patch pitch, advises us that the oil companies "see few alternatives to fossil fuels." Where did the *Times* find this guy? What else would those sitting on top of all the oil say, particularly if they wanted to scare away competition?

There seems to be a lot more oil out there and under our oceans than most so-called experts thought. Many of those experts have their own vested interest in the "peak, peak, peak" mantra. As Mouawad breathlessly relates, not only are new deepwater deposits being found, but new technology and techniques developed in the last decade are also discovering and bringing to the surface trillions more bbl still left in wells that have long been thought unrecoverable. Indeed, the Cambridge consultants now put recoverable oil reserves at 4.8 trillion bbl, and that's their low-end guesstimate.

Of course, die-hard peak oil theorists among petroleum geologists and those pundits with their own agendas won't face up to their errors. They continue to sound the alarm of shortages, price spikes, and economic decline just down the road. If this dubious line of reasoning sounds familiar, it is. Ever since oil was first discovered more than a century ago, alarmists have been forecasting its disappearance. Such stubborn wrongheadedness isn't winning any new converts these days; it's merely casting the naysayers in the dim light of the ill-informed.

There are the two things we must not lose sight of. First, OPEC, the Saudis, and big oil in general are not our friends. They're all in it for the money, no matter how their extreme greed harms the global economy and us. What is more, far too many of the billions upon billions of dollars we've shipped to the Middle East have bankrolled those who seek to destroy us. We have to free ourselves from their grasp. Second, if big oil doesn't bankrupt us and Islamic extremists don't kill us, we'll do the job for them unless we can wean ourselves off of fossil fuels. Global warming is no joke. Greenhouse gases are choking the life out of our planet. Our only hope for saving ourselves is to cut emissions and develop alternative sources of energy.

That means we mustn't be lulled by any temporary price declines or false hopes that the likes of ExxonMobil will find a conscience. The biggest of big oil admits that the planet is warming, but its response seems to be, "Hey, it's not my problem." Making obscene profits is ExxonMobil's be-all and end-all.

Now that the truth about oil resources has been revealed by America's most famous newspaper, we can at least hope that the scarcity threat has lost its punch. But if the truth is going to set us completely free, we have to keep the pressure on Congress to rein in our consumption of fossil fuels and give more support to the development of alternatives.

The House Acts with Authority, and the Media Remain Silent
May 28, 2007

Congress is now considering legislation that calls for a nearly fivefold increase in the use of ethanol. It's no surprise, then, that Jad Mouawad, the oil industry's plant at the *New York Times*, would deploy a front-page article ("Oil Industry Says Biofuel Push May Hurt at Pump," May 24, 2007) that is written with the authoritative hauteur that only the *New York Times* can pull off and promotes the self-serving received wisdom of such oil industry flacks as the American Petroleum Institute and the Energy Policy Research Foundation.

According to the article, it seems that the government's push to increase the supply of biofuels will inhibit the oil industry's decision-making toward building additional gasoline refineries, and that the program is already "forcing many companies to reconsider or scale back their plans for constructing new refinery capacity." Mouawad goes on to state the obvious by saying that, without this capacity, we will be more dependent on imported gasoline. It also notes that imported gasoline is "more expensive than fuel refined domestically." Mouawad's observation is patent nonsense. We are importing significant volumes of gasoline presently just as we import oil and other fossil-based fuels such as liquefied natural gas. Gasoline is shipped here from refineries both near and far, from points in the Caribbean and Canada, from refineries in Europe and elsewhere. These imports are priced at market levels that are competitive with domestic gasoline.

Not only is Mr. Mouawad's argument misleading, but he also chooses not to draw our attention to the fact that much of the fuel that is or would be refined domestically is cracked from imported crude oil on which our growing addiction is becoming clear to all. Nor does he mention that imports of crude oil will be significantly reduced through a domestically grown and formulated ethanol program.

Then, as though to raise the flag of caution and in all likelihood stitched together by his mentors in the oil patch, he informs his readers that some member of Congress would like to make the president's ten-year goal for biofuels mandatory. Rather than comparing the 2.3 million bbl per day goal as the equivalent of an integrated oil company's daily oil production (such as BP's or half of ExxonMobil's), he makes the ten-year goal as daunting as possible. He dramatically compares it to creating an ethanol industry "roughly the size of world-class oil producers like Kuwait and Nigeria."

Finally, Mr. Mouawad brings us near–crocodile tears by pointing out that the oil companies have "spent vast amounts—more than $50 billion the last ten years—to meet requirements to produce cleaner fuels" as well as, presumably, to add capacity. Now the adjective *vast* has never, to my knowledge, been applied by Mr. Mouawad to oil company earnings or to crude oil profit margins. Nor does he clarify that the fifty billion-dollar capital expenditure is a tax-deductible item and affects the bottom line by some half the flagged amount. Nor does he put the sum in perspective in a universe where the current quarterly earnings of the major integrated companies, say ExxonMobil (nine billion dollars last quarter alone), Shell, BP, ConocoPhillips, and so on would easily cover the net outlay of this vast ten-year expenditure in one quarter alone—so much for unbiased reporting.

In keeping with the spirit of the *Times*—reporting what is good for the oil folks and ignoring what oil news would be good for the rest of us—a deafening silence greeted what otherwise should have been hailed as a truly significant event. Last week, the House proactively voted to give the Federal Trade Commission the authority to bypass issues of sovereign immunity to sue members of OPEC for price manipulation. This news was buried by the *Times* in an article about the House's Price Profiteering Bill. The *Times* further diminished the House's action by brushing it aside with the observation that the Bush administration has vowed to veto the bill "because it could pinch supplies"—end of story (Chris Baltimore, "UPDATE 2-U.S. House Passes Gasoline Price Profiteering Bill," *Reuters*, May 23, 2007, http://uk.reuters.com/article/2007/05/23/usa-congress-gasoline-idUKN2324593220070523).

The rest of the press was no more forthcoming than the *Times*, and there's the rub. Here is an issue that needs be processed to its conclusion, and a responsible press would focus on it with laser-like intensity. Eventually, if the president vetoes the bill, so be it. We will all know where he really stands on the issue of oil independence, the lengths he is prepared to go to accommodate his friends in the oil patch, and the degree of nefarious Saudi influence upon this White

House. The process would be enormously instructive to the citizenry in understanding exactly how dependent we are and upon whom. It would also identify those in our government who, in the thrall of oil profits, are prepared to tolerate this stickup of the world's consumers without the least semblance of protest.

This time, the House has one of the major players of the oil price con game in its sights. Let's hope the House perseveres.

Peak Oil is Snake Oil!
June 25, 2007

Last Friday, I had occasion to do brief battle on CNBC's *Morning Call* with Steve Andrews, cofounder of the Association for the Study of Peak Oil and Gas, who strenuously defended the peak oil mantra that we are approaching the moment when we will no longer be able to replace the oil we are consuming. My argument to the contrary was that oil is far more abundant than peak oil theorists would like us to believe. Major finds and new drilling techniques have made ever greater reserves/supplies available. The Association for the Study of Peak Oil and Gas is widely considered the most influential organization supporting peak oil, the Hubbert curve theory that predicts future oil availability or lack thereof. Surprisingly, there is more than one such organization. Why should that be? The *Wall Street Journal* summed it up succinctly in a September 14, 2006 article (Bhushan Bahree and Jeffrey Ball, "Producers Move to Debunk Gloomy 'Peak Oil' Forecasts," http://online.wsj.com/article/SB115818976320462464-search.html?KEYWORDS=prod). The article goes on to say, "That argument known as 'peak oil theory' has provided intellectual backing for the boom in crude prices."

I contended that the fabricated drama of peak oil goes back to the very beginnings of oil history to 1855, when crude oil was bubbling to the surface in Pennsylvania and transformed into patent medicine as Samuel Kier's rock oil. The rock oil that people pointedly cautioned buyers about by saying, "Hurry, before this wonderful product is depleted from nature's laboratory." That refrain, in one version or another, has been a constant theme of the oil peak theorists for over a century now.

Mr. Andrews defended his peak oil theory by pointing to a study paid for and conducted in 2005 by this administration's ambassadorial mission to the oil industry, the Department of Energy. There was no mention of the Department of Energy commissioning another study by the National Petroleum Council, an oil and gas research organization, to investigate peak oil claims some months ago. Heading this new study was none other than the oil industry's "Gipper" himself, Lee Raymond, who tore himself away from counting his four hundred million-dollar golden parachute from ExxonMobil long enough to help the folks in the industry who made it all possible—so much for the Department of Energy's objectivity. Its concern for the sensitivities of the oil patch has far outweighed its concern for the nation as a whole.

There are others who are less invested in terrifying us into accepting higher crude oil prices and have different views. There is Michael C. Lynch (the noted economist associated with both Massachusetts Institute of Technology and the Fletcher School of Law and Diplomacy) and former president of the United States Association for Energy Economics (who has pointed out that Colin Campbell's research is simply sloppy). Campbell is among the most notorious of the peak oil doomsday scenarists and a founder of the Association for the Study of Peak Oil. Sloppiness is a common feature of these doomsayers; the patron saint of peak oil theory, former Shell geologist M. King Hubbert, had to revise his peak oil doomsday from the year 2000 to 2007 and again to 2010.

There have been recent massive oil and gas finds off China's northeastern coast, the Gulf of Thailand, the US and Mexican Gulf of Mexico, Sakhalin Island, Siberia, and the West Coast of Africa, as well as staggering increases in proven oil reserves in Saudi Arabia that have recently been announced by Aramco officials—these are attributable to new exploratory and recovery techniques. This increase in Saudi Arabia is from 260 billion to more than seven hundred billion bbl, with the potential the reserves might reach one trillion bbl. Interestingly, the *New York Times*'s article was dismissed by the Association for the Study of Peak Oil and Gas, which accused the *Times* of distorting news and suggested that perhaps its reporting "has something to do with the negative impact of soaring oil prices on a delicate stock market" (Association for the Study of Peak Oil and Gas Newsletter 76, April 2007, http://aspoireland.files.wordpress.com/2009/12/newsletter76_200704.pdf).

It seems Mr. Hubbert's predictions will have to be revised again and again by vast Arctic reserves of oil being made available by melting ice caps, for instance—talk about an industry having it both ways, helping to create global warming and then benefiting by its effects.

In this writer's opinion, the peak oil pranksters' zeal is closer to theology than it is to theory. They are aided by the oil companies' television advertisements that claim that half the planet's oil will be consumed in twenty year, or by studies such as the one released by BP that cautions us that available oil will be consumed in forty years. Oil interests are essentially permitted to tweet "peak, peak, peak," while stampeding us into higher and higher prices.

I have a final point. What we pay for fossil fuels urgently needs to be readdressed in terms of its cost to our environment, its cost to our national security, and its cost to our economic and future well-being. The oil and gas market as currently construed and managed is a manipulated and propagandized sinkhole that has enriched oil companies beyond the wildest dreams of Croesus while the rest of the nation absorbs the ancillary costs and is left to deal with the effect on our society. It is time we realized that what is scarce is not oil but honesty and transparency.

Peak Oil Theorists Gush Obfuscation
June 29, 2007

I know it's too much to expect that determined peak oil theorists like the Association for the Study of Peak Oil and Gas cofounder Steve Andrews will suddenly admit that they're wrong, no matter how many times their predictions of doomsday come and go without the world ending. Sometimes all one can do is shake one's head at their stubborn denials. But Mr. Andrews's rejoinder ("Rejecting the Real Snake Oil," HuffingtonPost.com, June 27, 2007) to my claim that peak oil is snake oil requires some untangling to get at the pertinent facts.

The first thing to note is that the Association for the Study of Peak Oil and Gas simply changed the text of its argumentation, whereby reference to flawed geological studies by the likes of Hubbert and Coleman are conveniently bolstered by geopolitical observations that have little or nothing to do with the purported science of peak oil. To quote Andrews, "Roughly two thirds of the world's oil lies in the Middle East—a cauldron for geopolitical, religious, cultural and military conflict" and "[o]ver 90 percent of the world's oil is owned by government-controlled companies." These truisms are abundantly clear to anyone focused on this issue. They don't take a degree from the Massachusetts Institute of Technology to grasp. Within their own parameters, they have a decided impact on the price of oil, but they are separate issues altogether. To wrap them up into the science of peak oil is a digression and a deliberate obfuscation that underlines the spuriousness of peak oil theology.

When I speak of the fabricated drama of peak oil, I am referring to the oft-repeated and overheated claim that the end is near even as the nearness of that *near* continues to drift just out of reach. Yes, some oil fields are diminishing. If the peak theorists miss the point, yes, they once panned gold in California, and yes, they once pumped oil in Pennsylvania. But new oil is to be found and is being found all over the globe; it is being made increasingly accessible by innovations in exploration and technology from deepwater fields in the Gulf of Mexico, in Cambodia, in Africa, in China, in India, offshore Sakhalin, in the marginally tapped Canadian oil sands, in the Venezuelan Orinoco deposits, in our Western shale, in our currently off-limits offshore and Alaskan deposits, and of course, potentially in the Artic and in a peaceful Iraq whose oil resources, were they ever to be fully developed, could conceivably challenge those of Saudi Arabia. The list could go on.

There is Mr. Andrews's argument that access to new sources, such as ultra deepwater fields, is costly. Yes, but that doesn't mean the oil isn't there. Even at half of today's prices for oil and gas, these difficult-to-access deposits offer windfall profits. Yet, once again, this argumentation has absolutely nothing to do with the science of peak oil.

As for what Mr. Andrews calls my "delusional notion" that the Association for the Study of Peak Oil and Gas USA is "in cahoots with the oil companies," I would point out that the Association for the Study of Peak Oil and Gas's propaganda furthers the price-gouging aims of the oil companies, even if no blood brother rituals were ever performed.

Is it curiosity or coincidence that, in 2005, the Association for the Study of Peak Oil and Gas's International Workshop on Oil and Gas Depletion was held in Lisbon under the auspices and sponsorship of the Calouste Gulbenkian Foundation, which known for its support of the arts and sciences. Calouste Gulbenkian, who was perhaps the richest man in his time, was known as Mr. Five Percent for the royalties he received on all the oil pumped in Mesopotamia as a stipend for having been the go-between for virtually all early lease negotiations in the region.

Just for the record, the preeminent peak oil theorists do indeed have strong ties to the industry; many of them having been on oil company payrolls as geologists and engineers. The peak theorist saint, M. King Hubbert, whose 1956 theory started all this oil patch piety, was a Shell geologist. His acolyte, Colin Campbell, worked for Texaco and BP. Jean Laherrere spent many years at Total.

Finally, Mr. Andrews says a "growing list of respected energy analysts" think the world peak is coming soon—where have we heard that before?—most likely between 2010 and 2015. Maybe so, but there is another list of high-profile industry figures who say otherwise. Robert W. Esser, director of Cambridge Energy Research Associates, says peak oil theory "is garbage as far as we're concerned" (Mark Morrison, "Plenty of Oil—Just Drill Deeper," *Bloomberg Businessweek*, September 7, 2006, http://www.businessweek.com/investor/content/sep2006/pi20060907_515138.htm). Richard Nehring, who was once described by Laherrere as the best expert in the United States on its reserves and one of the best in the world, has concluded that the Hubbert method clearly fails to predict future production accurately and substantially overstates the rate of decline in producing fields (in his articles on peak oil entitled "Hubbert's Unreliability," published in three parts in the *Oil and Gas Journal* April 3, 17, 24, 2006).

Fifty years ago, when Hubbert made his predictions—as did many others since that first well in Pennsylvania with varying peak dates along the way—that worldwide output would peak in 2000, he had no way of knowing what impact the new technologies would have on exploration and production. Today's peak oil spinmeisters have no such excuse.

The *New York Times*, Mouthpiece of the American Petroleum Institute
July 23, 2007

Once again, the *New York Times* has come to the defense of the oil industry by propagandizing a point of view that is certain to bring cheer to the American Petroleum Institute and everyone in the oil and refining business. See yesterday's first-page, right-hand column (Jad Mouawad, "Record Failures at Oil Refineries Raise Gas Prices," *New York Times*, July 22, 2007, http://www.nytimes.com/2007/07/22/business/22refine.html) for an article that could have been provided to them by the American Petroleum Institute.

To make sure we learn our lessons well about the hardships being encountered by the industry, the *Times* belittles any suggestion of profiteering. Of course, there is no mention of the manipulated supply of oil by OPEC, no hint of the possibility of manipulated futures trading on the commodity exchanges, and no reference to the possibility of purposeful restraint of gasoline imports to make up whatever shortfalls may actually exist. You see, according to the *Times*, it's about a litany of sad events rarely experienced before by a beleaguered industry, such as leaks, spills, breakdowns, power losses (sounds a bit like my mother's kitchen), and natural phenomena such as lightning strikes and—*sacre bleu*—"a midsize refinery in Kansas [...] flooded by torrential rains last month." That's to say nothing of hurricanes past; you do remember Katrina, and in case you don't, the *Times* is happy to remind you of its long-lasting impact on this beleaguered industry.

I must tell you, it's hard to fathom that so many disasters, both terrestrial and celestial, could be visited on one hapless industry that is doing its very best to supply us with its product at the highest price possible. But, according to the *Times*, the price is an element of circumstance, and the industry should be lauded for its Herculean efforts. The *Times* goes on to sing the oil patch lament, humming to us about the industry's difficulty in meeting environmental regulations, addressing safety concerns, and dealing with unfortunate, unforeseen circumstances. Almost incidentally, we learn from the Occupational Safety and Health Administration that "there is a lack of investments in modern equipment." This is an industry swimming in money with cracking margins at the highest levels ever—$25/bbl compared to "$5 a barrel just a few years ago" (Jad Mouawad, "Record Failures at Oil Refineries Raise Gas Prices," *New York Times*, July 22, 2007, http://www. nytimes.com/2007/07/22/business/22refine.html?pagewanted=print).

That said, leave it to the good old *Times* to spring to the defense of this beleaguered industry by noting admiringly in that same article that "[r]efiners spent $9 billion from 2002 to 2006 to make low sulfur diesel." There is no mention, of course, that ExxonMobil alone (they have extensive refinery operations) earned more than nine billion dollars in the last quarter (multiply that by four to see where one year gets you). For ExxonMobil, as but one player, this investment over four years could probably have been handled out of petty cash.

Neither is there any mention that a sizable portion of our gasoline needs is supplied by offshore refineries; that the shortfall after Katrina was quickly made up by imports; that any current production constraints could readily be offset by gasoline imports were there a willingness by the oil industry to attempt to rein in prices. Please remember that most of our refining capacity is in the hands of oil companies that are integrated from the well to the gas pump such as ExxonMobil, BP, Shell, ConocoPhillips, Total, and so on.

The dire circumstances described in the *Times* article are not in the least reflected in data collected by the Energy Information Administration. The Energy Information Administration allows that we have about twenty-one days of gasoline supply on hand, which is a fully normal inventory level. Further, according to the Energy Information Administration, the capacity utilization of refineries has been in the range of 88 to 91 percent over the past two months, which is at the high end of normal, and at 91 percent last week. So where's the beef, *New York Times*?

The *New York Times* has been unabashedly consistent in its defense of the fiction that the oil business is the reflection of unfettered market forces. To the American Petroleum Institute go my compliments—you pick your allies well.

The *New York Times*, the Oil Patch's Faithful Cheerleader, Trashes Ethanol
September 24, 2007

Perhaps it was inevitable that the New York Times, reporting on the world oil industry with rose-tinted glasses, should stand shoulder to shoulder with Hugo Chavez and his well-rehearsed aura of victimization, bashing ethanol and undermining its growing challenge to oil's perfidious hegemony.

Chavez's self-interest is clear: Use more ethanol, and you use less of his oil. The *Times*'s motivations are a little harder to fathom. Why does it persist in voicing oil industry platitudes, remaining delinquent in presenting any insightful or questioning reports on the acceleration of increases in world oil prices? Perhaps the corn growers and the agricultural cooperatives don't have the massive advertising budgets that the oil companies do, or maybe it's just a lack of market sophistication. But the bottom line is that, for Chavez and the *New York Times*, it makes good sense to pay more than $80/bbl of oil and get on with global warming. The *Times* seems to think it's fine to strangle economies and freeze households in winter with exorbitant fuel costs so that the good royals of Saudiland can roll around in Rolls-Royces and fund hatemongering madrassas or so Mahmoud Ahmadinejad can buy new parts for his nuclear erector set.

Yet making an otherwise abundant food product a touch higher in price so our farmers can buy a new John Deere is a grievous sin in the eyes of the *Times* and a misallocation of economic resources. As to the staggering disparity in feedstock prices, the price of oil is at more than $80/bbl after rising 800 percent in the past decade with production costs that are significantly less than $20/bbl throughout the industry and, in the case of Saudi Arabia, less than $1.50/bbl. That latter margin is more than 6,000 percent versus that of corn at $3.85 per bushel, on which our farmers are doing well if they have a 50 percent margin.

Aha, you say, but oil is a finite resource, whereas corn is a renewable one. If, for some reason, you don't say that, the oil boys will be quick to remind you. But consider this. To grow corn, sugar, or whatever crop with sufficient yields to meet the world's needs (think Green Revolution) requires vast inputs of such fertilizer elements as phosphates, potash, and nitrates—all of which, like oil, are finite. Without them, food shortages would have become commonplace years ago.

Last Wednesday, the *New York Times* instructed us in a lead editorial ("The High Cost of Ethanol," *New York Times*, September 19, 2007, http://www.nytimes.com/2007/09/19/opinion/19wed1.html) on the shortcomings of ethanol as an alternative fuel. Warily, the paper of record warned us that grain prices have been pushed higher and are threatening social unrest, though there was no mention of the social unrest in Myanmar that has been caused in large part by escalating energy prices and culminated in riots this weekend. The piece goes on, cherry-picking its references and presenting us with emotionally charged buzzwords, saying that growing corn and biodiesel feed stocks is "threatening natural habitats and imposing other environmental costs."

In July of 2007, I reported from an energy policy forum in Aspen attended by senior oil industry officials that it became chillingly clear that those with a vested interest in oil or oil production, oil and energy distribution, and oil governance are all for conservation and protecting the environment as long as it does not negatively impact the prices of oil or of other fossil fuel–derived energy. In his article entitled "Myth versus Reality" in the current issue of *Foreign Affairs* (September/October 2007), the former Senate majority leader, Tom Daschle, wrote, "As the public's attention has begun to focus on the need for alternatives to oil, the major oil companies have become concerned. Unsurprisingly, warnings of a looming food-fuel tradeoff have crept back into the national debate."

Unlike oil, corn is grown by farmers throughout the world to meet market needs; still, oil has its peak doomsayers and the production constraints imposed by OPEC (and cheered on by international oil companies and other major producers like Russia). According to Daschle, the US corn crop alone has increased from approximately seven billion bushels in 1980 to nearly twelve billion in 2006. Compare that to OPEC's oil production of thirty-one million bbl per day in 1979 to barely thirty million bbl per day today, which includes the production of its newest member, Angola, and of Iraq, where production is once again edging toward prewar levels. OPEC constrains oil production not because there is less oil but rather to manipulate prices higher. OPEC's acknowledged reserves today are significantly higher than they were in 1979, with Saudi Arabia alone revising its reserves from some 260 billion bbl then to more than seven hundred billion bbl now.

There are two additional points of particular significance. I quote again from Daschle's article: "An interesting analysis released by the Natural Resources Defense Council last May showed that corn-based ethanol outperforms gasoline when the two fuels' full production and use cycles are compared. Innovation in the biofuel industry is leading to even greater greenhouse gas reductions, regardless of the feedstock." He later writes that "[a]n acre of corn, one of the rare plant species to use a carbon dioxide–efficient photosynthesis system, removes more carbon dioxide from the atmosphere than does an acre of mature Amazonian rain forest, and the next generation of biofuel technologies—including those using nonfood cellulosic feed stocks—will increasingly contribute to the critically important goal of reducing, as the author Michael Pollan has put it, humans' 'carbon footprint.'"

It is clear that the oiligopoly and allies like the *New York Times* will do all they can to deflect our focus and confuse our goals to divest ourselves from dependence on fossil fuels. Yes, some of the current government programs supporting bio or ethanol fuels are overly generous. The fifty-four-cent per gallon import duty on Brazilian sugar-based ethanol is a particular blemish, especially in that gasoline can be imported duty-free. But, in all, they do not compare to the government largesse extended to the oil patch from near giveaways of oil drilling rights on federal land and offshore to tax incentives that are costing us billions before we even get to the pump.

Those Damnable High Oil Prices: Blame It on the Energy Hogs in Maine
November 13, 2007

Metaphorically speaking, that is just what the *New York Times* has done—blamed high oil prices on those consumers in Maine who will be near bankruptcy after paying their fuel bills this winter and on all the rest of us—you, me, and everyone else out there, both at home and abroad. In a bizarre article in last Friday's *Times* (Jad Mouawad, "Rapidly Rising Global Demand for Oil Is Provoking New Energy

Crisis," November 9, 2007, http://www.nytimes.com/2007/11/09/ business/worldbusiness/09oil.html), the consumers of energy—namely, you and me—are to blame for what the *Times* is defining as "the world headed toward its third energy shock in a generation." The producers and refiners of crude oil, the oil industry, and a compliant government are all innocent as lambs in this *Times* propaganda piece.

The high price of oil? Let's not mention the supply side; that could be embarrassing, especially with OPEC keeping literally millions of bbl of oil off the market in order to artificially induce inventory drawdowns and push prices ever higher. There was no mention of the manipulation of commodities markets, especially the ongoing investigations by the Commodity Futures Trading Commission and the Congressional hearings scheduled "to examine the role of speculation in recent record oil prices" by Senator Carl Levin's permanent subcommittee on investigations (Senate Committee on Homeland Security and Governmental Affairs, "Levin-Coleman Report Finds Speculation Adding to Oil Prices: Put the Cop Back on the Beat," June 27, 2006, http://hsgac.senate.gov/ public/index.cfm?FuseAction=Press.MinorityNews&ContentRecord_ id=648ca6ed-b5b0-46ef-82b3-19e69163592e).

The nonsense continues. We are told that oil prices are up 56 percent this year. Really? In mid-January, the price of crude touched $49.90/ bbl. The march to the recent $98/bbl brings the increase to nearly 100 percent in less than a year's time, an incredible jump for such a core commodity. But then the article goes on to inform us, incorrectly, that the price of crude oil has jumped 365 percent in the last decade. Wrong again. The price of oil some ten years ago was under $11/bbl, which comes to an increase this past decade not of 365 percent but of over 900 percent. Perhaps they have no calculators at the *Times*, only dictionaries.

The article makes no mention of the International Energy Agency's recent biting condemnation of the ongoing manipulation of the supply side of the oil price equation. On the subject of oil exporters from OPEC to Russia, the agency said, "[t]he greater the increase in the call on oil and gas from these regions the more likely it will be that they will seek to extract a higher rent from their exports and to impose higher prices in the longer term by deferring investment and constraining production" (International Energy Agency, *World Energy Outlook 2007*, Executive

Summary, China and India Insights, http://www.worldenergyoutlook.
org/docs/weo2007/WEO_2007_English.pdf).

To back up its argumentation, the article quotes the observations
of the Energy Policy Research Foundation of Washington, D.C., an
organization that is largely funded by the oil industry and is always
ready to give malleable reporters sound bites (such as "This is the world's
first demand-led oil shock") that are supportive of the oil patch—so
much for objectivity.

But that's not all. The article introduces two observations that have
become refrains of the oil industry and its comrades-in-arms.

First, feeling our pain, the article informs us that the price of oil has
not yet reached the inflation-adjusted peak, touched during the 1980
Iranian Revolution, of $101.70/bbl. Hey, up there in Maine, everyone
feel better now? This ludicrous point of reference has become a staple
of *Times* reporting on oil prices. Then, quite unbelievably for a paper of
purported seriousness, the article trots out the tired line that, even at
today's prices, oil is cheaper than imported bottled water, as though the
economy of a nation would come to a screeching halt without access to
Evian, Perrier, or Pellegrino. Perhaps this is news to the editors of the
Times, but the rest of us do have access to tap water, supplied by our
municipalities at costs not very different from those of ten years ago.
Perhaps there is a lesson here when it comes to pumping oil from the
nation's public lands.

But wait, it's not over yet. While predicting significant increases in
oil demand by 2030 and in lockstep with the industry's major concern,
which is the growth of alternative fuels, the article has ominous words of
warning. It calls on us be it policy makers or investors thinking of making
commitments to alternative energy (be it solar, wind, biofuel, thermal
power, hydro power, tidal power, nuclear power, coal conversion, flex
fuel vehicles, electric cars, or rail and mass transportation), the message
loud and clear is "stop, stop, stop!" The *Times* is asking us, by innuendo,
"Don't you understand the danger, and the risk to the investments you
are making?" The article continues, "Economic slowdowns in China
and the United States […] would probably send prices tumbling […] it
happened a mere decade ago after the Asian financial crisis […] global
oil prices fell to $10." So now that you understand the risk, put those

plans away, because if you don't, the oil industry may not reach that wondrous state of nirvana predicted for it by 2030.

The Gray Lady should be ashamed of herself and, at the very least, help pay for the fuel bills in Maine this winter.

The *New York Times* Wins the Alfred E. Neuman Award for Its OPEC Coverage
November 19, 2007

I know that commenting about the *New York Times* is getting tiresome. But the *New York Times* is relentless in its "coverage" of the oil industry, shoveling OPEC alibis at us by the truckload. Its coverage is worthy not only of the Alfred E. Neuman "What, Me Worry?" award but also of the even higher-degree ribbon "What, Me Think?"

This weekend, covering the OPEC heads of state meeting in Riyadh, the *Times* reached a high point of journalistic laziness and naïveté (Jad Mouawad, "OPEC Gathering Finds High Oil Prices More Worrisome than Welcome," November 17, 2007, http://www.nytimes. com/2007/11/17/business/17opec.html). Only a *Times* oil industry reporter could quote verbatim the nonsense served up by Prince Abdel Aziz bin Salam, Saudi Arabia's deputy petroleum minister, when he said, "We are so perplexed and so frustrated with the idea we have anything to do with these prices." That the *Times* reports this sickening bit of disingenuousness in total earnest is breathtaking. The reporter does so without ever informing readers that the prince's frustration could easily have been alleviated if Saudi Arabia, together with its OPEC brethren, reinstated the 1.2 million bbl per day that they cut from their production quota a year ago.

For those not following the bouncing ball—that's not your job, but from the *New York Times,* one might have expected professional pride and a responsibility to inform its readership—a short explanation is in order. In November of 2006 with prices above $50/bbl, OPEC cut its production quota by 1.2 million bbl per day. This cut was followed in February of this year by an additional cut of five hundred thousand bbl per day. As prices escalated past $80/bbl in August and September, OPEC announced, graciously in the cartel's view, that the five hundred thousand bbl-per-day-cut would be reinstated but not until November.

That still leaves the perplexed and frustrated Prince Abdel Aziz bin Salam 1.2 million bbl per day short of his and OPEC's production quota of a year ago. Could this be the reason oil prices have escalated? Given this irrefutable statistic, only in the never-never land of the *Times*'s oil patch reporting would the prince's confusion be presented with deadpan seriousness and without further query.

The article goes on to advance the OPEC party line, intoning the usual concern about the falling dollar. It then continues reporting that, at the Riyadh gathering, "fears are rising that that high oil prices will help throw the global economy into recession." This while OPEC members go skipping to the bank. The *Times* quotes such sound bites as one from the oil minister of the United Arab Emirates, Mohamed bin Dhaen al-Hamli, who said, "These prices are potentially dangerous especially if they remain high [...] We cannot remain complacent."

A shivering resident of Maine couldn't have said it better.

The *New York Times*'s Hidden Hand on Oil's Agenda
April 25, 2008

Last Sunday, a *New York Times* front-page headline read, "Behind TV Analysts, Pentagon's Hidden Hand" (April 20, 2008). On the front page of the "Week in Review" section, energy reporter Jad Mouawad set out to instruct us that oil's future is murky ("The Big Thirst," April 20, 2008, http://www.nytimes.com/2008/04/20/weekinreview/20mouawad. html). Mouawad would be a standout candidate for the oil patch's Golden Goose Award for espousing the preprogrammed pieties that encourage soporific acceptance of the greatest transfer of wealth in human history. Wherever there are arguments to be contrived and oil patch rationalizations to excuse the heist represented by today's oil prices, there one will find the *New York Times* and Mouawad to confer its imprimatur of what once passed for serious journalism upon this greatest of all con games.

Mouawad has never been held to account by either the *Times*'s editors or by its editorial page. His writings could easily be attributed to an OPEC or oil patch pitchman. In Mouawad's view, it is never the industry, its willing allies in and out of government, or the perverting hand of OPEC that is to blame. It is us and a host of reasons that he and others repeat ad nauseam that are the cause of what has become a dysfunctional oil market. Let me explain by citing a few examples from his article "The Big Thirst." More would run me out of ink and you out of patience.

"[N]o exporter [is] turning off the spigot.[...] Producers are struggling to pump as much as they can." There alone, the full dimension of Mouawad's biased reporting is laid bare. Clearly and seemingly purposefully, no mention is made of the fact that OPEC has, by its own admission, held 1.2 million bbl per day off the market since the end of 2006; that is oil it could readily produce. Nor is there mention of the fact that Saudi Arabia and OPEC have turned a cold shoulder on President Bush's lame entreaties, as well as on those of the International Energy Agency, to produce more, not because they can't but because they won't.

"The North Sea and Alaska are slowly running out of oil, and producers there are struggling to keep production from falling. Russia's phenomenal surge is coming to an end." Ah, shortages on the horizon—one of the oil patch's banner headlines to ratchet up the price another notch. There is no mention of the new finds offshore Brazil, the massive upward revision of Saudi Arabia's reserves, the burgeoning oil development activities in Iraq, whose reserves are estimated to be comparable to those of Saudi Arabia with barely 10 percent of its landmass having been prospected for oil. As for Russia ... there's no explanation that the slowing of the oil surge is structural and hardly due to an inherent diminishment of oil potential under the right rules and management. But that is how the oil boys and the *Times* try to scare us into higher prices.

We are not running out. There are still trillions of bbl of oil around to be found and tapped from offshore Alaska in the Chukchi Sea to coastal Africa, from the South China Sea and the Gulf of Siam to Greenland, as well as in the Arctic, offshore Sakhalin, in Kazakhstan, and in Uzbekistan. There are untapped reservoirs offshore the United States, the Gulf of Mexico, and elsewhere. At current and significantly lower oil prices, all are economically viable. But leave it to Mouawad to pull out the arm's-length opinion from his friends at BP that "Another 1.2 trillion barrels of known conventional oil reserves wait to be tapped [...] But given the current rate of growth in demand, a trillion of those barrels will be used up in less than 30 years." Feel better now? Once upon a time, the same argumentation was flagged to oil consumers, and yes, we did run out of oil in Pennsylvania. You all remember that, don't you?

Mouawad goes on and on, giving praise and glory to the heroic efforts of the oil companies (and advertisers in the *New York Times*?), ExxonMobil, BP, and Chevron. The *Times* tells us of their magnanimity, because they, together with the two other of the largest international oil companies ("the five largest international oil companies") had spent one hundred billion dollars on exploration last year—by implication, to ease our pain at the pump. Of course, there is no mention that one hundred billion dollars after tax credits is closer to fifty billion dollars in bottom-line money or the approximate earnings of ExxonMobil alone. In typical *Times* fashion, it was a nice plug for the oil companies as to what they sow with no mention of the egregious profits they reap.

Then, throwing caution to the wind, Mouawad cites the benefits of high oil prices, saying, "High oil prices might end up forcing people to conserve and encourage the development of alternatives." There's no argument there. All that cheering you hear in the background are the oil companies and oil producers chanting, "Go, Jad, go," and reminding him not to mention the enormous transfer of wealth that these high oil prices have facilitated; the risks to our security given the nature of the regimes benefiting from it; the crippling impact on our currency (since 2007, the price of oil has advanced more than 110 percent, whereas the dollar has depreciated less than 30 percent. Correlation?) or on our balance of payments; on steadily engulfing stagflation; and on our economic well-being.

Mouawad cites John Hess, chief executive of the Hess Corporation. At a recent energy conference, Hess reportedly warned that an oil crisis was looming if the world didn't deal with runaway demand and strained supplies. Mouawad would have given us an especially instructive insight into what is happening had he quoted John Hess's father, Leon Hess, the legendary founder of Hess Oil. Hess Sr testified before the Senate Committee on Government Affairs in a hearing on the role of futures markets in oil pricing back on November 1, 1990 (no mistake, yes, 1990). At that time, he said, "I'm an old man, but I'd bet my life that if the [the New York Mercantile Exchange] was not in operation, there would be ample oil and reasonable prices all over the world without this volatility."

Mr. Leon Hess, where are you? We need you now. But please don't apply to the *New York Times*. Your incisiveness and clarity of vision would only confuse them.

Paul Krugman and the *Times*'s Pious Pontifications at the Pump
May 16, 2008

On May 12 upon reading Paul Krugman's bizarre op-ed "The So-Called Oil Bubble" in the *New York Times*, they must have been popping champagne corks at the American Petroleum Institute. The *New York Times*, which is consistently off base when reporting on oil markets, permitted its resident economic guru to hit one out of the *Alice in Wonderland* ballpark.

In an extraordinarily jejune piece of analysis, Mr. Krugman tells us that the rise in oil prices isn't the result of runaway speculation but rather of fundamental factors; he then repeats the standard oil patch response by citing the growing needs of emerging economies, the difficulty in finding oil, and so on. Therefore, "there's no good evidence that prices have gotten out of line." These words, coming from the hallowed pages of the *Times*, are an oil flack's dream come true.

The nonsense continues as speculation in oil markets is dismissed. According to Krugman, higher prices due to excessive speculation would result in a situation "in which supply exceeded demand. This excess supply would, in turn, drive prices back down." So according to Krugman, since this hasn't happened, the vertiginously high oil prices as we now know them are a legitimate reflection of market forces—simple as that, Economics 101. Oh, for the good old days.

That trading markets can successfully be manipulated is dismissed. Think of Enron and the California utilities. Think of the Commodity Futures Trading Commission investigation of BP's alleged manipulation in crude oil trading. Look at India suspending futures trading in foodstuffs markets because of the distortions that have resulted. Think of the firepower inherent in Middle East SWFs, which gives them the

176

capacity to move oil and energy markets if they chose to do so. Are they or aren't they? It's an open question.

Then Mr. Krugman continues as though he had landed on this planet from some distant celestial body made of blue cheese. He makes not a single mention—not one—of OPEC, which controls 40 percent of the world's oil supply and willfully and collusively keeps millions of bbl off the market each day. There's no comment on what that has done to distort oil markets. In repeating the oil industry mantra about the difficulty in finding oil, Mr. Krugman supplies no coherent examination whatsoever of the veracity or accuracy of the statement. He never takes into consideration the development and exploration work being done around the world from offshore Brazil to the South China Sea and elsewhere.

He goes on piously to inform us that "France consumes only half as much oil per capita as America," and voilà, the last time he turned his gaze toward it, "Paris wasn't a howling wasteland." What our good instructor overlooked in his lesson is that more than 80 percent of France's power grid has nuclear energy as its source—ah, details. The good editors of the *Times* dare not contest the anointed wisdom of their economics professor.

Finally, and most dangerously, Krugman gives a baleful whitewash of high oil prices. He says high oil prices are okay because "energy conservation becomes increasingly important [...] people may even"—gasp—"take public transportation."

That is the extent of the discomfiture of the nation's citizenry as far as Mr. Krugman is concerned. There is certainly no heads-up from Krugman that the issue here is not energy conservation, which is essential and which must be acted upon with or without high prices. The issue here is the price of oil and his whitewash of a corrupted market (our OPEC friends, were they American or chargeable under American law, would all be sitting in jail as massive violators of antitrust laws). What Krugman has done is given legitimacy to a massive heist of billions of dollars out of our pocketbooks into the voracious treasuries of the oil industry and the transfer of our nation's wealth to malign regimes that present a danger to our values and future.

Mr. Krugman, you should be ashamed of yourself.

The *New York Times* Pipes the Saudi Production Polka
June 15, 2008

Can't you hear it now? The drums and hosannas around the energy desk at the *New York Times*? The high fives and the backslapping? Their guys did it. The Saudis are going into high gear and are going to pump more oil. All their buddies at the *Times* are going to make sure that we know about it with a front-page headline instructing us clearly, "Plan Would Lift Saudi Output to Highest Ever" (June 14, 2008).

To make us understand the profound sense of responsibility and the shared pain emanating from the Saudis, the article informs us that Saudi Arabia was uncomfortable with oil prices and quotes Saudi sources that "Our goal is to bring stability to the oil market." Now that is a gracious, caring gesture from a supplier who has brought the world's economy to the brink of ruin, causing untold damage to the daily lives of people around the world and placing a grievous burden on those least equipped to pay for the palaces and yachts, the princely and national boondoggles of the oil-producing states, of which Saudi Arabia is the chief cheerleader.

The irony, as always, is lost on the *Times* and its editors, who are forever at the ready to do the Saudis' bidding and to render them praise for being "concerned that today's record prices might eventually damp economic growth"—*eventually* is not a typo—when opprobrium would be more in keeping with the reality of events. Thus, Saudi Arabia is pictured as always looking after our interests. We are told that Saudi Arabia is pumping 9.45 million bbl per day as of May, and with the new increase of five hundred thousand bbl, the Saudis will be producing just about ten million bbl per day—the "highest ever." Bravo for Saudi Arabia.

Both increases come after months of stonewalling the world community's pleas to increase production as prices escalated dramatically. What the *Times* doesn't tell us is that even with this increase, under Saudi Arabia's suzerainty, OPEC's quota still has not made up the full cut of 1.7 million bbl per day made in early 2007. This additional production of four hundred thousand bbl per day reinstates the total level of production to the 1.3 million bbl level: five hundred thousand bbl per day last November; three hundred thousand last month; five hundred thousand next month. A report has just come across the wires that, according to Saudi oil minister Ali al-Naimi, the increase for next month has been set at two hundred thousand bbl (Ane Penketh, "Saudi King: 'We will pump more oil,'" the *Independent*, June 16, 2008) not five hundred thousand bbl as reported by the *Times*. Are you surprised?

By the way, in case you missed it, in case you don't think OPEC and its production constraints have much impact on prices, and in case you feel the price of oil is determined by the unencumbered forces of supply and demand or the erosion of the dollar (dollar index down about 25 percent; oil price up 160 percent over the period between January 2007 and June 2008), please take note. Before the Saudi and OPEC cut in daily production by 1.7 million bbl per day in early 2007, the price for crude was in the low fifties compared to today's price of roughly $135/bbl. Given their proclivities, if you asked the oil desk at the *Times* why there was this massive jump in price, they would probably attribute it to astrological forces.

Has the *New York Times* Finally Recognized that the Concept of Peak Oil is Snake Oil?
August 25, 2009

This is a day of deep gloom for the McPeaksters, those preaching the gospel of peak oil. The *New York Times*, which is otherwise deeply sympathetic to oil patch pseudoscience, today burst one of the most entrenched of the oil patch's nuggets of disinformation: the theory of peak oil.

There it was in the op-ed section of the hallowed pages of the Times and three columns wide: "'Peak Oil' Is a Waste of Energy," by Michael Lynch, a former director at the Center for International Studies at the Massachusetts Institute of Technology. His tone was unequivocal as he said, "[P]eak oil theory has been promoted by a motivated group of scientists and laymen who base their conclusions on poor analyses of data and misinterpretations of technical material." He goes on to say that "most arguments about peak oil are based on anecdotal information, vague references, and ignorance of how the oil industry goes about finding fields and extracting petroleum."

After expanding on these points, he goes on to conclude that "[o]il remains abundant, and the price will likely come down closer to the historical level of $30 a barrel as new supplies come forward in the deep waters off West Africa and Latin America, in East Africa, and perhaps in the Bakken oil shale fields of Montana and North Dakota."

Mr. Lynch's "revelations" in the Times are especially gratifying in that at last, one of the greatest and most dangerous pieces of public disinformation—which borders on brainwashing—has been deflated. All of this may be gloom incarnate for the McPeaksters. For the rest of us, it is a breath of fresh air, and as Mr. Lynch clearly puts forward, "This is not to say that we shouldn't keep looking for other cost-effective, low-pollution energy sources—why not broaden our options?"

Methane Oozing in Alaska, Cows Jumping Over Mars, Dinosaurs in Arabia: Peak Oil Pranksters Don't Read This
March 30, 2010

The oil industry and its complicit profession of English-speaking geologists, many of whom are on oil industry staff, have been working for several generations to make us believe unquestioningly that oil and gas are of biological origin. It is a cornerstone of the peak oil dogma that has indoctrinated us into the belief that oil is consummately and imminently finite; that belief permits the oil industry and its allies to drive all over us, setting prices beyond the wildest dreams of Croesus. You see, if oil supply is running out quickly—as we are taught by the oil industry and geological gospel ever since that first well in Pennsylvania in the 1850s—a lesson that the oil industry wants us to learn each and every day is that we will have to pay, pay, pay.

Well, just suppose we have been purposely misled, that the peak oil pranksters and their geologist sidekicks have been the purveyors of one of the great con jobs in history, that oil and gas is not the biological phenomenon that has been drummed into us, rather that oil and gas are a geological phenomenon inherent to the geological construct of the earth and all that means to its expanse and availability. Just recently the *Wall Street Journal* published an eye-opening article informing us that a large sector of the Arctic seabed, which is sitting on a methane reservoir, has become unstable and is releasing methane into the atmosphere (Gautam Naik, "Arctic Site is Oozing Methane," *Wall Street Journal*, March 3, 2010). The article goes on to say "Of the roughly 500 million tons of methane emitted annually world-wide, an estimated 40% has a natural origin, such as wetlands and the digestive processes of termites."—I kid you not; he said "the digestive process of termites"—"while the rest results from human activities including cattle farming" Then, quoting a researcher at the University of Alaska, the article says, "This particular source has never been taken into account in tallying methane emissions."

Well, bravo. That gives us an important clue for solving another newly evolving mystery. You see, last year a team of NASA and university scientists achieved the first definitive detection of methane in the atmosphere of Mars. This discovery indicates, according to NASA, that the planet is either biologically or geologically active. Giving credence to the idea that the existence of methane might indeed be of geological origin rekindles the question of whether the theory attributing the origins of oil and gas to biological (fossil) origins on earth is a myth, in large measure.

Our friends in the oil patch and their geologist allies would, in all likelihood, have a very focused explanation that aligns them with biological phenomenon. Perhaps it would flow along the lines that we have gotten it wrong for generations, that "Hey diddle diddle,\The Cat and the Fiddle,\The Cow jump'd over the Moon" was, in fact, altogether incorrect. It was not "over the Moon" but rather "The Cow jump'd over Mars." Perhaps they would say that it was in fact many cows—all leaving a trail of methane-rich flatulence while jumping over Mars, ergo—hocus pocus—methane's presence in Mars' atmosphere. Far fetched? Not if you try to envisage the huge size of the dinosaur farms in Saudi Arabia and Texas that were needed to turn up as the hundreds of billions of bbl of oil all these eons later.

The methane oozing in Alaska and its presence in the atmosphere of Mars seems a dead giveaway that the theory of biological origins of oil and gas is deeply flawed. Please understand that methane with its four atoms of hydrogen bound to a carbon atom is the main component of natural gas on Earth. Given methane's existence in such nonbiological environs as Mars and conceivably the Arctic seabed brings into question once again the facile dismissal of abiotic oil theory by our oil industry and its OPEC allies.

Why has so little has been published on this issue in English-language scientific or geological journals in spite of the rigorous work done by the Russian and Ukrainian geological community, which is highly supportive of the theory of the geological origins of oil and gas? It is time to revisit this issue, especially at this moment when we find an oil market awash with oil but with oil prices at levels leaving all semblance of market reality. Natural gas prices are touching six-month lows, and oil prices are now a whisker from six-month highs. Given the traditional relationship between these two fuels, wherein one would closely track the other, there is something clearly and profoundly amiss. It is long past time that our media and our government agencies begin to deal with the plethora of misinformation emanating from the oil industry and its allies, who have reduced the consuming public to being passive and paralyzed bystanders in one of history's great swindles.

The *New York Times* Slays the Peak Oil Dinosaur
August 4, 2010

Well, there you have it, right in the opening sentence of an eye-opening article in this Sunday's *New York Times* ("Tracing Oil Reserves to Their Tiny Origins," August 2, 2010): "If you believe petroleum came from dinosaurs, think again and look toward the seas." Here, in the science section, the *Times* tells us that the emphasis on the saurian origins of fossil fuels all these many years "turned out to be wrong." The article goes on to detail the evolution of vast reservoirs of oil that owe their origins to microscopic life that fell into the sea over the ages and was cooked into oil through the earth's core heat. More than 95 percent of the world's oil, it seems, "traces its genesis to the sea." The article notes that "Restrictions on watery flows turn out to have played starring roles in determining where oil formed, scientists say. The Tethys Sea—an ancient ocean that girded the equator in the Cretaceous period some one hundred million years ago in the heyday of the dinosaurs—became a sprawling factory.

"Its most productive regions centered on shorelines, coastal regions, and shallow seas," said Dr. Stow of Heriot-Watt University, whose new book describes the secret life of the Tethys. He identified broad shelf areas as some of the best "factories for biogenic proliferation." When the Tethys mostly closed up (its remnants include the Aral, Black, Caspian, and Mediterranean seas), its fertile southern shores formed the dozen or so nations of the Middle East that produce two-thirds of the world's oil."

Similar Cretaceous period events, we are now learning, may have yielded munificent reservoirs of oil. As an example, when the mass of Africa pulled away from South America, "Big rivers poured in nutrients. A biological frenzy on the western shores of the narrow ocean ended up forming the vast oil fields now being discovered." It is not for nothing that Brazil alone has unveiled a five-year, $224 billion investment plan to tap and develop these vast oil deposits. Combine this information with some equally impressive work done by Russian and Ukrainian geologists on the theory of abiotic oil—the hypothesis that oil is inherent to the geological makeup of the earth—and the dimensions of extant oil begin to look very, very different.

Our previous conception of those dimensions has been the cornerstone of peak oil dogma, which has indoctrinated the American and global public into believing that oil is imminently running out. It has permitted the oil industry to get away with setting prices wholly unrelated to the forces of supply and demand, prices achieved by having successfully lulled the oil-consuming public and governments into a trance of blind acceptance of more and more costly oil.

The peak oil geologists and their prediction of the imminent arrival of the peak is science paid for in large measure by the best geology that oil money can buy. One after another, the peak oil pranksters fall all over themselves, fine-tuning their prophecies of physical depletion to, "Well, it's not so much that there is a physical shortage but that it is more difficult and costly to access." That may be the case—especially with regard to offshore reservoirs as we all now know. But that is a very different argument than the oil industry's self-serving cries of, "There just ain't no more, so please pay, pay, pay."

PART VI

An Economy in Crisis

The Beginning of the Eclipse of American-Style Capitalism
January 28, 2008

Consider that Citigroup ended last year holding at least eighteen billion dollars in mortgage-backed junk, which it has had to write off. Its share price has been halved in a year, which has cost its shareholders billions in losses. It has been reduced from a venerable bank to a tin-cup institution, selling parts of itself at fire-sale prices—all this while recent legal discovery has increased its liability exposure to the Enron bankruptcy.

For their management skills, awards have been visited on Citigroup's visionaries. Vikram Pandit, Citigroup's new chief executive officer, has been awarded a $26.7 million stock bonus and three million dollars in stock options after just six weeks on the job. This was given to a man who, when he was appointed to run trading, investment banking, and alternative investments at Citigroup in early October, caused Deutsche Bank analysts to pronounce that "to restructure the investment bank means that changes in the office of the chairman, which we feel are needed, are unlikely to be forthcoming" (Landon Thomas Jr. and Eric Dash, "Shake-Up at Citigroup," *New York Times*, October 12, 2007, http://www.nytimes.com/2007/10/12/business/worldbusiness/12iht-citi.4.7870967.html). Thus, according to Deutsche Bank's prescient assessment, Pandit's appointment showed nothing more than that the past was prologue.

For his brilliance in 2007, chief executive officer Charles "Chuck" Prince, who was replaced by Pandit in December, was awarded $10.7 million in stock in addition to a $13.2 million cash bonus. Wrecking franchises seems to be nice work if you can get it.

After pocketing one hundred million dollars over the last nine years for being asleep at the switch, Robert Rubin, Citigroup chairman and former US Treasury Secretary, told the Citigroup board's compensation committee that he didn't want a stock bonus this year (the previous year's payout was $6.81 million in stock plus $8.4 million in cash). A true *geste* from someone of Rubin's public profile would have been to return the full one hundred million dollars. Now that would have sent an undeniable message and set a new standard of public responsibility and accountability.

Here is the key. While all these executives were wallowing in gravy, Citigroup had the effrontery to announce almost simultaneously that it was cutting 4,200 jobs—that's 4,200 jobs lost and 4,200 families in distress. *Shameless* is hardly too strong an adjective. By proceeding with such unfairness in such a one-sided and callous manner, Citigroup has become the poster child for much that is happening in—and much that is wrong with—corporate America.

What we are seeing are foreclosures, lost jobs, and lost futures for the middle class and the unempowered while the corporate bigwigs dance off richer than ever before. It is a sign that American capitalism has grown rotten at the core. The capitalist impulse—the kind that made a Bill Gates possible, that nurtured his exemplary vision, making him rich and all of us, as a society, richer—is under attack by vested and influential interests that have stacked the game to such one-sided advantage. It is on the verge of losing all credibility and crushing our confidence in a system that once was a meritocracy and a beacon unto others. This is obscene, and a healthy society cannot permit it to continue.

Your Troubled Asset Relief Program Money Is Being Used to Prop Up the Price of Oil
January 23, 2009

No, it's not about your local gas station not getting a loan from its bank to keep it in business. It is far more insidious. It is about hundreds of millions in Troubled Asset Relief Program (TARP) monies being spent on oil speculation. Billions upon billions of TARP dollars have been made available to the likes of Morgan Stanley. You know what that money was intended for: to finance business and to take pressure off the housing market by helping homeowners avoid foreclosure.

But then again the first $350 billion was released virtually without strings by the Bush administration and its appointees, and you can well imagine the winks and nods that went on behind closed doors:

"Mortgages? C'mon. I've got a better plan. And it's going to be a big help to all the fans of Bush and Cheney in the oil patch. We're going to do our damnedest to prop up the price of oil, and if we buy enough, we'll keep the price from falling and push up the price of gasoline as best we can. Just think of all those dummies out there. We take in their tax bucks and hit them again with higher oil and gas and heating oil prices. Guys, we're on a roll here."

Is that fantasy? How about this *Bloomberg* news item, entitled "Morgan Stanley Hires Supertanker to Store Oil" (January 19, 2009), from Monday of this week that says, "Morgan Stanley hired a supertanker to store crude oil in the Gulf of Mexico, joining Citigroup Inc. and Royal Dutch Shell Plc. in trying to profit from higher prices later in the year, two shipbrokers said." What does all that mean exactly? Well, Morgan Stanley, as but one example, simply took off its banker's hat and donned its speculator's hat, putting down some eighty million dollars (at today's prices) to buy two million bbl of oil. No, they didn't store the oil in their bank vaults. They went out and chartered a supertanker, the *Argenta*, at some sixty-eight thousand dollars per day, and they just have it sitting out there, floating at anchor for day after day. That cost doesn't include finance charges, insurance costs, and all those other ancillary costs. But hey, finance charges? That's cheap, if you have a friendly government agency to fork over the loot.

How many home mortgages could have been salvaged from foreclosure? How many businesses could have been saved by the banks making liquidity available? How much lower would the price of oil have tumbled without Morgan Stanley and other banks' intercessions? In case you need a reminder, the Bush years made it possible for ExxonMobil and their oil company brethren to clock the largest profits ever for any corporations in history. This happened while most everyone else was hurting. Even now, the price of oil is some 100 percent higher than when Bush first took office. Let us hope the Obama administration is not so pliant to the bankers' whims.

Billions for AIG to Protect the Speculative Profits of Goldman Sachs & Morgan Stanley
March 5, 2009

The dysfunction of our financial institutions is almost beyond belief. In November of 2008 with the nation's economy unraveling, Morgan

Stanley and Goldman Sachs (one of the top five US municipal bond underwriters) were infuriating politicians and public finance officials by recommending the purchase of credit default swaps, thereby betting against the debts of eleven states, including New Jersey, California, Wisconsin, Florida, Ohio, and others. Many of these were municipal bonds that they had originally underwritten. Thus, through an act of blatant opportunism, they were contributing to the destabilization of the financial markets already at the edge.

Credit default swaps are, in effect, insurance policies. Insurance policies are normally taken out to cover loss against the occurrence of an event such as fire, flood, accident, and so on. But credit default swaps, rather than being called insurance, became "derivatives" in the parlance of Wall Street, making them much more elegant to deal with and, for the rest of us, much more difficult to understand. They were, in this case, simply insurance bets on the bankruptcy or inability of municipalities throughout the country to meet their debt obligations. It's a bit like taking out insurance against fire on the house next door and having a lottery on the proceeds should it burn down.

Now, to buy insurance, one would naturally go to an insurance company to cover the risk. The insurance company would sell the person a policy and would set an amount on its balance sheet that would represent a reserve against the potential loss and payout. An insurance company likely to write a policy covering this would be AIG. After all, AIG became the king of credit default swaps. This was probably the case for the likes of Goldman Sachs and Morgan Stanley.

Except that it gets worse. You see, in the mumbo jumbo of credit default swaps, the word insurance is not mentioned. According to the good souls at AIG, if you don't use the word insurance, you don't have to set aside any reserves in case of loss. If you don't set aside any reserves, you can issue all the credit default swaps the market can bear (which is understood at AIG to be in the range of four hundred billion dollars) and cash in the policy premiums as an enormous supplement to your usual insurance business, allowing for zillions in paychecks and bonuses. Of course, if it all comes crashing down, you can put up the systemic risk flag, and your Wall Street friends in Washington will charge to the rescue with taxpayer dollars.

During his testimony this week, Federal Reserve Chairman Ben

Bernanke felt compelled to say, and I quote, "AIG exploited a huge gap in the regulatory system; there was no oversight of the financial products division. This was a hedge fund basically that was attached to a large and stable insurance company, made huge numbers of irresponsible bets [and] took huge losses" (David Stout and Brian Knowlton, "Fed Chief Says Insurance Giant Acted Irresponsibly," *New York Times*, March 3, 2009, http://www.nytimes.com/2009/03/04/business/economy/04webecon.html).

One knows the folks at Goldman Sachs are no fools. Were they going to put good money down for credit default swaps that their counterpart (AIG) might not be able to honor because it made no reserve provisions? Or was the temptation of another big payday just too great not to risk other people's money to play the game?

To date, we have poured $160 billion into AIG while others see the values of their homes cut in half, the better part of their 401(k)s wiped out, their government services significantly reduced. Other lending institutions try diligently to work out past-due credits, taking significant markdowns and extending due dates to keep industries and corporations alive.

Goldman Sachs and Morgan Stanley are being covered one hundred cents on the dollar on their speculative positions of intrinsically flawed credit default swaps derivatives, on which they gorged themselves to the bursting point. It is past time that a distinction be made between that part of AIG's business that was a "large and stable insurance company," and that part that was a hedge fund, or better put, a casino. So the big question becomes, why should AIG's credit default swaps be paid down one hundred cents on the dollar when the rest of the country is taking at or near a 50 percent haircut on the value of its assets?

Then again, the rest of the country doesn't have those well-oiled K Street lobbyists pursuing their special interests in Washington. The rest of the country just votes and pays.

Banks, the Oil Market, and the Next Financial Meltdown
May 1, 2009

Yesterday the *Wall Street Journal* reported ("Citi Seeks Approval to Pay Out Bonuses," April 29, 2009) that Citigroup is seeking the US

Treasury's approval to pay special bonuses to key employees. According to the *Wall Street* Journal, the focus of this request is the highly profitable Phibro trading division, whose energy-trading unit is at the point of losing key employees because of federal pay restrictions. Aside from receiving forty-five billion dollars in TARP funds, Citigroup is now 30 percent government-owned.

With the current focus on whether or not to pay bonuses, a much larger and more ominous issue is being overlooked. It highlights the massive distortions in our financial system and the grave potential to repeat the massive risk and leverage blunders taken on by the behemoths of the banking world—blunders that have come frighteningly close to destroying the financial system. Once upon a time, banks played a significant role in aiding the flow of trade both domestically and internationally. A bank would open letters of credit that would permit trade to flow between buyers and sellers in different parts of the world. They would finance the inventory or storage of goods and commodities, thereby assisting the smooth functioning of markets. They would provide loans for the expansion of production capacity. In other words, they would function as banks did once upon a time.

But now, for Citigroup, Morgan Stanley, and many others, such stolid, unglamorous contributions to the world's economy have become too mundane. No, better they risk their depositors' monies, their capital, their TARP infusions (ten billion dollars for Morgan Stanley) by opening oil-trading casinos and forgoing their traditional functions as lenders and facilitators of trade. *Shazam.* They have transformed themselves into oil traders or, simply put, principals, taking title to the physical product by taking delivery, storing it, and thereby foisting on their fiduciary depositor base and shareholders the enormous risks attendant in trading oil (not simply oil futures on the exchanges but an important part of the billions of bbl of crude oil being shipped all over the world). The risks are enormous, and the rewards can be, as well, as they have been for the last few years. But the same could have been said, if anyone had been paying attention to the risk side, to the reckless compounding of credit instruments, the morphing of home finance loans into bank bonds, and the plunge into and packaging of credit default swaps. Banks ceased to function as banks but became traders and gamblers with other people's money, which provided enormous individual payouts while the going was good.

Where we probably do not need any more credit default swap instruments, for which there is no insurable interest at hand, thereby making them pure speculative products, we probably do need oil traders for the smooth functioning of markets. But we need traders who do so at their own risk with their own capital. Leaving it to the banks portends another financial disaster because they tie their viability to the highly volatile world of commodity trading, most especially of crude oil.

It is long past time that the bankers got back to banking the old-fashioned way. We would all be the better for it, and it is time for our government to do what is necessary to ensure that bankers keep to their knitting.

Is J.P. Morgan Chase a Bank or a Government-Funded Casino?
June 9, 2009

CNBC reported yesterday that up to nine banks would soon be allowed to pay back their TARP loans. J.P. Morgan Chase has received some twenty-five billion dollars from the TARP program, has petitioned the government to permit repayment, and will, in all likelihood, be among the banks permitted to do so. Yet that is hardly the end of the government's involvement with J.P. Morgan Chase. The government stood ready and able to assist the financial sector through probably the most difficult crisis since the Depression, and J.P. Morgan Chase was among the primary beneficiaries of those actions. The twenty-five billion dollars may no longer be needed now, but it was certainly crucial then to reestablish public confidence in the system and in each bank's viability. The ultimate aim was, and is, to permit these banks to function as banks, by making it possible for J.P. Morgan Chase and others to continue lending to businesses and consumers, thereby unfreezing the credit markets and returning badly needed liquidity to the system. That was what was meant to be.

Just last week, *Tanker Operator* reported ("VLCC to Store Heating Oil," June 5, 2009) that the good people of J.P. Morgan Chase had hired the good ship or, better put, the very large crude carrier, *Front Queen* f~~or~~ *Liberal Idiot* months—to carry two million bbl of h~~eating oil off~~ ~~M~~alta. One is compelled to wonder how many homes in California, in Michigan, or anywhere in the United States could have been saved from foreclosure or how many payrolls could have been met with the hundreds of millions poured into an oil-trading gambit sitting off the coast of the distant Mediterranean island of Malta. Is this why J.P. Morgan Chase is rushing to repay its TARP monies, so that the freewheeling ways of the past can resume without the possibility of TARP constraints?

The very least one can ask is that the banks act as banks and not as trading houses that make casino-like bets and expect that, should they go sour, the taxpayers will pick up the pieces. By playing the oil game, J.P. Morgan Chase bilks taxpayers twice. First, because it is in part taxpayers' own money being played against them, and second, because they are forced to pay more for their oil, gas, and heating oil. The kind of transaction entered into by J.P. Morgan Chase provides a phony market for oil in that, had the physical product entered the marketplace and not been stored away, it would have weighed on the price of oil and heating oil, pushing prices down. It is exactly these moneyed players and speculators who are keeping oil prices at their gamed level.

It is untenable for banks, whose responsibility it is to provide the liquidity needed for the economy to prosper, to use depositors' monies to delve into the trading of all manner of ancillary risk-laden products, be they derivatives, credit default swaps—and on to title shipping documents attaining to cargos of oil, heating oil, and (eventually, if not already) bananas.

There is nothing wrong with a world-class bank helping in the financing of trade, and that is as it should be. But here the determinants are the competence of the parties to the transaction and their business viability, a determination that banks are normally schooled to make. In doing so, they provide a healthy measure of oversight as to the viability of the trade in question. But when the bank itself becomes the principal, the next financial crisis is just around the corner.

Are our banking regulators truly going to wake up to the profound dangers of the current structure of our banking institutions, or are they too closely aligned with the powers that be to change it in a meaningful way?

Wall Street Stampedes to the Aid of the Oil Speculators!
July 12, 2009

Here we go again. The same financial class that brought us to the edge of economic meltdown is now pressing its well-connected pals and cronies on Wall Street, in Congress, in the press, and in our OPEC-cheering oil industry to keep their hands off the continued stripping of America's wealth through the gamed and egregiously profitable racket of oil futures trading.

This week the Commodity Futures Trading Commission responded to a national and international outcry that enough is enough and, in keeping with the Obama administration's goal of tougher oversight, has finally decided to act. Reacting to Congressional pressures, a struggling industrial landscape, and a beleaguered public, the Commodity Futures Trading Commission announced that a series of restrictions on energy trading would be set forth.

The Commodity Futures Trading Commission and the American public are not alone in their outrage. Earlier this week, the *Wall Street Journal* printed an op-ed ("Oil Prices Need Government Supervision," July 8, 2009) jointly written by Prime Minister Gordon Brown of Great Britain and President Nicolas Sarkozy of France calling for "transparency and supervision of the oil futures market in order to reduce damaging speculation" (signaling its own take on the issue, the *Wall Street Journal* placed the piece at the bottom of page fifteen).

To arrest the clear evidence of speculation-driven trading by financial and noncommercial interests (by *noncommercial* I mean neither oil producers nor oil users) speculating heavily and erratically, pushing markets higher (usually), the Commodity Futures Trading Commission has committed itself to take the issue in hand. A glaring example of runaway speculation was reported on July 3 by the *Financial Times*; a rogue trader in London had moved the market by more than $2/ bbl "without apparent justification" (read, without any commercial interest other than rank speculation; Javier Blas, "PVM Blames $10m Loss on Unauthorized Trades," July 3, 2009, http://www.ft.com/cms/ s/0/48365f5c-676a-11de-925f-00144feabdc0.html#axzz1Gz8U8ozB). The trader, PVM Oil Futures Limited's Stephen Perkins, was fined seventy-two thousand pounds and a minimum five-year ban in trading.

On July 7, 2009, the Commodity Futures Trading Commission announced its readiness to place volume limits on energy futures by pure financial traders and investors, as well as to create tougher information requirements to identify the role of hedge funds and traders who swap contracts on the barely regulated or transparent over-the-counter markets. Almost immediately thereupon, the *New York Times* ("U.S. Ponders New Curbs on Speculators," July 8, 2009) cautioned that "proposals could encounter fierce opposition from big banks and Wall Street firms, which each are big traders in the commodity markets."

Who are these "big traders in the commodity markets"? They include Morgan Stanley and Goldman Sachs, both colossi in the field. Both were once investment banks and are now bank-holding companies, having turned themselves into the same with the Federal Reserve's blessing on September 22, 2008, in the wake of the finance world chaos after Lehman's demise. As bank-holding companies, these entities became eligible for TARP funds and other emergency loan programs set up by the Federal Reserve and the US Treasury, an array of new Federal Reserve lending facilities, including access to the Federal Reserve's discount window and to bank deposits that would be insured by the Federal Deposit Insurance Corporation.

Both banks reported enormous gains from their trading activity over this second quarter, enough for Goldman Sachs, according to the *Wall Street Journal* ("Big Pay Packages Return to Wall Street," July 2, 2009) to be on track to pay out twenty billion dollars this year or seven hundred thousand dollars per employee—nearly double the firm's $363,000 average last year.

All of this happened after it was reported that Goldman Sachs received billions in counterparty funds from AIG, which the Federal Reserve made available to AIG to permit it to bail out Goldman Sachs' speculative derivative positions of credit default swaps and similar toxic paper, which were probably worth less than thirty cents on the dollar at the time, for one hundred cents on the dollar. This covered what otherwise would have been billions and billions of dollars in Goldman Sachs losses—talk about a good ol' boys network. How many homeowners were as fortunate and escaped foreclosure? How many small businesses could have made their payrolls had they had equally accommodating banking relationships?

This raises an even bigger question. What are these bank-holding companies doing, using Federal Reserve monies and programs with access to the Federal Reserve's discount window and Federal Deposit Insurance Corporation—insured deposits, to speculate in the commodity futures markets? The irony is that Federal Reserve monies, instead of going to business lending and real estate mortgage financing—what the economy really, desperately needs—provide exceedingly cheap, voluminous liquidity to play the commodities casino.

It's clear that, given the prodigious profits they enjoy from the current system, the casino players will fight tooth and nail to turn back the Commodity Futures Trading Commission initiatives. They will be allied with the oil industry in espousing the need for a futures market as a tool to manage price risk, never whispering their delight in a market that assigns their product immeasurably more value than is fair or sensible. Our sad Congress, while paying lip service to the best interests of the nation's citizens, will be swayed in too many cases by the influence and campaign largesse of K Street lobbyists.

At present, bank-holding companies like Citigroup, J.P. Morgan Chase, Morgan Stanley, and Barclays are exercising their *banking responsibilities* to assist this difficult economy by playing what is termed the contango game. Acting as principals (i.e., for their own account) and using their access to cheap money, they are loading themselves to the brim with hundreds of millions of bbl of crude oil and oil products supertankers that are kept at anchor for months to a year at a time. Taking the oil and oil products off the market helps to sustain ever-higher oil prices at vast additional cost and burden to the nation's consumers. The oil is held at sea for months—thereby tying up hundreds of millions of dollars—in anticipation of higher prices for the cargo at the end of the tanker charter period. What does this have to do with banking as we came to understand it, especially in this time of crisis?

There is too much at stake here, not least of which is the need to determine the role of banks, especially bank-holding companies, after the disasters of the past year. Are banks meant to help the economy or to go back to business as usual in helping to destroy it?

Question for the Federal Reserve and G-20: Why Are Our Banks Running Commodity Casinos?
September 25, 2009

In an article in Wednesday's *Financial Times* (Gregory Meyer, "Banks Braced For Fed's Commodities Decision," September 22, 2009, http://www.ft.com/cms/s/0/90514590-a79d-11de-b0ee-00144feabdc0. html#axzz1Gz8U8ozB), an issue was raised that has been swept under the rug by the banking community and, I'm sad to say, by our government since the repeal of the Glass-Steagall Act in 1999. A plethora of banks and bank-holding companies such as Goldman Sachs, Morgan Stanley, J.P. Morgan Chase, and Citigroup have been actively trading physical commodities and paper commodity derivatives (i.e., oil, natural gas, an array of agricultural commodities, metals, and so forth). According to the *Financial Times* article, several banks have entered the commodity business in recent years as guided by "an increasingly permissive [Federal Reserve]."

What a time to be permissive! The likes of Goldman Sachs, Morgan Stanley, and J.P. Morgan Chase slunk their way onto a commodity trading platform some years ago by acquiring interests in power plants and oil tankers, giving them a rationale to deal in physical commodities.

Divestment was envisaged as companies became financial holding companies. But a knowing banking community, aided by moneyed lobbyists, created an accommodating loophole in the Gramm-Leach-Bliley Banking Reform Bill of 1999. This loophole allows proprietary trading such as using the banks' assets and deposits to speculate in commodity markets and other financial instruments.

One need raise a question again and again. What is a bank or bank-holding company doing using Federal Deposit Insurance Corporation–insured deposits, access to loans at the Federal Reserve window, access to myriad Federal Reserve and governmental loan and support programs, and the implied government guarantee of "too big to fail," to play casino, gambling with commodity positions with both physical product and paper derivatives? They are buying and selling commodity derivatives far beyond their in-house needs and, in most cases, based on pure speculation. This continues even after the egregious and disastrous speculation of the all-too-recent past.

In the title, I have used the word *our*, because these banks would very likely not be in existence were it not for the government's massive interventions, ranging from handing out TARP funds to guaranteeing dubious asset holdings to—as in the case of Goldman Sachs—providing third parties (AIG) with counterparty liquidity to cover billions of what otherwise would have been massive losses on speculative derivatives. In a sense, a strong case can be made that they have become morally beholden to us as our banks.

It is one thing for banks to finance the trade in commodities by establishing letters of credit and providing third-party financing for inventories and production. But it is sheer madness, after recent history, to permit banks to become commodity traders, especially with our money.

Goldman Turns into a Financial Frankenstein While the Federal Reserve Snoozes Away
October 17, 2009

Before the financial crisis, before Goldman Sachs was the recipient of billions in TARP funds, before the rescue of AIG and their derivative contracts representing thirteen billion dollars (that we know about), before the myriad telephone calls at the height of the crisis between Lloyd Blankfein, chairman of Goldman Sachs, and Treasury Secretary Henry Paulson, former chairman of Goldman Sachs—before all that, Goldman Sachs was a tried and true investment bank that was active in proprietary trading and investments and battling away in the realm of you-win-some,-you-lose-some with its own money (Gretchen Morgenson and Don Van Natta Jr, "Paulson's Calls to Goldman Tested Ethics," *New York Times*, Aug 8, 2009).

Then, as the crisis peaked, financial wizardry reached a new apogee. *Abracadabra*—the Federal Reserve, in concert with the US Treasury, waved its magic wand and Goldman Sachs was magically transformed almost overnight into a bank-holding company to ensure that it had access to varied government lifelines during the heavy weather of what many feared was an incipient financial meltdown. Further, it sent a crystal clear signal to the world marketplace that, after the collapse of Lehman Brothers, Goldman Sachs was too big to fail, and the government wouldn't allow its failure to happen. At that moment of financial havoc, it was a priceless endorsement.

Now what does that mean? Goldman Sachs not only received the government's implied guarantee that it was too big to fail—which was essential to Goldman Sachs, given the financial turbulence at hand—but also many other benefits. For example, Goldman Sachs got access to the Federal Reserve window, where banks borrow money from the Federal Reserve Bank at a deeply discounted interest rate, and dirt cheap money (less than 1 percent interest on borrowings); access to money from bank deposits that would now be guaranteed by the Federal Deposit Insurance Corporation; and myriad Federal Reserve programs in support of the banking system.

The *Financial Times*, commenting on Citigroup's sale of its oil-trading unit to Occidental Petroleum ("Citi Bows to Pressure by Selling Phibro," October 10, 2009), made a fundamental observation that applies in spades to Goldman Sachs. The article said, "The divestment of Phibro [...] enables the bank to redeploy billions in capital the unit needs but deprives it of a big profit engine." An even more accurate observation would have changed the text to read "a big profit/risk engine," because that is the nature of oil trading and virtually all proprietary trading—be it in bonds, currencies, financial derivatives, or all manner of commodities from copper to soybeans. Here lies the core of the financial Frankenstein that the Federal Reserve, our oversight agencies, and our government have created and continue to nurture.

You see, Goldman Sachs was not assisted by the government to become a voracious and even heftier investment bank. One must assume that the government's assistance was to prevent systemic failure and to enable Goldman Sachs and others to function as banks in order to assist in the restructuring of the American economy. One must assume that it was the US Treasury and the Federal Reserve's intention and expectation that, given the extraordinary assistance extended to Goldman Sachs, it would pitch in toward calming the nation's economic turbulence by assuming many of the responsibilities attendant on being a bank—extending loans to businesses large and small and to homeowners, doing what banks do to help communities throughout the land. One might have expected Goldman Sachs to redeploy a large measure of the government's largesse to the less profitable, less risky, but urgently needed retail banking and to spur local economies.

Would it have been too much to ask that Goldman Sachs do this out of a sense national obligation and perhaps an ounce of gratitude, that it not simply siphon hundreds of billions out of the economy for proprietary trading. Goldman Sachs gorged itself on government-funded programs with practically the sole purpose of enhancing its bottom line (with the result all too often of increased prices for the consumer). One can seriously ask if Goldman Sachs' trading in oil played an important role in pushing the price of oil to $147/bbl, thereby helping to crush the economy?

It could be said that what we are seeing is a gross misallocation of government funds and programs. It stands to reason that the purpose of Goldman Sachs' transformation from investment bank to bank-holding company was not to enhance its ability to trade and profit. There is a moral obligation here that goes far beyond turning a buck.

Citigroup, Goldman Sachs, Wall Street, and the Tolling of the Bell for America's Meritocracy
October 22, 2009

In late 2007 and the early days of 2008, Citigroup announced that it was cutting 4,200 jobs. This happened shortly after Vikram Pandit— just six weeks on the job as Citigroup's chief executive officer—was awarded a $26.7 million stock bonus and three million dollars in stock options. It also happened as the bank was set to announce that, by the end of 2007, it had held eighteen billion dollars in mortgage-backed toxic assets. The share price had halved already while Citigroup was led into the abyss by a management team that included its previous chief executive officer, Charles Prince, who was given a golden parachute of $10.7 million in stock and a $13.2 million cash payout. Things have deteriorated dramatically since January of 2008. By early 2009, the job cuts at Citigroup climbed beyond seventy-five thousand, and what happened at Citigroup was only the beginning of the one-sided unfairness that has become the shameful norm in the way we now do business.

Now it is no longer Citigroup and the then 4,200 layoffs; millions nationwide have lost and are losing their jobs and their futures. Families and communities are overwhelmed by foreclosures, and far too many are losing hope along with their homes. This is happening while the likes of Goldman Sachs, Morgan Stanley, and their brethren on Wall Street are dancing off richer than ever before. Consider that, just a short while back, the likes of Lee Raymond, the chief executive officer of ExxonMobil, retired with a four hundred million-dollar golden parachute. This was the culmination of a career presiding over the largest cog in an industry whose rapacious profits resulted from Americans paying more than $4/ gallon for their gasoline, even while many were unable to meet the cost of heating their homes.

American capitalism was becoming and has now become rotten to the core. Gone is the unique sense of fair play and adherence to a level playing field, accessible to all. Gone is that formidable confidence in our system as being a meritocracy, which was quintessentially American in its nature and very nearly devoid of envy and resentment. I'm talking about the American capitalist impulse that made a Bill Gates not only possible but also downright probable. Ours was a land that nurtured and celebrated his exemplary vision, making him rich and all of us, as a society, richer. That land is now being overwhelmed; its creative vision and sense of fair play are being destroyed by vested interests that have stacked the deck so consistently and successfully as to destroy the meritocracy's credibility altogether.

In January of 2008, I asserted that "the Citigroup bell has tolled" ("Citigroup's Self-Immolation and the Beginning of the Eclipse of American-Style Capitalism," *Huffington Post*, http://www.huffingtonpost. com/raymond-j-learsy/citigroups-selfimmolation_b_83518.html). Today, struggling with some $350 billion in government bailout loans and guarantees and covering hundreds of billions in toxic assets, the bell has indeed tolled for Citigroup. Now, sadly, the bell is tolling for the spirit and brilliance of what once was American capitalism and its sense of fairness and free enterprise. What has come to pass is obscene, and a healthy society cannot allow it to continue.

Is There a Change in the Weather at Goldman Sachs?
October 26, 2009

Perhaps, just perhaps, the opprobrium heaped on Goldman Sachs these many weeks and months has begun to have an effect on its tone-deaf leadership and its bizarre rationalizations, such as those of Lord Brian Griffiths, vice chairman of Goldman Sachs International, who instructed us last week that "[w]e have to tolerate the inequality as a way to achieve greater prosperity for all" (Kathryn Hopkins, "Public Must Learn to 'Tolerate the Inequality' of Bonuses, Says Goldman Sachs Vice Chairman," Guardian.co.uk, October 21, 2009, http://www.guardian. co.uk/business/2009/oct/21/executive-pay-bonuses-goldmansachs). This statement was made at a time when millions had lost their jobs and had their homes foreclosed. No, I am not making this up. Given Goldman Sachs' way of dealing with the issues at hand—the issues of reward and fairness, the potential of it all becoming a total disaster to its public image and reputation—even the unbelievable has become sadly believable.

A news item appeared this week that seems to offer at least reasonable hope that Goldman Sachs is beginning to use its good fortune to help remedy the foundering fortunes of Main Street America. Helping institutions that deal directly with America's day-to-day economy is where Goldman Sachs could play a truly constructive role. If the news item in question is being read correctly, it appears that is what may be happening.

On Friday, October 23, 2009, CNBC reported, "CIT Reaches a Tentative Deal with Goldman" (http://www.cnbc.com/id/33444384/ CIT_Reaches_Tentative_Deal_with_Goldman_Report). Now CIT is a financial institution on which myriad small and midsize American businesses depend to finance their working capital. CIT provides businesses with funding against accounts receivable and inventory of goods and materials, without which many small and midsize firms could not operate, especially in the current fractured banking environment. These are businesses and companies to which Goldman Sachs would normally have little or no access, no commercial interface. Yet, through working with CIT, Goldman Sachs would be able to assist a core part of the American economy that needs all the help it can get.

Because of the economy, CIT is struggling to restructure billions of dollars in debt and to stay out of bankruptcy. Unlike the cases of Goldman Sachs, Morgan Stanley, AIG, and Citigroup, its failure might not present a systemic and catastrophic risk to the entire financial system. For that reason, government assistance for a CIT restructuring has not been as freely forthcoming as it has been for the large banking/insurance/speculation entities. That is where Goldman Sachs is about to play a highly purposeful role. By assisting CIT, it will be assisting main street businesses the length and breadth of the land.

According to the news report, Goldman Sachs and CIT have reached a tentative agreement over a disputed maturation of a three billion-dollar loan. Goldman Sachs' accommodation on this issue would open the door for CIT to get billions of dollars in new financing from its bondholders, which it could then use to reorganize. In so doing, a vital financing link on which many small to midsize American businesses depend would continue to play its key role. The alternative would add enormous additional stress to the American economy.

One hopes Goldman has come around to understanding that, given the public support it has received and the government's implicit guarantee that it is too big to fail, it has responsibilities and, at the very least, moral obligations that go beyond the bottom line and maximizing the bonus pool. How this all plays out remains to be seen, but if nothing else, we will learn a great deal about the players.

The Key Question No One Asked about Goldman's Role in the AIG Bailout
November 20, 2009

A critical and fundamental issue was not brought up during the fierce interrogation of Treasury Secretary Timothy Geithner during Thursday's hearings before Congress's Joint Economic Committee. The contentious subject at hand was the Fed Reserve and the US Treasury's role in AIG's multibillion-dollar bailout. The key question neither asked nor answered was what was the nature of the myriad discussions, at the height of the crisis in September 2008, between the treasury secretary and former Goldman Sachs chairman, Henry Paulson, and the Goldman Sachs chairman, Lloyd Blankfein?

It is hard to imagine that the issue of AIG was not broached, that information was not exchanged. Most tellingly, Geithner's testimony yesterday reiterated the fact that the Federal Reserve and the US Treasury viewed the prospect of AIG's failure as posing a highly significant risk to the economy, and after what happened to Lehman, AIG's failure would not be permitted to happen. That morsel of information, had it been made available to Goldman Sachs in September of 2008, would have been worth tens of billions of dollars to Goldman.

Goldman Sachs was AIG's largest counterparty; its holdings, directly or indirectly through credit default obligations and credit default swaps, made up one third of the sixty-two billion-dollar counterparty trades on AIG's books. Given Goldman's know-how and connections, it would seem probable that it also played a leading role as enabler in what Federal Reserve Chairman Ben Bernanke described to a Congressional committee in March of this year. He said, "AIG exploited a huge gap in the regulatory system [...] There was no oversight of the financial products division. This was a hedge fund, basically, that was attached to a large and stable insurance company, made huge numbers of irresponsible bets—took huge losses. There was no regulatory oversight because there was a gap in the system" (David Stout and Brian Knowlton, "Fed Chief Says Insurance Giant Acted Irresponsibly," *New York Times*, March 3, 2009, http://www.nytimes.com/2009/03/04/business/economy/04webecon.html).

During the subsequent rescue of AIG, a game of high-stakes poker evolved, perhaps with a touch of outright extortion. The New York Federal Reserve, which Geithner headed at the time, was charged with negotiating with AIG's trading partners to try to modify their counterparty contracts with AIG to levels more closely approaching their real-time value—at the time, that was considerably less than face value. At one stage, discussions took place between the trading partners and AIG about writing down AIG's obligations to some forty cents on the dollar—without success, as Goldman Sachs refused to budge.

Here is the crunch and the key to the question, did Goldman Sachs and the other banks know for certain that the bankruptcy of AIG was no longer a risk for them, that the Federal Reserve and the US Treasury were irrevocably committed to saving AIG, that Goldman Sachs and the other banks, with that foreknowledge, were empowered to take—risk-free—the inflexible position that "it would be improper and perhaps even criminal to force AIG's trading partners to bear losses outside of bankruptcy court" (Mary Williams Walsh, "Audit Faults New york Fed in AIG Bailout," *New York Times*, November 16, 2009, http://www.nytimes.com/2009/11/17/business/17aig.html)? Goldman Sachs et al would have been playing poker with a clear view of the Federal Reserve's hand. That raises the serious question of what Goldman Sachs knew and when it knew it and whether it played the AIG derivatives card with inside information about the Federal Reserve's intentions. If so, what might be the legal ramifications?

Mr. Paulson is a valuable man to know. Pimco, an international investment management firm, pocketed $1.7 billion (Pimco's single largest payday ran the proud boast) by taking positions in underwater Fannie Mae and Freddie Mac paper, which were then surprisingly redeemed at full value, piggybacking on the taxpayers' more than one hundred billion-dollar bailout of those institutions. When the big guys were in trouble because of the public's perception of greed and funny games, there was Henry Paulson to tell us, while en route to Saudi Arabia with oil on its way to $147/bbl, that it was all about supply and demand. We should thank Mr. Paulson for making us all feel better about paying more than four dollars per gallon at the pump and watching our economy go down the pipeline.

Securities Investor Protection Corporation: The Grinch That Grotesquely Stole Christmas
December 22, 2009

You've probably seen the television ad. A young girl is given a bicycle set in a white painted rectangle that's, say, eight by four feet. Delighted, the young girl sits on the bicycle and starts to ride, but after barely getting started, she's stopped at the white line. "That's as far as you can ride," scolds an austere gentleman (a banker, we are given to understand). Stunned, the young girl gazes at him, befuddled and sad. "Didn't you read the fine print?" he asks. "It says you can only ride the bicycle in a predetermined space." Welcome to the world of the Securities Investor Protection Corporation (SIPC). Protection?

The Madoff calamity touched thousands of individuals and families, many of whom lost what amounted to their life savings. Many had gone to bed one night last December confident that their financial future was secure only to wake up the next day to find their lives devastated and their savings worthless. Many were then without so much as the means to pay their monthly bills, and many, given their ages, had no hope of finding a job ever again.

Confronted with disaster, all the Madoff account holders believed that the SIPC seal prominently displayed on their brokerage statements—the seal of an organization created by an act of Congress—would protect them at least up to the five hundred thousand dollars SIPC was authorized to pay out. SIPC, in its brochure "How SIPC Protects You" (http://www.sipc.org/how/brochure.cfm), brayed about its insurance coverage, saying, "SIPC replaces missing stocks and other securities," while the Financial Industry Regulatory Agency (FINRA) would point out in its literature, "Your Rights under SIPC Protection," that "SIPC's coverage also includes protection against unauthorized trading in customers' securities accounts" (http://www.finra.org/Investors/ProtectYourself/AfterYouInvest/YourRightsUnderSIPCProtection/). With input like this, even a highly sophisticated investor would have taken comfort in the SIPC seal.

Yet, perversely and after the fact, SIPC sniffed out a legal loophole that imperiled probably the most vulnerable, the longest standing, and the oldest of Madoff's victims. They adopted a bizarre method of determining claims, namely the "cash in/cash out" method, that repays customers the money invested minus the cash they'd withdrawn from their accounts, thereby seeking, where possible, to avoid the maximum five hundred thousand-dollar obligation. It makes as much sense as if the Federal Deposit Insurance Corporation denied paying out the bank statement balance of an interest-bearing account in one of its failed banks because the customer withdrew more funds than he deposited over the years the account was active.

Instead of finding a solution that would uphold its moral and legal obligation and return credence to SIPC—and what were once thought to be bankable government guarantees—it was with brazen callousness that SIPC's deputy solicitor dismissed the last hope of thousands of claimants. "The claims of the Madoff investors cannot be valued based on the balance shown on their account statements" (Michael A. Conley, "SEC Statement before the Capital Markets, Insurance, and Government-Sponsored Enterprises Subcommittee, United States House of Representatives," December 9, 2009, http://www.sec.gov/news/testimony/2009/ts120909mac.htm). That might be true in some measure in bankruptcy court, but SIPC was specifically created to deal with issues of failure and fraud with a five hundred thousand-dollar account limit, and if that was the amount lost by the customer, then that was the amount on which SIPC was expected to make good. All sums above that figure would be between the account holder and the bankruptcy court.

Testimony before the House Financial Services Committee on December 9 bore out the callousness of SIPC and the terrible straits in which the victims had found themselves. "The money I had invested with Madoff represented thirty years of my life savings," Jeannene Langford from San Rafael, California, told the committee. "This was my retirement, a down payment for a house, investment for the business I was starting, and it was money for my daughter's education... I do not have 30 years to earn this money again" (Testimony of Jeannene Langford, December 6, 2009, http://www.house.gov/apps/list/hearing/financialsvcs_dem/langford.pdf).

According to some, SIPC's hard line is conditioned in part by a perception that it is grossly underfunded and hamstrung by a concern that paying out troublesome claims may not leave enough funding for future claimants. In testimony before the US House of Representatives, the Subcommittee on Capital Markets, Insurance, Government-Sponsored Enterprises, and the Committee on Financial Services, Stephen P. Harbeck, president and chief executive officer of SIPC, testified that the balance of the SIPC fund was $1,188,000,000 (note: that's less than 10 percent of the Goldman Sachs 2009 bonus pool, which exceeds twenty billion dollars). He also advised that SIPC "may borrow $1 billion line of credit from the United States Treasury," and went on to proclaim proudly, "In its nearly forty-year history, SIPC has never drawn upon the credit line." In doing so, Mr. Harbeck clearly revealed he is not the man for the job. Instead of doing his utmost to calm the turbulent waters caused by the greatest economic crisis since the Great Depression at a time of massive claims occasioned by the Madoff, Lehman, and Stanford bankruptcies and myriad others, he is busy pinching pennies.

Where is the Treasury, which was so eager to bail out or make whole the likes of Citigroup, AIG, Morgan Stanley, Goldman Sachs, and so on with billions upon billions in cash loans, infusions, and guarantees of otherwise toxic loans and derivatives? What would the prospects have been if, as a condition of the billions going to the banking and Wall Street crowd, they would have been persuaded or coerced to use some of their bumper profits to come to significantly increase their fees to SIPC so it could substantially increase its lines of credit and conduct itself in a way that would be of real assistance to those victims of financial mismanagement and fraud, not to mention to regain the respect and confidence of the nation's stockholders? In the meantime, Mr. Harbeck better watch out; that little girl may indeed be riding off on that bicycle.

Taxing Wall Street's Bonuses Should Focus on Clawbacks
December 29, 2009

The *New York Times*, in a recent editorial entitled "Taming the Fat Cats" (December 19, 2009 http://www.nytimes.com/2009/12/20/opinion/20sun1.html), called on President Obama to impose Britain's special 50 percent tax on all bank bonuses greater than forty thousand dollars this year. Concurrently, Senator Charles Schumer of New York voiced his outrage that AIG executives have not returned the major portion of the forty-five million dollars they agreed to by the end of the year, in spite of the $183 billion they received from taxpayers in order to keep their company afloat.

In the meantime, Goldman Sachs has set aside a bonus pool of twenty-three billion dollars for 2009, even after receiving billions in TARP funds (which it has since paid back to the government, much in the manner of a rescued drowning man returning a life preserver to the ship's crew after it had served its purpose); after having been given a free pass to change its corporate moniker from investment bank to bank-holding company, with all its attendant access to federal programs and near-costless money; after having been showered with giveaway billions of government counterparty funding that permitted Goldman to be made whole on credit derivative bets that otherwise would have been worth next to nothing.

As pointed out in the *Times*'s editorial, this catalog of excess is the result of "the way America's voracious bankers leveraged hundreds of billions in taxpayer bailouts to line their pockets with multibillion-dollar bonuses while American businesses starve for credit"—not to speak of the millions of unemployed and the millions who have lost or will lose their homes. The rage is widespread, and to the financial community's great relief, it is grossly misdirected. Focusing on bonuses to come has taken the eyes of the public, the media, Congress, and the president off the ball. To the bankers, the issue of primary concern is the specter of clawbacks of the hundreds of billions of bonuses and salaries paid out in these past years against illusionary profits from trading value-destroying derivatives, from opaque market instruments, from accounting practices bordering on the spurious, from off-the-book entities, from vastly inflated balance sheets resulting in bonuses that were based largely on erroneous information and calculations if not outright fraud.

Being taxed on or reducing this year's bonuses is but an irritant if the hundreds of billions paid out over the past few years can be held free and clear by their recipients in the financial world in spite of their bringing the economy to the brink of catastrophe through "their foolhardy bets that tipped the world into the worst economic crisis since the 1930s, ("Taming the Fat Cats," *New York Times,* December 19, 2009, (http://www.nytimes.com/2009/12/20/opinion/20sun1.html). Had these banks and financial institutions gone bankrupt, as indeed many technically would have without the government's bailouts, the trustee in bankruptcy would have deemed the bonuses paid out to be fraudulent transfers and would have forced their repayment to the estate in bankruptcy, namely the myriad banks and financial institutions that received government help both directly and indirectly. Certainly, given the billions it is costing the public purse, it is incongruous in the extreme that those who caused the disaster should retain the spoils of their irresponsibility and mismanagement.

Back in March, Senator Schumer minced no words. In a letter dated March 17, 2009, to the then AIG chairman, Edward Liddy, he wrote:

> We write today to express our outrage at [AIG]'s recently revealed multimillion-dollar bonus payments.

In these perilous economic times, it is unconscionable for the American taxpayer to find out that the very employees responsible for running the company into the ground have now received 'performance-based' awards that are hundreds of times as large as the average American's yearly salary. If these contracts are not renegotiated immediately, we will take action to make American taxpayers whole by recouping all of the bonuses that AIG has paid out to its financial products unit, which, by all accounts, is primarily responsible for the near-failure of the company and the devastating impact on the global financial markets.

Senator Schumer was on the right track, but why limit the focus to AIG? The same could be said for just about all of the entities that received assistance from the Federal Reserve and Treasury over the past sixteen months. This has crippled the national budget and the economy both here and throughout the world. In the spirit of Senator Schumer's admonition, it is past time to right a great wrong perpetrated on the American taxpayer by designating the bonuses paid out from the illusionary profits in trading these financial products as fraudulent transfers and to demand the recapture of all bonuses derived from trading in such financial instruments as credit default swaps, collateralized debt obligations, or derivatives per se. It is time for Congress to act. As the *New York Times* pointed out in its editorial, the "constitutional ban of bills aimed to punish a specific group—so-called bills of attainder—is unlikely to apply because a tax would not be aimed to punish named people but an economic class."

Congress should now forcefully take the matter in hand and act to remedy one of the greatest con games ever visited on the American public. It would in large measure restore the nation's confidence in its financial markets and their governance; that confidence has been shaken as never before.

Wall Street Triage: Was Lehman Sacrificed So AIG Had to Be Bailed Out?
January 10, 2010

To date, the American taxpayer has pumped $180 billion into AIG to spare it from insolvency. That's a huge sum, especially considering that many of these billions were used to pay down exotic derivatives to the likes of Goldman Sachs and a bevy of foreign banks. The derivatives were paid out at one hundred cents on the dollar when their market value, before the government's intervention, was perhaps forty cents and probably a great deal less. Now we learn, through recent access to New York Federal Reserve documents and e-mails (Hugh Son, "Geithner's Fed Told AIG to Limit Swaps Disclosure (Update 3)," Bloomberg.com, January 7, 2010, http://www.bloomberg.com/apps/news?pid=newsarch ive&sid=aXIvW4igKV38), that the New York Federal Reserve, which was headed at the time by Timothy Geithner, actively withheld details about those counterparty payments and advised AIG not to reveal the recipients or the counterparty billions disbursed. Only much later did a Congressional committee override the Federal Reserve's guidelines and force AIG to make this information public.

At the height of the crisis, Timothy Geithner was working closely with then-Treasury Secretary Henry Paulson. Between September 18 and 21, 2008, Paulson called Geithner twenty-eight times. Over a seven-month period, Paulson and Geithner spoke 416 times, whereas Paulson's contacts with Federal Reserve Chairman Ben Bernanke counted some 286 calls (Nomi Prins, "Paulson's Revealing Phone Records," the *Daily Beast*, October 12, 2009). Paulson was also in very close contact with Goldman Sachs Chairman Lloyd Blankfein; they had nineteen telephone contacts over the period between September 18 and 21 alone. Geithner also had frequent phone contact with Blankfein.

Given the outcome of events—the blow-up of speculative bets on housing mortgages, the billions at stake in counterparty obligations—and the direction and immensity of the government's support for AIG, as well as the question of who ended up being the ultimate beneficiaries, much still needs to be explained. To quote Edolphus Towns, chairman of the House Committee on Oversight and Government Reform:

More than one year after the first federal bailout of AIG, the American people continue to question where their tax dollars were really sent when the government rescued this company. I continue to believe that a comprehensive review of the rise and fall of AIG, and of the involvement of counterparties, can provide a useful vehicle to understanding how inadequate regulations, cheap money, risky business deals, and in some instances, corruption led to the current economic crisis.

The prospect that favoritism, collusive practices, or outright corruption actually took place is underscored by the recent revelations that the Federal Reserve actively sought to hold back information on the billions of counterparty funds that went out of AIG's back door.

It raises the troubling question of whether the powers that be—the US Treasury and the New York Federal Reserve—played a lethal yet clandestine form of Wall Street triage. To arrive at the point where AIG presented the government and the economy with a systemic risk of bringing down the whole system, could the scenario have been orchestrated willfully, whereby everyone was too concerned or frightened to ask hard questions as billions were being dispensed to those with friends in high places? The specter of disaster was served by the bankruptcy of Lehman, which shook the financial world to its core. Lehman provided the ideal head fake, giving all that would be done to rescue AIG with an air of timely and necessary intervention.

But wait. Suppose all this was orchestrated first and foremost to spare the billions at risk by those holding AIG counterparty obligations. Would that not be tantamount to fraudulent conspiracy? What was the context of the many phone calls between Henry Paulson, US Treasury secretary and former chairman of Goldman Sachs, and current Goldman Sachs Chairman Lloyd Blankfein, especially at the height of the dramatic events of September 2008? Was AIG discussed? Was counterparty exposure discussed? Was the bankruptcy of Lehman discussed?

How much was communicated between the lines—the symbolic equivalent of nods and winks—given that Paulson, with his prior association with Goldman Sachs, probably knew as much about

Goldman Sachs' book as Blankfein did? Is this all conspiracy theorizing, at worst? I would like to hope so, but with scores of billions at stake, funny things can happen. These are all questions that should be asked both specifically and generally of the four pooh-bahs, Lloyd Blankfein of Goldman Sachs, Jaimie Dimon of J.P. Morgan Chase, John J. Mack of Morgan Stanley, and Brian T. Moynihan of Bank of America, who will be appearing before the Congressional Financial Crisis Inquiry Commission later this week.

I have a final question. At Goldman Sachs, how were the year-end bonuses affected by including the profits generated by those traders who arranged the Federal Reserve and AIG's buyback of those nearly worthless collateralized debt obligations at full price—with taxpayers footing the bill?

Our Banks Become Casinos, and Washington Yawns
January 20, 2010

Today, we learn that J.P. Morgan Chase is in exclusive talks to buy RBS Sempra. Sempra, together with energy interests, mostly trades in a full range of commodities from oil and gas to metals and agricultural products. Sempra is owned 51 percent by the Royal Bank of Scotland, which is being forced by European regulators, given the nature of the market's turmoil, to divest its holdings in the company. Where are our regulators? Why is a bank such as J.P. Morgan Chase, supported by myriad government programs and, under the guise of being a bank, with access to virtually cost-free money at the Federal Reserve window, permitted to gamble that money in the commodities arena?

Banks are supposed to be lending money vigilantly to support a badly debilitated economy. That is meant to be their mandate and why heaven and earth were moved to rescue the banking sector. Instead, public policy permits those with banking charters to use their depositors' money—deposits in many ways guaranteed by taxpayer programs such as the Federal Deposit Insurance Corporation, as well as by access to myriad Federal Reserve programs—to play commodity casino. Who is served when a bank such as J.P. Morgan Chase takes these funds, charters supertankers, fills them with millions of bbl of oil, and keeps those ships at anchor for months at a time?

Among other things, such activity ties up hundreds of millions of dollars that float idly at sea when industry, homeowners, and main street are clamoring for help and financial sustenance from the likes of J.P. Morgan Chase et al, and affects the day-to-day traded price of oil by taking oil off the market and thus supporting higher price levels. The upshot of this is that the consumer pays twice in higher prices for oil and oil products and by funding the programs that support the banks' places at the roulette table.

Here we have a clear example of the breakdown of our financial sector's priorities. J.P. Morgan Chase, instead of positioning itself to be of maximum aid and assistance to the economy at large, seeks to add to its existing commodities business to challenge market leaders Goldman Sachs and Morgan Stanley. Is that what our banks have come to? Isn't it time to reconsider their qualifications as bank-holding companies, or as banks at all, if playing commodities casino is their focus rather than functioning as banks? Is it not time for Washington and its hapless regulators to wake up?

The Question Unasked Again and Again of Goldman Sachs, Lloyd Blankfein, and Henry Paulson
February 8, 2010

A stunning and disturbingly informative front-page, Sunday *New York Times* article was written by the *Times*'s business columnist, Gretchen Morgenson, with Louise Story ("Testy Conflict with Goldman Helped Push AIG to Precipice" February 6, 2010). It quotes Bill Brown, a Duke University law professor and former Goldman Sachs and AIG employee, as saying that the dispute between the two companies "was the tip of the iceberg of this whole crisis."

The article details the demand for billions of dollars made against AIG's complex insurance derivatives (credit default swaps and obligations) by Goldman Sachs and claims that paydowns were triggered as the housing mortgage market collapsed. All the while, Goldman Sachs was taking proprietary positions and, in effect, shorting the housing-backed mortgage instruments, allegedly pushing their values down and setting the stage for a rancorous dispute with AIG. The dispute centered around establishing the values being assigned to the underlying instruments and, in consequence, the level of paydown owed to Goldman Sachs.

According to the article, Goldman Sachs resisted letting third parties value these securities, even though third-party price determination was required by the contract documents. Nonetheless, with the housing market melting away, billions were transferred by AIG to trading partners—especially Goldman Sachs—before September 2008, when AIG was on the verge of collapse. In the year before the AIG bailout, Goldman Sachs had already collected seven billion dollars from AIG, and of course, Goldman Sachs received many billions more after the bailout. This happened in spite of a determination by Black Rock, one of the nation's leading asset management firms, that Goldman Sachs' valuations of the AIG derivatives were "consistently lower than third-party prices," thereby making the paydowns from AIG to Goldman Sachs greater than they needed to be. Further, according to the *Times*, the Securities Exchange Commission is investigating whether any of Goldman Sachs' demands improperly distressed the mortgage market, meaning that Goldman Sachs would stand to gain handsomely from the implosion of the housing market and the crash in value of housing-backed mortgages.

In 2006, Henry Paulson left Goldman Sachs to become secretary of the US Treasury in the Bush administration. Morgenson's article states that, during the same year, Goldman Sachs began to "make huge trades that would pay off if the mortgage market soured. The further mortgage securities fell, the greater were Goldman's profits." Consider that you own your home, and here is a financial behemoth doing everything in its power, through its trading strategies, to make your home worth as little as possible—ah, the wonders of creative finance.

After the conclusion of hearings by the Congress Joint Economic Committee, I wondered, "What was the nature of the myriad discussions between Treasury secretary and former Goldman Sachs chairman Henry Paulson and Goldman Sachs Chairman Lloyd Blankfein at the height of the crisis?" I wondered this again during the hearings of the House Oversight and Government Reform Committee on January 27, 2010. Yet, again, to the best of my knowledge, even with Blankfein and Paulson testifying to the panel along with the current Treasury Secretary Timothy Geithner, the nature of the direct interchange between Paulson and Blankfein, the gist of their telephone calls, and whether AIG was discussed between them then or before, was not touched upon specifically by the committee apart from some muted questions on staff contacts.

Clearly, with the information we now have from the *Times*'s reporting, the contact and the content of the communication between the two Goldman Sachs chairmen becomes ever more significant.

- Was AIG brought up during their discussions in September?

- Given that Goldman Sachs' trading strategy of betting against the mortgage market dated back to 2006, was AIG discussed between the two prior to September 2008?

- Was the nature of AIG's exposure to Goldman Sachs known to Paulson or anyone on his staff?

- A question posed in a Goldman Sachs report in August 18, 2008, was quoted in the *Times* article: If a trading partner "is not in a position of weakness, why would it accept anything less than the full amount of protection for which it had paid"? This sounds as though the condition of the insurer who covered these speculative bets was of no merit. Was Goldman aware that a badly damaged and bleeding AIG would be resurrected by the government and that it would be paid in full? If so, was that information, which was worth billions to Goldman Sachs, a point of conversation or of winks and nods between Paulson and Blankfein?

- Might Blankfein have known that Paulson, as events demonstrated, considered AIG too big to fail and that it was not a decision arrived at in the penultimate moment but one held in the offing all along? Was it the case—one certainly hopes not—that Paulson found Goldman Sachs too intertwined with AIG to permit it to happen?

- Were the Treasury and the Federal Reserve aware that the French bank Société Générale's exposure to AIG was largely at Goldman Sachs' behest and that AIG's paying down its counterparty obligations to Société Générale after receiving its own government bailout was putting additional money into Goldman Sachs' pocket?

All of these questions boil down to one issue: What was the exchange of information between Paulson and Blankfein and/or their staff, and what impact might it have had on Goldman Sachs' intransigence vis-à-vis AIG? If inside information may have been exchanged, inadvertently or otherwise, what redress is there to the public that footed the bill for these many billions of dollars?

Goldman Sachs and Wall Street Profit from Housing Market's Collapse, Erosion of Municipal Bonds, Explosion in Oil Prices
April 26, 2010

Well, the beat goes on. A Sunday *New York Times* article (Louise Story and Sewell Chan, "Goldman Cited Serious Profit on Mortgages," April 24, 2010, http://www.nytimes.com/2010/04/25/business/25goldman.html) goes into detail about the profits Goldman Sachs made by shorting the housing markets with positions taken as far back as 2007; e-mails boast that "some serious money" would be made from betting on the market's deterioration. Certainly, these directional bets on a housing market collapse helped achieve exactly that.

One need recall that, after September 2008, Goldman Sachs became a bank-holding company with government guarantees of being "too big to fail" inherent in that designation and with access to nearly limitless funding at the Federal Reserve window at close to zero cost. Isn't that what a bank is supposed to do—profit from loans that were made to millions of homebuyers and that have gone sour and may enter foreclosure? That is, in essence, what Goldman Sachs and several other bank-holding companies were doing.

But it wasn't just shorting the housing market. In November 2008 with the nation's economy unraveling, Morgan Stanley and Goldman Sachs, wearing the mantles of bank-holding companies, were recommending the purchase of credit default swaps and themselves placing proprietary bets against the municipal bonds issued by eleven states, including California, Florida, New Jersey, Ohio, Wisconsin, and others. Given that they were among the largest US municipal bond underwriters, many of these bonds were underwritten by the very banks that were shorting them through the purchase of credit default swaps, which are essentially insurance policies. They became, in the parlance of Wall Street, derivatives. They were insurance against the bankruptcy or inability of municipalities throughout the country to meet their debt obligations. It's nice work if you can get it and if you're so inclined. First you unload the municipal bonds as underwriter. Then you bet against them. In a time of crisis, as was and is the case, it's not very different from pouring kerosene on a fire.

Interestingly, the insurance company that stood ready to sell the likes of Goldman Sachs these insurance policies (credit default swaps) was none other than AIG. We all know that, as the markets collapsed, it was good ol' Uncle Sam who rode the cavalry over the hill to save the day and make sure that Goldman Sachs collected the billions of dollars owed to it on its credit default swap bets with AIG. As Frank Rich pointed out in his Sunday *New York Times* op-ed ("Fight On, Goldman Sachs!," April 24, 2010), "That we still haven't seen the e-mail and documents that would illuminate [AIG]'s machinations with Goldman and the rest of its counterparties amounts to a cover-up."

But being aware of counterparty trading positions can bring huge profits as well as disaster. There is the case of Semgroup Holdings, a private firm in Tulsa, Oklahoma, that entered into some enormous trades with J. Aron & Co, Goldman Sachs' oil-trading arm. In February 2008, Semgroup made available a massive position in oil purchase options to Aron for delivery in July 2008 at $96/bbl. As prices shot past that mark in June 2008 on their way to $147/bbl on July 12, Semgroup was caught in a massive short squeeze to the point that *Forbes* (Christopher Helman and Liz Moyer, "Did Goldman Goose Oil? Black Gold: How Goldman Sachs Was at the Center of the Oil Trading Fiasco That Bankrupted Pipeline Giant Semgroup," April 13, 2009) would comment "there was the smell of blood in the water." Then, John Tucker, attorney for one of the interested parties, commented that "Nothing's been proven, but if somebody has your book and knows every trade, it would not be difficult to bet against that book and put the company into a tremendous liquidity squeeze."

The *Forbes* article goes on, saying, "What's known for sure is that Goldman Sachs, through J. Aron & Co, its commodities trading arm, was in prime position to use such data—and profited handsomely from

Semgroup's fall. J. Aron & Co was Semgroup's biggest counterparty, trading both physical oil flowing through the pipelines and paper oil in the form of options and futures." Here's a thought: Did we see $147/bbl oil and four-dollar per gallon gasoline in 2008 because of Goldman Sachs' short squeeze on Semgroup?

Unfortunately for our once respected and emulated financial system, playing a double-sided game for single-sided profit seems all too often the norm of the day. It just seems that some are better at it than others.

The Decline of the Middle Class as Metaphor for the Decline of America
August 8, 2010

Over the last decade, this nation has experienced a massive loss of productive and high-value jobs in manufacturing, trade, and the professions. Many have been sent overseas. Many others have been destroyed through the self-serving and misdirected priorities of our financial institutions, which have encumbered viable companies that are making real goods and services with untenable debt. These institutions have leveraged their assets in order to maximize profits for the financial engineers before flipping a company or taking it to market as an IPO, or initial public offering. All too often, the workers who created the company are left with little or nothing; the Wall Street whiz kids march off with a bundle, after destroying the vision, imagination, and hard work that went into creating these companies.

Disproportionate is the freighted word that shackles our society. Over the past few years, some two thirds of the gain in national income has gone to the top one percent of Americans—mostly those in the financial industry who are harbored in such government-protected entities as bank-holding companies and are part of something that has ominously come to be called the "shadow banking system." They bring virtually nothing viable to the economic landscape other than egregious speculation that gorges on complex derivatives; they enrich the financial players, but through their malign impact, the financial hierarchy impoverished great swaths of the American and world economy (e.g., by betting on the collapse of the housing market).

When these bets go dramatically wrong and also collapse the institutions that took the long side of the bets, the institutions are then bailed out by the government, which makes good the value of these betting instruments, whose function had no greater economic justification than a compulsive gambler's casino bets. The grim irony is that, when red comes up instead of black, it's the casino's next-door neighbors who are asked to pay to keep the casino afloat while the casino lets the gambler keep his chips. Those neighbors pay dearly. Their services are curtailed; their stores are forced to close; their local banks are driven to the edge; the values of their homes plummet, or their homes are repossessed. Since they don't have insider status, the neighbors' financial assets deteriorate dramatically; even if, in desperation, they want to get back into the casino to try their own luck—their new world being bereft of all other opportunity—the house refuses to extend them credit. It's just as well, because they won't have to see our compulsive gambler swilling Dom Pérignon and downing a small mountain of pâté de foie gras after having feasted on beluga caviar at the casino's resplendent restaurant.

The gambler is there, and he or his proxy will always be there. The town and its inhabitants, tattered and poorer, are still there trying to make do as best they can and to contain their simmering anger at the unfairness of it all; they don't quite know what to do. Some join in the regional meanderings of the Tea Party or some equivalent movement that promises to address the clear wrongs that are being inflicted and tolerated by those in charge. When all is said and done, it becomes apparent that it is the casino that needs fixing, because it is the casino that set the rules, the casino that has permitted the outrages that have resulted in the destabilizing of the norm and the sanctioning of the unexpected and unfair.

Now, with a very small leap of imagination, let us substitute our government for the nefarious casino. Clearly, it needs new management or a new way of managing. What has come before is not functioning, and major changes are called for. The locals need a voice in running the casino, a voice that has been denied them, in a sense, because they are unable either to pay the entry fee or to pony up the cash to play at the tables. That is what it has come to. If you lack access and money, no one at the casino pays the least bit of attention to you. All that must change for the locals ever again to have a chance to rectify the wrongs imposed by the casino's management and to participate in an equitable distribution of benefits, should they accrue in the future.

Today, too much of our political system is bought and paid for. Too much of our political system is self-serving, responsive to our two parties and indifferent to the day-to-day concerns of middle-class Americans in spite of the incessant lip service extended to them. Yes, there is limp Wall Street reform, but there is no clawback of the exigencies that drove the nation to the brink. Yes, there is a stimulus program, but it is faltering shamelessly through lack of clear direction. Yes, there is an alternative energy program, but without clear mandates or meaningful results, the transfer of billions of dollars to oil providers continues unabated.

Our soldiers are dying in fragmented nation-states far away without a modicum of sacrifice being asked of our home front. There are moneyed interests, both domestic and foreign, that have limitless access to those who govern and to a shameless Congress ready to do their bidding in spite of the promises made during the presidential campaign to curtail their influence.

We have courts of law that, through the study of judicial minutiae rather than a pragmatic sense of national welfare, have given these moneyed interests even greater influence by striking down financial restraints on the powerfully funded in election laws, thus leaving the middle class even more disenfranchised. Yes, there is talk of restraining government spending, but special interests with access to government and its earmarks are encumbering the nation with ever greater debt.

While main street and middle-class Americans continue to lose jobs, while middle-class Americans absorb pay cuts or shortened workweeks (if they have any jobs at all), while teachers—the backbone of the nation's future—and police and firemen are losing their employment, the paychecks on Wall Street and in corporate boardrooms continue to grow unabated. And so it goes, eventually leaving the nation with a Frankenstein system whose core objective of governance has become the preservation of power and personal influence. Governing for the greater good of the nation has become a secondary and distant gerrymandered priority, which leaves the great body of the American electorate virtually without meaningful representation and forestalls and diminishes the

American middle class's engagement with its government with each and every passing day.

Yet something is stirring. People understand that the political system is broken; Americans the length and breadth of the country know that their government no longer speaks for them, no matter which party happens to be in power. They feel the system is gamed from within for those who have access and the money to follow through to ensure that their parochial interests are taken into account and acted upon. How those interests affect the greater good has become a dangerously secondary consideration. Checks and balances seem to have gone by the wayside long ago.

Wall Street Guiding America toward Third-World Status and Instructing China as Well
August 31, 2010

Wall Street will not let up. In spite of the financial regulation bill passed last month, the Wall Street casino continues at full tilt. Just last week, the *New York Times* reported (Nelson D. Schwartz and Eric Dash, "Despite Reform, Banks Have Room for Risky Deals," August 25, 2010) that the likes of J.P. Morgan Chase and Goldman Sachs are continuing to squander hundreds of millions of dollars on bets, although purportedly on transactions handled for their customers. They are now passing themselves off as croupier at the roulette wheel. These bets seem to serve little or no economic purpose other than to pressure an economy already in distress and push a deeply burdened American middle class further into third-world status and take the rest of the nation along for the ride. It is an all-too-real phenomenon and has been described authoritatively in Arianna Huffington's recent book, *Third World America: How Our Politicians Are Abandoning the Middle Class and Betraying the American Dream.*

Among the most malicious effects of Wall Street's workings on our economy have come from the ruthless focus on the bottom line and Wall Street's own enrichment irrespective of the cost to workers, communities, or the nation's economic sinews and its entrepreneurial vision. Millions of workers have lost high-value and productive jobs in manufacturing, trade, and the professions. Many of these were at enterprises with years of tradition that were created by the hard work of entire communities. Many have now closed down entirely or moved offshore after dismissing their workers en masse—all to the rapacious benefit of the Wall Street mergers and acquisitions teams, their banking enablers, and the hedge fund honchos.

But our friends on Wall Street need not despair about how they are perceived. They have their admirers, or better put, emulators, in Beijing of all places. Heartlessness in the name of capitalist efficiency makes strange bedfellows. As in so many endeavors, China will not be left behind. Just yesterday, August 29, 2010, the *New York Times*'s lead article by Michael Wines blared "China Fortifies State Businesses to Fuel Growth." The article informs us that China, which calls itself socialist, is often perceived as brutally capitalist. Once eager to learn from the United States, "China's leaders during the financial crisis have reaffirmed their faith in their own more statist approach to economic management." Yet some of the lessons learned under Wall Street tutelage continue to linger on to our shame.

Some weeks ago an illuminating article, again in the *Times* (Andrew Jacobs, "Workers Let Go by China's Banks Are Putting Up a Fight," August 15, 2010), reported on the single largest public offering ever—a twenty-two billion-dollar IPO of the Agricultural Bank of China— which resulted in windfalls for the well-placed in China and overseas. But wait—having learned a thing or two from Wall Street, the bank "slashed payrolls and restructured to raise profitability and make themselves more attractive to outside investors." Where have we heard that before?

Of course, in China, nothing is small. Some seventy thousand people among those laid off by the bank are seeking to regain their old jobs or to receive fair monetary compensation. There are differences, naturally. Here we do not, as yet, place recalcitrant laid-off workers into labor camps or have them do jail time without having been prosecuted. But then again, here as in China, the financial upheavals of these last years are tearing at the very fabric of our society. In China, dozens of former bank staffers that have been unsuccessful at finding new jobs have committed suicide. Where will it all end for China and for us as the excess of the few trumps the welfare of the many?

The President's Misguided Class Warfare
October 8, 2010

President Obama's struggle against the extension of the Bush tax cuts for those families earning over $250,000 has become the banner issue of a cumulatively focused campaign, one perceived by more and more Americans as stirring up the dangerous specter of class warfare. According to Martin Feldstein, the noted economist and Harvard University professor, "The president has given the impression that he just doesn't like business. That's not his constituency. He doesn't like high-income individuals, and he makes that very clear" (Alex Kowalski and Tom Keene, "Feldstein Says Dollar to Weaken, Boosting Exports," *Bloomberg Businessweek*, October 7, 2010, http://www.businessweek.com/news/2010-10-07/feldstein-says-dollar-to-weaken-boosting-exports.html). He wants to extend the tax cuts for households earning under $250,000 dollars and to permit the cuts to lapse on December 31 for those earning more. Yet according to Feldstein ("Feldstein Says Dollar to Weaken, Boosting Exports," *Bloomberg*, October 7, 2010), the economy is too weak to raise taxes on anyone. In two years, perhaps, one could revisit the issue but not now.

After hearing Obama's Labor Day speech, in which he stated "Anyone who thinks we can move this economy forward with a few doing well at the top, hoping it will trickle down to working folks running faster and faster just to keep up, they just haven't studied our history," one can understand where Feldstein is coming from (Daniel Henniger, "A President's Class War," *Wall Street Journal*, September 9, 2010, http://online.wsj.com/article/SB10001424052748703453804575479831591176068.html).

Yet, in a way, both miss the mark. There is anger at those few who did well but who did it unfairly and destroyed our faith in what was once our vaunted "American meritocracy." By painting all with the same brush, Obama is plumbing the dangerous depths of the nation's psyche: the politics of envy. A far better strategy would be to focus his recriminations on those who warrant the anger. How many Americans feel anger toward the likes of Bill Gates? Very few, I would venture. Most celebrate him for his achievement and vision and are proud of his example of what can be realized in America. Far better to vent on those who, through greed and influence, have played the system to their own benefit at a painful cost to the livelihoods, homes, and sense of self-respect of so many millions of Americans.

In a lucid article in the *New York Times* ("Still Stuck in Denial on Wall St.," October 1, 2010), Joe Nocera clearly spelled out Obama's failings, citing Roosevelt's 1936 comments about Wall Street, "They are unanimous in their hatred for me and I welcome their hatred." Nocera goes on to say, "The big banks aren't being broken up the way they were in the 1930s. Bankers aren't being hauled off to jail. No serious effort has been made to rein in executive compensation or even to claw back millions of dollars in bonuses that were based on what turned out to be illusory profits. Most of the financial practices and products remain legal under the new Dodd-Frank legislation, though they will finally be regulated. All things considered, Wall Street has gotten away pretty easy."

And there's the rub. Instead of class warfare, Obama could harness the rightful indignation and anger against a financial system that made literally billions selling products that were ticking time bombs, which exploded all over Main Street America. Middle-class Americans have seen the values of their homes, if they still have homes, of their investments, and of their livelihoods diminish drastically or vanish. If any of them can pick themselves up and rekindle the American dream by becoming millionaires or billionaires ... why, more power to them. They should be held up as examples of what can be accomplished in this nation not dismissed as "a few doing well at the top." But the excesses and abuses of Wall Street, with its multibillion-dollar bonus pools divvied up while families all over America are being evicted from their homes, are another matter altogether.

Perhaps the action most feared by those who gamed the system and one that would be cheered the length and breadth of the land would be the clawback of the billions of dollars that were disbursed as bonuses (twenty-three billion dollars at Goldman Sachs alone) to the Wall Street multitude who feasted on those illusory profits. Their payouts were made possible by placing taxpayer monies at grave risk through TARP and other governmental programs. These programs saved the banks, which would otherwise have brought the whole system down. That these banks turn around and reward themselves is what Americans find so deeply grating.

No, it is not whether families earning $250,000 are paying more or less in taxes, that is of visceral concern. The public feels they have been victims of a holdup and that the perpetrators are laughing all the way to bank. Said bank, by the way, is probably still in business thanks to the bailout risks undertaken by the taxpayers. The very taxpayers, who received little or no benefit, received instead foreclosed homes and lost jobs.

Bravo, J.P. Morgan Chase. Just What We Need, Another Wall Street Casino
October 12, 2010

The French have an expression that says "Plus ça change, plus c'est la même chose," which means "the more it changes, the more it's the same thing." After the Financial Regulation Bill, after crassly challenging the president's policies, after the near collapse of the financial markets, and after the debate over the Volcker amendment that would separate banks from their proprietary trading desks, J.P. Morgan Chase knows better.

Given the financial calamities we've endured, it was head-spinning to read an article in this weekend's *Wall Street Journal*, entitled "J. P. Morgan's Commodities Chief Takes the Heat" (October 9, 2010). The article by Dan Fitzpatrick and Carolyn Cui details J.P. Morgan Chase's full court press ambitions "to build and finish building the No. 1 commodities trading franchise on the planet." This came from staff who were "in the eye of the controversy over derivatives when they helped trigger the 2008 financial crisis" and who were viewed as being among those who "built financial weapons of mass destruction."

Hardly deterred by the events of 2008, J.P. Morgan Chase has been assiduously buying commodities trading assets, spending more than two billion dollars sopping up the trading operations of Bear Stearns and UBS Commodities (2008) and Sempra Commodities (2010), poaching traders and executives from rivals, and boosting its workforce from some 125 in 2006 to 1,800 today.

When J.P. Morgan Chase executives were confronted in a private meeting with US Senators in the summer of 2008, they pointedly disagreed with the contention that J.P. Morgan Chase had an incentive to drive oil prices higher. Yet they chartered very large crude carrier supertankers to sit at anchor for months at a time, filled to the brim with crude oil and tying up hundreds of millions of dollars that were badly needed by a desperately sinking economy. They did this even months after having cashed in billions from the TARP program.

J.P. Morgan Chase's fig leaf for this exercise—given the Financial Regulation Bill's pointed restriction on proprietary trading by banks and bank-holding companies—is that it's mostly about providing a service for its customers and "focusing on client fees" (Dan Fitzpatrick and Carolyn Cui, "JP Morgan's Commodities Chief Takes the Heat," *Wall Street Journal*, October 9, 2010, http://online.wsj.com/article/SB10 001424052748703927504575540241298913962.html). Yes, but not to the point where a proprietary trade can go badly off the rails, as when a $130 million loss was booked this year betting on coal prices—$130 million on a single trade. This is an institution whose depositors' monies are guaranteed by the Federal Deposit Insurance Corporation and which, through its ownership of Chase Bank and Washington Mutual, has ultimate oversight responsibility for tens of thousands of mortgages throughout the country. How many homes might not have been foreclosed on had that $130 million been available for mortgage loan workouts? Heck, that's dull work. Better to blow it at the casino.

America's Anger at the Great Financial Bailout, and the Press's Ongoing Inability to Understand It
October 31, 2010

Just last week, two of America's leading newspapers, the *New York Times* and the *Wall Street Journal*, presented opinion pieces discussing why Americans remain bitter about the federal bailouts.

In the *Wall Street Journal*, Matthew Winkler's "Time for Bailout Transparency" (October 28, 2010) lamented that the public outrage centers on the government's lack of transparency. The government has refused to disclose all facts attendant to the bailout, like how public funds were disbursed, which firms borrowed from the Federal Reserve and accessed the Federal Reserve discount window, and who made the decisions. All are interesting, which is well and good. The answers could even be embarrassing to the likes of J.P. Morgan Chase, Citigroup, and Wells Fargo, who are suing to have recent rulings mandating transparency reversed.

Just a few days earlier, Ross Douthat of the *New York Times* weighed in with "The Great Bailout Backlash" (October 25, 2010), declaring that "[n]othing this election season, no program or party or politician is less popular than the [TARP] of 2008." Douthat quotes Matthew Yglesias of the Center for American Progress Action Fund, who wrote that the Wall Street rescue package is "one of the most unfairly maligned policy initiatives of all time." He continued to put us at ease by stating, "As it stands, the government may actually end up turning a modest profit on the money injected into Wall Street's failing banks."

There is much in each piece about the necessity for TARP, without which the nation would have slid into depression and far greater unemployment. That is understood by most Americans. What they can't abide is the patent unfairness of it all. The financial engineers who very nearly sank the ship of state were permitted to reward themselves munificently, while the public bailout brigade that did the bailing was left holding rusty buckets. Then, if the bailers didn't bow humbly and accept the financial engineers' admonitions, even those rusty buckets were taken from them (along with their homes, in some cases). The financial engineers, meanwhile, were still able to take shore leave from their rescued ship and tear up the town.

What galls most Americans is the manner in which Wall Street rewarded itself after the public took the risk of bailing it out. While millions of Americans were losing their homes and their jobs, Wall Street was setting aside huge bonus pools, such as Goldman Sachs' twenty-three billion dollars in 2009. Earlier this month, we learned that Wall Street would achieve a record in 2010 by setting aside some $144 billion as compensation (Rappaport, Lucchetti, and Grocer, "Wall Street Pay: A Record $144 Billion," *Wall Street Journal*, October 11, 2010).

Had the companies been permitted to fail or had they been administered under some form of managed bankruptcy, the bonuses of the failed companies would never have been paid out; had they been, the bankruptcy courts would have recaptured them as fraudulent transfers. Only a vigilant government initiative to claw back these dubious payouts would have assuaged the public's feeling that it was being taken for a ride and gamed by well-connected insiders.

Sadly, our government—probably under pressure from Wall Street lobbyists and the meek of heart—did practically nothing. Yes, they did delegate that *stalwart fighter* for all things fair and equitable, Ken Feinberg, as the administration's "Pay Czar," but he came away soft-pedaling the outrageous bonuses as "ill-advised" and left matters at that. The issue may have come to an end for the administration, but Americans are still seething. Yes, more openness will be helpful, but that is not the core issue. The Wall Street perpetrators were rewarded while Main Street and the rest of America paid the price. Is this the new American way?

Time to Dismiss the Commodity Futures Trading Commission Chairman and His Commissioners
December 27, 2010

The Dodd-Frank Act gave the Commodity Futures Trading Commission until January 2011 to set mandatory position limits to curb pervasive and excessive speculation in the energy markets. Lo and behold, on December 15, the Goldman Sachs alumnus and chairman of the Commodity Futures Trading Commission Gary Gensler told congressional lawmakers that the Commodity Futures Trading Commission wouldn't meet the deadline "because it doesn't yet have sufficient data" (Asjylyn Loder, "Commodity Speculation Divides CFTC as Deadline Looms," *Bloomberg Businessweek*, January 13, 2011, http://www.businessweek.com/news/2011-01-13/commodity-speculation-divides-cftc-as-deadline-looms.html). A few days earlier, Commissioner Jill Sommers, who is always happy to lend a word in support of delay, delay, delay, instructed us that it was "bad policy to promulgate regulations that are not enforceable" (Commodity Futures Trading Commission speech and testimony, "Opening Statement, Open Meeting on the Eighth Series of Proposed Rulemakings under the Dodd-Frank Act" by commissioner Jill. E. Sommers, December 16, 2010). In turn, Chairman Gensler—as part of the Sommers/Gensler duo, the Commodity Futures Trading Commission's own Abbott and Costello act—intoned, "It's just appropriate to let this one ripen a little more." Just "ripen a little more" (*Reuters*, "CFTC Delays Tough Commodity Speculation Crack-Down," December 16, 2010)? Really?

In remarks made on September 19, 2008, before the First Asia Derivatives Conference in Tokyo, Ms. Sommers is quoted as saying:

> The US futures markets have been the focus of intense scrutiny by law makers, the press, and the public over the past year as prices for crude oil and many agricultural products reached record highs. The question on everyone's mind is whether trading is responsible, especially with the influx of new traders into the markets.[...] One of the primary tasks of market regulators is to foster a high level of market integrity necessary to preserve the important management and price discovery the futures markets perform.

Those are succinct words from a commissioner whose formative experience included service with the International Swaps and Derivatives Association as head of the government affairs and policy department and working closely with congressional staff as well as time spent responsible for oversight of regulatory and legislative affairs with the Chicago Mercantile Exchange. Talk about putting the lady fox (the reverse would be inappropriate) in the hen house. This past week, as the Commodity Futures Trading Commission proposed a rule to restrict the number of contracts a firm can hold, and called for a sixty-day public comment period, Ms. Sommers let it be known she would vote against the rule (now some two years since her Tokyo dissertation), thereby assuming the mantle of the "Queen of Delay and Obfuscation" on issues relevant to reforming our severely tainted commodities-trading institutions and procedures.

In the meantime, Chairman Gensler has been busy passing himself off as a reformer. Gensler is a former Goldman Sachs partner; he worked at the firm for eighteen years and was brought into the Treasury by former Goldman chairman and Treasury secretary Robert Rubin. Rubin is perhaps best remembered for his defense of the trading of unfettered derivatives with minimal government oversight. The derivatives market now reaches some three hundred trillion dollars, or twenty times the nation's annual output. Gensler was quoted extensively in a *New York Times* article ("Goldman Dealmaker Now Advocates Regulation," March 10, 2010) as saying, "Wall Street's interest is not always the same as the public's interest.[…] Wall Street thrives and makes money in inefficient markets, and I am creating efficiencies in the market." This came from a man who, according to the *Times*, "in 2000 played a significant role in shepherding through Congress deregulation measures that led to explosive growth of the over-the-counter derivatives."

When Gensler assumed his post in May 2009, the price of oil was $60/bbl at a time when, according to a then-current interview in the *Financial Times* (Javier Blas, "Recovery in Oil Prices Ignores the Fundamentals," May 20, 2009, http://www.ft.com/cms/s/0/34f66ec4-44d7-11de-82d6-00144feabdc0.html#axzz1Gz8U8ozB), "the fundamentals of supply and demand are weak—much weaker than current prices imply." Today, prices are at $90/bbl, and fundamentals are still glaringly weak with inventories near all-time highs and refineries working under capacity; his "efficiencies," or lack thereof, are draining six hundred million dollars per day from the economy. We consume some twenty million bbl per day at $30/bbl (the difference between $90/bbl and $60/bbl), a staggering tax on the economy of eighteen billion dollars per month with gasoline prices again over three dollars per gallon and heating-oil costs spiraling out of control.

In his remarks this December 15, Mr. Gensler went on to observe that 148 days had elapsed since the Dodd-Frank Act had been signed into law, calling for trading limits to be in place for oil contracts come January 2011. He assured us that his staff had worked assiduously, saying, "They have had more than 475 meetings with the public on rulemaking, had more than 300 meetings with other regulators, and organized seven public roundtables."

All of that sounds very impressive but less so if you turn back the clock. Mr. Gensler has had much longer than 148 days to deal with this issue. On July 27, 2009, beneath the headline "Traders Blamed for Oil Spike" (Ianthe Jeanne Dugan and Alistair Macdonald), the *Wall Street Journal* advised that the Commodity Futures Trading Commission was to issue a report in August "suggesting speculators played a significant role in driving wild price swings in oil prices." We are still waiting.

In July 2009, the Commodity Futures Trading Commission also

announced that it was considering volume limits on energy futures by financial/proprietary traders, as well as tougher information requirements. That wasn't 148 days ago; that was nearly five hundred days ago, and now they want even more time. Or to quote Gensler once again, "It's just appropriate to let this one ripen a little more." All the while "it" is ripening, we are paying through the nose.

Who has access to the Commodity Futures Trading Commission while the issue is ripening? A plethora of industry lobbyists, such as the CME Group Inc., the world's largest futures/derivatives trading marketplace (which is pushing the Commodity Futures Trading Commission to defer setting limits), and Gensler's professional alma mater, Goldman Sachs, do. A *Forbes* article from April 13, 2009 (Christopher Helman and Liz Moyer, "Did Goldman Goose Oil?"), hypothesized that Goldman Sachs played a key role in the massive short squeeze on Semgroup Holdings, whose oil positions amounted to 20 percent of the nation's crude oil inventories. The squeeze itself was deemed to have had a dramatic impact on the price of oil moving up to the $147/bbl price on July 12, 2008. Semgroup Holdings filed for bankruptcy on July 22, 2008.

Then there are the likes of the Vitol Group, the oil trading behemoth that held oil contracts equal to 57.7 million bbl in August 2008 according to the Commodity Futures Trading Commission. At the time, the *Washington Post* (David Cho, "A Few Speculators Dominate Vast Market for Oil Trading," August 21, 2008) noted that the Commodity Futures Trading Commission also determined that a massive amount of oil-trading activity was concentrated with a handful of speculators, and at that time alone, 81 percent of the New York Mercantile Exchange was held by financial firms speculating for their clients or on their own accounts. This did not seem to be enough to light a fire under Mr. Gensler or the Commodity Futures Trading Commission so they would do the needful: set trading limits post haste. It is clear that letting themselves be stonewalled by industry lobbyists was a greater priority than were bringing transparency and making constructive limits to what had become a trading racket that was leaving the nation's consumers to stake the chips of the financial casino's high rollers.

Meanwhile, the economy staggers under indefensibly high prices while our Commodity Futures Trading Commission commissioners delay and delay, running out the clock on a gullible Congress and Department of Energy. *Bloomberg* reported (Asjylyn Loder, "US Regulator to Consider Measures to Limit Oil, Gold, Wheat Speculation," December 16, 2010) that) "Scott O'Malia and Michael Dunn said they will vote today in favor of publishing the rule for comment" but that "Dunn and O'Malia said they may not ultimately support imposing position limits." Is this the open-mindedness we look for in our public servants?

There seems to be but one forthright voice on the commission—that of Mr. Bart Chilton, who stated earlier this month that the Commodity Futures Trading Commission is "facing pressure from inside and outside the agency" to find a way around the implementation deadlines, saying, "First, we have no legal authority to do so. Second, that is exactly the type of dancing on the head of a legal pin Washington-speak that folks in the country are tired of—and they should be."

Mr. Gensler may be a good man. He may be sincere in his efforts. He may truly have distanced himself from his formative underpinnings on Wall Street and the influence of power. Perhaps, perhaps not.

If you'll permit me a baseball analogy, this is the eighth inning. The Commodity Futures Trading Commission All-Stars are playing the Oiligopoly All-Stars. The Commodity Futures Trading Commission All-Stars have their ace pitcher, Gary Gensler, on the mound, facing the Oiligopoly batters. They have already scored six runs this inning and have the bases loaded. The Oiligopoly All-Stars have nine points; the Commodity Futures Trading Commission All-Stars have six. No matter Gensler's previous record, he now needs to be pulled from the game. It's high time for Obama to play Yogi Berra, "the manager," and get that guy off the mound—maybe even cashier the whole team. He might want to keep Chilton in the dugout, at least, so that he could give instruction and guidance to the new players coming on board. If something isn't done soon, the bleachers may collapse, because those are the only seats anyone will be able to afford.

SECTION III

How We Can Fight Back

Part VII

The Strategic Petroleum Reserve
and When We Should Use It

The Department of Energy Gets It Right ... For Once
October 3, 2006

Election Day must be getting close. The US Department of Energy just announced that it would put off replacing eleven million bbl of crude oil for the nation's 680 million-bbl-strong strategic petroleum reserve. The department had sold the crude to oil companies for some six hundred million dollars in the wake of Hurricane Katrina and the BP Alaska debacle—sales that were completely in keeping with the strategic petroleum reserve's mandate. The stated aim of the delay is to keep more oil on the market through the winter heating season. For once, the Department of Energy is acting in the interest of the country and is not simply supporting the oil industry and its egregious excesses as it has for years now.

The Department of Energy was always happy to be the oil industry's handmaiden in milking the public. This is how it worked: The Department of Energy has been buying oil for the strategic petroleum reserve willy-nilly, despite the fact that prices have been escalating to undreamed of heights. There was no consideration for how these purchases would exacerbate the country's cumulative oil bill, the prices allocated to oil producers, the price of oil itself, and product prices at the pump and home. Neither was there any thought to using the strategic petroleum reserve's vast purchasing power to talk down the price of oil. The Department of Energy never seemed to fully understand that *strategic* also applies to the enormous transfer of American wealth to malign regimes. The high prices it has countenanced and helped along enriched those who wish us ill.

All the same, bravo to the Department of Energy for once. How long beyond Election Day will this allegiance to the consumer—rather than the oil industry—last?

Our Strategic Petroleum Reserve—Iran's
Weapons of Mass Destruction
February 6, 2007

Iran's weapons of mass destruction is our strategic petroleum reserve. How so? Allow me to explain. First, let me state categorically that, in this unstable world, having a strategic petroleum reserve is a decided plus. But filling the reserve blindly without considering the ramifications filling it has for markets and policy makers, echoes the one-dimensional thinking inherent in so many of this administration's policies. That's the best interpretation, lest one permit oneself to think that it's all in the interests of the oil boys back down in Texas. Nah, that couldn't be.

In its management of the strategic petroleum reserve, the administration has shown not the slightest understanding of the political or market impact of its actions. The strategic petroleum reserve has a major influence in both respects. In November of 2001, President Bush announced his decision to fill the strategic petroleum reserve to its seven hundred million-bbl capacity. At the time, 545 million bbl of oil had been stockpiled. Over the next several years, an additional 155 million bbl of oil were added, plus another twenty-seven million bbl, which brought the total to 727 million bbl.

Purchases have been made as "royalty in kind" purchases, meaning that royalties were previously collected in cash. Think about it. The oil companies, instead of putting the oil on the market where it might depress prices, turn their oil over to the government in lieu of royalties, which would otherwise be paid by them in cash. The government gives them credit for the full market value for a product it costs them a small fraction to produce. It's like paying your gambling debts with plastic chips. The trouble being, in this case, that we all own the house.

In November 2001, the free on board spot price for crude oil, according to the government's Energy Information Administration, was about $17.03/bbl. After that it began its inexorable rise, touching more than $78/bbl on the New York Mercantile Exchange in July of 2006 and decreasing to $59/bbl today. Never, it seems, was any thought given either to the impact that these purchases for the strategic petroleum reserve had on the psychology of the oil markets or for the signals they sent to producing nations, validating them and giving Washington's blessing to the upward creep in prices. They gave no thought to the foreign policy consequences of those higher prices.

Let me give a quick, thumbnail review of oil pricing history these past years. Shortly after the president's announcement, the price of oil started its ascent. By April 2002, it had surpassed $24/bbl. According to press reports at the time, OPEC and other producers were intent on keeping the price of crude in the range between $22/bbl and $28/bbl. There was much hand-wringing by OPEC and other suppliers when the price popped above that level. Our government could have sent a meaningful signal to those other governments that were limiting the supply of oil by a simple declaration that we would desist purchases for the strategic petroleum reserve until the price fell back below $28/bbl.

Perhaps needless to say, that was not done, and in not doing anything, Washington validated the price creep and the billions of dollars of wealth transfer it represented. Would such a declaration have changed the price? As you will see below, probably it would have. At the very least, it would have shown the government's displeasure at the manipulated direction of the oil market. Not taking any action sent a signal of validation. It said, in effect, "It's okay to push prices higher." The political ramifications of wealth transfer were ignored, as was the question of what that wealth was being used for. The oil industry was probably popping bottles of champagne.

When the price headed to $40/bbl in late 2004 amid OPEC expressions of concern and yet OPEC decided to cut production to push the price ever higher, we blindly continued filling the reserve. In April 2005, with then-Crown Prince Abdullah at Crawford, Texas, holding hands with President Bush and the price of oil approaching $50/bbl, a discreet word in the crown prince's ear—"Your eminence, if the price of oil continues to rise we can no longer justify filling our [strategic petroleum reserve]"—might have made some headway. But certainly the conversation never got around to that, and the price of oil continued to climb above and well beyond $50/bbl.

With the coming of Hurricane Katrina, not a word was heard from the Department of Energy that it stood ready to release oil from the strategic petroleum reserve to becalm the market and to cover any shortfall that might result from the storm. Only after the storm hit and the markets had already gone into overdrive was an announcement made about releasing reserves. By then, the price of oil had jumped some ten percent. Nonsense, you say. The market is simply reflecting higher demand, limited supply, political uncertainty, stormy weather, and so forth—the usual litany. I would like to add an additional and very important element: the management of the strategic petroleum reserve.

Just over a week ago when word got out that the president was going to double the oil stored in the strategic petroleum reserve to nearly 1.5 billion bbl, the price of oil jumped by some 6 percent ($2.40/bbl on one day alone) to $55/bbl. It has continued to climb and has now reached $59/bbl. That price means a transfer of wealth to the oil industry of some forty-two billion dollars in what the government will pay or credit for oil. With financing costs, custodial costs, transport, and handling, the total cost to taxpayers will approach sixty-five billion dollars.

Since the president's announcement, the price of oil has jumped nearly 15 percent. The advent of cold weather at this late stage of the winter had but a minimal impact on storage conditions that were brimming to capacity, even to the point that ships at sea had to cut steaming speed because offloading capacity was limited at their destination ports. Prior to the president's announcement, the price of oil was reeling and heading below $50/bbl. Many predictions were made of levels between $40/bbl and $45/bbl.

The president's announcement dramatically changed the psychology of the market. The psychology and perceptions of those who trade and consume commodities are some of the key elements in pricing. Suddenly, in view of the marketplace, there was support under an eroding price structure, and the market, the hedge funds, and the oil consumers piled in. At the time of the Department of Energy's announcement that it would begin purchases of oil for the strategic petroleum reserve, the price hovered around $52/bbl, and now it's at $59/bbl.

That's a $7/bbl difference. Americans consume some twenty-one million bbl of oil a day. That means that, in the United States alone, an additional $150 million per day or one billion dollars per week is transferred to the oil industry and to oil interests in this country. It represents a tax on each and every one of us, and the irony is that we are being taxed by a runaway industry (see ExxonMobil's last year's profits, which have just been announced) while our dollars go to pay for the oil in the strategic petroleum reserve stockpile. In other words, they have us coming and going.

But if that's not enough, consider this. That seven-dollar increase means a transfer of wealth to Iran of some one billion dollars in value and revenues every month. Iran produces over four million bbl of oil per day and is dependent on that revenue. Much of that money is going to fuel insurgencies all over the Middle East and to supplying militias in Iraq. Had there been any interest by this government in holding the price to, say, $35/bbl—a reasonable and very healthy commodity price increase over 2001 prices—Iran's current account wealth would have been curtailed by some three billion dollars each month or thirty-six billion dollars per year.

An already shaky economy like Iran's does not have the luxury of exporting hundreds of millions to stir up trouble around the Middle East and elsewhere in the world. As for the Saudis and their flow of oil cash, the billions that radicalize schools and mosques throughout the world and fund, in part, the Sunni insurgency in Iraq ... well, let's not go there. The numbers are too enormous.

Mr. President, the oil industry, Iran, Saudi Arabia, even Mr. Chavez (he's a devil of a guy), and President Putin thank you.

By the way, to talk about injustice, Lee Raymond, former head of ExxonMobil, was handed a more than four hundred million-dollar golden parachute last year. And yet President Bush, Vice President Dick Cheney, and Secretary of Energy Samuel Bodman did more to help ExxonMobil's bottom line than Lee Raymond could ever have dreamed of doing. Wouldn't it be gracious if he carved up the pie between them and maybe saved a few crumbs for the Department of the Interior?

Should it ever become the government's agenda to curtail consumption of fossil fuels through higher prices, let's make sure those increased prices aren't just for the benefit of the oil patch.

What Is Our Strategic Petroleum Reserve For, Anyway?
March 30, 2007

The price of oil has jumped more than 10 percent or more than six dollars toward $67/bbl since the abduction by Iran of fifteen British Royal Marines, and gasoline prices are veering to more than three dollars per gallon. Oil traders are hanging on every news bulletin from the Arabian Gulf. The oil patch is celebrating the transfer of $125 million per day to its interests both here and overseas. President Chavez, who is now rolling in even more dough, will be going for an extended visit to Cuba, and our friends in Saudi Arabia will have even more money to transfer to Wahhabi madrassas and prayer halls to propagate their poisonous fundamentalism.

The key concern in the oil pits is that, should the Iranian-British standoff spin out of control, Iran's oil would be affected, the Iranians would cease oil exports, and its daily loadings of over two million bbl would be lost to the world market. All of this while we are sitting on 721 million bbl of oil bought and paid for by American taxpayers, the equivalent of a year's total Iranian exports. An additional seven hundred million bbl are being held by the International Energy Agency, and commercial stocks throughout the world bring total stocks (commercial and government-held) to some four billion bbl.

Were this administration not so wedded to high oil prices and to the oil industry, were it not so indifferent to the high price of energy irrespective of its impact on the economy, the Department of Energy would be directed to issue the following proclamation:

> We consider the recent run-up in crude oil prices to be without justification. Commercial oil stocks in the United States are currently over 6 percent higher than their five-year average. We understand the concerns occasioned by the political tensions in the Persian Gulf, and we wish to assure the market that if there is any interruption of oil shipments from Iran we stand ready to immediately release oil from the strategic petroleum reserve.

Don't hold your breath waiting for that proclamation to issue from President Bush's Department of Energy. Were it only the nation's Department of Energy, things might be different.

Time to Tap the Strategic Petroleum Reserve as Pipeline Explosion Cuts US Supplies
November 29, 2007

This morning we woke up to the news that a pipeline explosion in Clearbrook, Minnesota, cut 1.5 million bbl per day of Canadian oil imports. The explosion killed two workers, and the price of oil catapulted up by nearly $4/bbl at the time. The pipeline company said the resulting fire is still burning. Enbridge spokeswoman Denise Hamsher advised that "all our lines are shut down until we can safely start up the system. At least one or two lines will be shut down for quite some time" ("Oil Prices Spike as Fire Shuts Pipeline to U.S.," *New York Times*, November 29, 2007, http://www.nytimes.com/2007/11/29/business/worldbusiness/29iht-oil.1.8525998.html?scp=3&sq=enbridge%20pipeline%20explosion%202007&st=cse).

With prices escalating by nearly $4/bbl or a transfer of wealth from American consumers to oil interests of some eighty-five million dollars per day, this supply interruption classifies as a national emergency. It is exactly the type of contingency for which we have a strategic petroleum reserve in place, and release of oil to the market would abate the supply disruption caused by this event. Will the administration, that is to say President Bush and Secretary of Energy Bodman, do the needful thing and immediately announce a release from our 750 million-bbl strategic petroleum reserve to compensate for the Canadian shortfall? It stands to reason that they should. But then again this is an administration so wedded to oil interests that they might well want to continue adding to the stockpile rather than to release supplies to stabilize market disruptions. This while American consumers, who paid for the strategic petroleum reserve in the first place, continue to have their pockets picked. Here we have a real test of whether we have an administration more concerned with serving oil interests than our own.

The Strategic Petroleum Reserve Follow-Up
November 30, 2007

Since yesterday's pipeline explosion in Clearbrook, Minnesota and the $4/bbl spurt in the price of oil to $95.17/bbl, the price of oil has retreated by some $6/bbl to a level under $90/bbl for the first time in over a month. Two significant changes took place. First, the pipeline operator of the largest Canadian oil pipeline to the United States advised that repairs—first reported as potentially problematic—were underway, that oil had resumed flowing, and that the pipeline would be in full operation within three days. Second, and significantly, the Department of Energy announced that it was prepared to open the emergency stockpile to compensate for the disruption.

That the price of oil retraced its initial spurt can well be attributed to getting the pipeline back into operation. That the retracement in price went beyond the initial $4/bbl jump can well be attributed to the Department of Energy's response. It was a signal to the market and to oil traders that they can no longer rely on temporary disruptions—real or imagined—to support their pricing strategies to push prices ever higher. Our strategic petroleum reserve stands at the ready to compensate for temporary dislocations.

The Department of Energy's actions and the reaction of the marketplace give clear evidence as to how valuable a tool the strategic petroleum reserve can be in containing the hysteria of the market and the excesses of the traders. Let us hope the lesson learned is applied more consistently in the future.

Hugo Chavez, ExxonMobil, and the Misuse of Our Strategic Petroleum Reserve
February 18, 2008

With a slowing economy and rising inflation, the *S* word (*stagflation*) is being bandied about. Now Hugo Chavez is threatening to cut off oil shipments to ExxonMobil in retaliation for ExxonMobil's twelve billion-dollar court-ordered freeze of Venezuelan assets for alleged breach of contract and confiscatory actions against ExxonMobil in Venezuela. The imbroglio involving Venezuela and ExxonMobil (since last week, Venezuela has actually begun cutting oil shipments to ExxonMobil) is said to have helped oil prices bounce back from a low of $86.11/bbl this year to near $96/bbl today—a rise of over 10 percent or, in dollar terms, a transfer of more than two hundred million dollars per day from American consumers to oil interests around the world.

Now for questions all Americans should be asking. Where is our Department of Energy? Where is the White House announcing that our strategic petroleum reserve, which is currently holding some seven hundred million bbl of oil bought and paid for out of the Treasury, is available and at the ready to make up for any of Hugo Chavez's extortionary tactics?

One now has the feeling that the strategic petroleum reserve has been created as a boondoggle for the oil industry exclusively, whereby purchases for the strategic petroleum reserve help escalate prices as they are made. Yet releases from the reserve that would help stabilize prices or even push prices down are anathema to our government. If the Venezuelan government's actions are not reason enough for our government to proclaim loud and clear that the strategic petroleum reserve is at the ready to iron out any supply discrepancies, the question becomes what, exactly, would it take?

It is high time Congress looked into this matter. The management of the strategic petroleum reserve under this administration defies comprehension and raises the worst suspicions.

Obama Nails It: Calls for Release of Seventy Million Barrels from the Strategic Petroleum Reserve
August 4, 2008

Finally, we have someone on the national presidential stage willing to confront the staggeringly high oil prices at their core. Nothing would be more immediately effective at reining in runaway prices than a willingness to release oil from the strategic petroleum reserve. It would immediately affect the psychology of the traders in the sense that it would encourage them to make a run for the exits. It would be a signal to oil producers, most especially OPEC, that our days of being patsies to their cartel corruption are at an end. It would have an immediate and salutary impact on the price of oil. Witness today that simply mentioning the possibility of a strategic petroleum reserve release decreased the price of oil by more than $5/bbl to less than $120/bbl, thereby ending the day a shade under $4/bbl lower.

Of course, the airwaves were immediately filled with talking heads and in-house commentators, who were telling us that Obama's talk of a release of seventy million bbl was not the cause of the price retreat. It was, they said, all about Tropical Storm Edouard bypassing the offshore production platforms—you could almost hear the sounds of "Damn it!" rising from the trading floors—and Iran's signaling a more accommodating response to the United Nation Security Council's threat of sanctions. Then there was the aha! moment when one of the CNBC commentators instructed us that seventy million bbl was but a drop in the "barrel" given that we use twenty-one million bbl every day.

There was no sense of appreciation of or insight into what the release of one or two million bbl a day would accomplish when released over a one- or two-month period. It would wreak havoc on oil trading futures and probably bring down the price of oil by $20/bbl or more in short order in and of itself and especially now that demand destruction is taking hold and the tendency is for the price of oil to erode in any case. The release from the strategic petroleum reserve would accelerate that decline dramatically. It would be a mirror image of what OPEC has done to us. As prices escalated, the cartel withheld millions of bbl from the market, pushing prices ever higher. Now that consumption is declining, we would be putting more bbl into the market to make prices decline even faster.

All this would be perfect were we able to combine policy with an absolute ceiling on fossil fuel consumption for the nation as a whole so that lower prices would not lead to higher consumption but rather to lower oil prices, thereby stopping the bleeding of our wealth to oil interests both here and abroad.

Stop the Department of Energy from Hiking Oil Prices by Reinstituting Purchases for the Strategic Petroleum Reserve
January 4, 2009

There they go again. It's the Bush administration's last bonanza for the oil industry. Samuel Bodman and his minions at the Department of Energy couldn't even have waited the nineteen days for the Obama administration to take office in order to permit them to deal with this issue from their perspective.

This administration hasn't passed up a single opportunity to further enrich the oil industry or to keep a free market from functioning in the oil industry when there is downward pressure on the price of oil. With its price cascading downward from $147/bbl in July to $35/bbl by Christmas, leave it to this administration and its newly recruited ally, Representative Edward Markey, chairman of the Select Committee on Energy and Global Warming, to do whatever was in their power to halt the slide in oil prices. On December 26, the price of oil (West Texas

Intermediate crude [WTI]) ended the day, as quoted on the New York Mercantile Exchange, at $37.58/bbl.

The Department of Energy was prohibited by law from adding to the strategic petroleum reserve through the end of December 2008. With the statutory moratorium coming to an end, it became clear that the Department of Energy was ready to gear up prices once more by preparing to reinstitute purchases for the strategic petroleum reserve. Just the whisper of the Department of Energy's planned action started to move prices.

Then, to cover themselves, they obtained the blessing of none other than Edward Markey, the congressman from Massachusetts, who had been a vocal critic of the Department of Energy's policies in the past. That was then, but now, spurred on either by a sad misreading of the dynamics of the oil market or by a highly successful campaign of the overly powerful oil lobby, Markey's attitude has changed. It flies in the face of what was once his clearly expressed outrage at unconscionable oil and product prices and his support for cogent oil policies (see Markey's comments in "Oil Speculator Cost Consumers $31 Billion this Summer," the *Huffington Post,* August 22, 2008). In any case, the day after Markey's very public support (December 30, 2008) of the Department of Energy's planned actions to reactivate strategic petroleum reserve purchases, the price of oil jumped by more than $5/bbl. If you're counting, that's more than one hundred million dollars out of American consumers' pockets each day and day after day). Of course, on the very first business day of the new year (the first day it was able to do so), the Department of Energy made it official, trumpeting that it would issue solicitations to purchase oil for the strategic petroleum reserve.

What did that do for the price of oil, which until then was on the ropes and flailing? Well, between Markey and the Department of Energy's strategic petroleum reserve initiative, by the close of business on January 2, the price of oil had enjoyed its biggest weekly gain since 1986, increasing to $46.34/bbl. This with some forty very large crude carrier class oil tankers carrying up to two million bbl each anchored off various ports and holding well over fifty million bbl of oil at sea alone. The reason oil is being held in tankers at sea is because there is virtually no independent land storage available. The world is awash in oil such that, without the strategic petroleum reserve lifeline, the price of oil was primed to drop even lower—please remember that the price of oil was about $22/bbl when President Bush took office.

Yes, there is the issue of Gaza (this all transpired before the land incursion) and the Russian-Ukraine gas imbroglio, but to those dealing with oil on a day-to-day basis, these were no more pertinent than the oil price frights that were so prevalent and so masterfully orchestrated by the industry's flacks and a hyper press. The issues were certainly not, given all the other exigencies over that period, worthy of the largest weekly jump in prices since 1986.

In essence, the strategic petroleum reserve has become a welfare program for the oil industry and one of the nation's most outrageous boondoggles, rather than being our oil safety valve. The last time the strategic petroleum reserve was invoked, it cost us enormously. In January 2007, President Bush announced, during his State of the Union address, the doubling of the strategic petroleum reserve. At that moment, the price of oil was crumbling; it had touched under $50/bbl just a few days before. Bush's announcement gave heart to the oil patch, their friends at OPEC, the oil price speculators, and anyone and everyone else who might benefit from higher oil prices. Invoking the doubling of the strategic petroleum reserve was the signal that set off the greatest price escalation in oil's commercial history. Barely eighteen months later, we were to hit a price of $147/bbl oil—a price never attained in the wildest and most seductive visions of a desert mirage. Yet, stubbornly, the Department of Energy continued to fill the strategic petroleum reserve, irrespective of price and the psychological impulse it sent to the markets. For the US government to purchase oil at these prices was tantamount to extending its blessing.

It literally took an act of Congress to override the administration in order to halt purchases as of May 2008. Other than releasing small amounts of oil from the strategic petroleum reserve for short-term climatic or pipeline disruptions, high prices risking a national economic calamity were never adequate cause to tap the strategic petroleum reserve in this administration's view. The oil barons would not have been pleased. It is a scandal, with the nation hurting in so many areas, that we are once again dedicating federal funds to the one industry that has benefited most shamelessly under the Bush administration. It is past time for this administration and its welfare policies for the oil industry to come to an end. It's time to send the hacks at the Department of Energy packing.

Gulf Oil Disaster: And the Winner Is ... the Oil Companies
June 9, 2010

Everyone seems to be the loser in the gulf oil spill, with one exception—the oil companies themselves, especially those with major production facilities onshore. The uncertainty of the government's policies toward offshore drilling and the temporary moratorium that is shutting down dozens of offshore rigs pending further study is beginning to put serious upward pressure on oil prices. Today alone, the price of oil has jumped by nearly $2/bbl.

Meanwhile, sitting there staring the government in the face are 727 million bbl of oil in our filled-to-the-brim strategic petroleum reserve. This lifeline sits there while our oil world is navigating, perhaps better said stumbling, through an unparalleled disaster. The strategic petroleum reserve exists, according to the Department of Energy's statement of purpose, "first and foremost, as an emergency response tool the President can use should the United States be confronted with an economically threatening disruption in oil supplies" (Department of Energy, "U.S. Petroleum Reserves: Releasing Crude Oil from the Strategic Petroleum Reserve," http://fossil.energy.gov/programs/reserves/spr/spr-drawdown. html). If not now, then when? Economically threatening? Can our precarious recovery, if it really exists, survive another tax in the form of higher oil and gasoline prices at this time on top of the enormous economic disruption along the gulf coast?

If the strategic petroleum reserve is not put into play to balance out the distortions in oil prices resulting from the gulf catastrophe, what is the sense of the billions upon billions of dollars expended in purchasing and storing that oil in the first place? The strategic petroleum reserve should be drawn down until, at the very least, firm policies are formulated for future drilling and until we have a full accounting of the current damage incurred and a resolution of the massive mess now spewing forth.

Further enriching the oil companies through higher oil prices is not the answer. It becomes a self-inflicted wound—a particularly foolish one, given that our strategic petroleum reserve is an insurance policy bought and paid for in the billions of dollars to head off exactly this kind of economic threat.

As Oil Pierces $90/bbl, It's Time for the President to Act—Finally
December 22, 2010

Since the beginning of the Obama presidency, the price of oil has nearly tripled from slightly over $30/bbl in February 2009 to over $90/bbl on the New York Mercantile Exchange today. To date, the president has barely dealt with this malignancy, which threatens to destabilize the feeble economic recovery he has sponsored. Yet during his presidential campaign, Obama presented himself as resolute on the issue of oil prices and their impact on the nation's well-being.

In August 2008, much to the dismay of the oil companies and most especially the oil speculators—including many of the major bank-holding companies such as Morgan Stanley, J.P. Morgan Chase, Citigroup, and Goldman Sachs—candidate Obama proposed releasing seventy million bbl of oil from the strategic petroleum reserve. The mere idea that someone with potential access to the White House was willing to deal with the issue of oil prices had an immediate effect, especially by contrast with the shameful oil patch–coddling policies of the Bush administration. On August 4, 2008, after Obama aired his proposal, the price of oil fell by some $4/bbl.

The talking heads went into action immediately. No, it wasn't the candidate's suggestion that caused the price of oil to fall, but rather the then-gathering Tropical Storm Edouard's change in trajectory, since it was meant to bypass production rigs in the Gulf of Mexico. They said anything to put the possibility of using the strategic petroleum reserve to combat excessive oil prices back into the box—and not a word about what the mere specter of releasing millions of bbl of oil would do to a market riven with speculation. There was nary a mention of the fact that releasing one or two million bbl per day over a one- or two-month period would wreak havoc on oil-trading futures and probably bring the price of oil down by $20/bbl or more by chasing scores of speculators out of the market. This is especially true now with commercial oil inventories close to their all-time highs and the strategic petroleum reserve bulging with some 750 million bbl in storage.

For those who take solace in high oil and gasoline prices because they reduce demand, and thus mitigate global warming, please understand that it is madness to reduce consumption by lining the pockets of oil producers here and abroad. It is long past time for our government to take this issue in hand and act forcefully to reduce oil consumption by fiat and not by transferring billions upon billions of dollars to the oiligopoly. We did it once before. It was called World War II.

PART VIII

Curbing Our Appetite for Consumption

A Forceful and Immediate Antidote to Our Oil Dependence
March 7, 2006

It has become clear to all of us that the nation's dependence on imported oil presents an immediate and exponentially growing risk to our national and economic security. Even President Bush has cautioned that "tyrants control the spigots" (Caroline Daniel, "Bush Steps Up Rhetoric on Foreign Oil Dependency," *Financial Times*, February 28, 2006, http://www.ft.com/cms/s/0/a84d9eca-a7fe-11da-85bc-0000779e2340. html#axzz1Gz8U8ozB). These are strong words, especially from a Texas oilman, but hardly extravagant in light of the recent failed attack on the Abqaiq oil facility in Saudi Arabia, the general state of the world from Nigeria to Venezuela to Iran, and new threats over the weekend from al Qaeda deputy Ayman al-Zawahiri. As reported by John F. Burnes, Al-Zawahiri urged Muslims in an audiotape posted on the Internet on Saturday, March 4, 2006, to "inflict losses on the crusader West, especially to its economic infrastructure with strikes that would make it bleed for years [...] to prevent [it] from stealing the Muslims' oil" (March 5, 2006 *New York Times,* World section).

Given the seriousness of the threat, it is essential that the United States act now to moderate the price of oil and to ensure an equitable distribution of available supply, no matter what the circumstances. But what the president has proposed are, at best, vague and underfunded alternative-energy initiatives, ranging from biofuels to clean coal to nuclear power, whose promised benefits are years away. The will to take quick and forceful action appears to be lacking. Most glaringly, there has been no mention of controlling demand, that shoved-aside, neither-seen-nor-heard stepchild of the energy debate. Indeed, the deafening silence lends an almost heretical aura to the question of mandating constraints on demand. Yet, such constraints are the most immediate and effective way for us to gain control and a modicum of self-respect on this issue.

Ironically, we needn't look any further than the cap and trade Clear Skies Initiative for a viable and very successful example of what can and should be done to take control of oil consumption. The federal Clear Skies Initiative permits cleaner-operating power companies to sell emissions credits to heavier polluters, thereby keeping total emissions within government-mandated levels. In spite of early criticism, the program has worked admirably and has reduced total pollution. A similar program incorporating a national system of tradable gasoline vouchers could be instituted almost immediately. Every car owner would be entitled to a designated number of vouchers based on geographical location, vocational need, transportation options, and so on—the idea being to meet a national target for gasoline consumption. The target would be revised, say, every three months or as contingencies necessitated. A driver who needed more gas than he or she was allotted could buy vouchers from drivers who needed less than the average. The price would be set by the market, with rights traded through classified ads, online bulletin boards, or local markets accessed at filling stations. Widely available tech products such as the versatile debit card could greatly facilitate this system.

The effects of the Cap and Ride Open Road Initiative—let's call it that—would be immediate, and the burden, if that is the right word, would be shared fairly. Everyone would be free to choose how little or how much gasoline to use, and no one would be unduly penalized. But more to the point, oil consumption would be controlled effectively in a way that would also encourage more fuel-efficient use of cars, trucks, and public transportation. Equally importantly, we would have a system in place that ensured equitable distribution of available fossil fuels in case a major displacement or emergency occurred.

Unlike an across-the-board gas tax, which would set the antitax folks to howling while unfairly punishing the poor and those living in rural areas (and in cities and towns without public transportation options), a voucher system would give all Americans a chance to pitch in to avert a national crisis. It would also set an example for other oil-importing nations to institute similar programs and would give our government valuable negotiating leverage with oil producers (i.e., if a producer threatens to cut supply, we retaliate by mandating a cut in consumption). In the end, a voucher system would allow us to regain our energy self-reliance.

Can we do it? Yes, but only with visionary political leadership and forceful political will. Just don't expect the oil patch to lend a hand.

Capping Our Gasoline Consumption through a Manageable Eco-Fuels Program
January 8, 2007

Greenhouse gases and their impact on global warming endanger not only our future but also our present. it's long past time for us to take a new look at the nature of our twin addictions to fossil fuels in the form of gasoline and the obsession it supports—our love affair with the automobile. By separating these intertwined dependencies, we might just find a workable cure for our afflictions. My two-part prescription involves weaning the automobile away from gasoline and putting policies in place to curb open-ended access to petroleum-based gasoline. These steps are essential to substantially diminishing our dependence on fossil-based fuels.

To begin, I believe we must create an infrastructure to power vehicles that use no or only minimal amounts of gasoline—that is, hybrids/plug-ins or flex-fuel cars and trucks. This changeover would require:

- an electric grid system that would be based on power generated from the traditional sources but increasingly supplemented by nuclear, wind, and solar power generation combined with greatly expanded delivery capabilities to permit the widespread use of plug-in hybrid vehicles;

- broader cultivation and land use that would target greater production of ethanol from both corn and biomass to power flexible fuel/biodiesel vehicles (think of Brazil's astounding success with ethanol made from sugar cane);

- a national program to facilitate distribution of eco-fuels to a new generation of vehicles that would access alternative fuels—plug-in stations for city dwellers, ethanol-pumping facilities, and so on—must be as widespread as gasoline pumps are now;

- policies designed to bring about an orderly conversion from gasoline-powered vehicles to hybrid, flex-fuel, and plug-in ones, including help for Detroit, car owners, and refiners that would be called upon to produce ethanol-rich gasoline formulations.

All of this would take time and investment, but with a combination of national volition, incentives, and Congressional leadership, it should be achievable within five years—an adequate period for the government to firmly establish the program and permit the changeovers necessary.

Then comes the hard part: a step that will take great political courage and leadership and a government willing to face down powerful vested interests. In five years' time, the Department of Energy would be called upon to establish a maximum quantity of petroleum-based gasoline available for national consumption in perpetuity over each six-month period (ideally, this would be an amount equivalent to the domestic production of oil and corresponding refining capacity; note that 60 percent of our oil is currently imported). Over time, the cap would be reduced as alternative, ecologically sounder fuels became more prevalent.

Each car owner would receive a magnetic debit card entitling that individual to a specific allocation of gasoline. These allotments, let's call them eco purchase permits, could be used on a free market basis or freely traded to others who want or need additional hydrocarbon gasoline for any reason. The buyers could obtain part of someone else's allotment through online bulletin boards, gas station–sponsored markets, personal transactions, and so forth. The key point is that those consumers wanting more gasoline could get it without increasing the overall consumption of gasoline. The beauty of such a system is that it would allow the open-ended consumption of ethanol, biodiesel, and plug-in energy power. Consumers using gasoline and ethanol blends would be debited for the gasoline-based content alone. In other words, only petroleum-based fuel would be limited, and that cap would remain in place irrespective of the price of gasoline—whether high or low— owing to its well-documented contribution to environmental pollution and to protect the viability of the alternative energy infrastructure that will have been established in its place. While ethanol and electric power would be freely sold at market prices, as is presently the case, gasoline would also be priced according to market conditions but within the cap parameter. Under this program, the only thing being regulated would be the national cap on gasoline consumption.

Writing in the *Wall Street Journal* on December 30 ("Gentlemen, Start Your Plug-Ins"), James Woolsey laid out the encouraging prospects for hybrid plug-in and flex-fuel vehicles. Woolsey, the former director of the Central Intelligence Agency, cited the National Energy Policy

Commission and its studies on the prospects for improved efficiency in biomass cultivation and production. The commission projected that the price of cellulosic ethanol could be headed down toward seventy cents per gallon.

Whether or not the National Energy Policy Commission's prediction comes to pass, it is now clear that we can no longer depend on the world oil market to supply the nation's needs in a rational and dependable way. To quote the Energy Security Leadership Council from its report ("Recommendations to the Nation on Reducing US Oil Dependence December 2006", secureenergy.org, http://www.secureenergy.org/sites/default/files/147_Recommendations_to_the_Nation.pdf):

> Oil prices may be a function of supply and demand, but the American people must also recognize that the twenty-first-century global oil market is well removed from the free market ideal. At least 75 percent—and by some estimates as much as 90 percent—of all oil and gas reserves are held by national oil companies (NOCs) that are either partially or fully controlled by governments. Oil markets are not only politicized, they are also distorted by the presence of large economic externalities such as military expenditures that are not factored into final pricing. Consequently, we must accept that market forces alone will not solve our oil problems.

The program proposed will go a long way toward reestablishing our energy self-reliance. We are up against a problem that will continue to bedevil us and future generations if it is not met with courage and vision. It's been said that energy is the new weapon of mass destruction. Here is one solution but certainly not the last word. If you've got a better idea, America is all ears.

The Vision Thing: Shortchanging Amtrak, Coddling the Oil Patch, and Building a Stealth Superhighway Nightmare
March 20, 2007

Last month, President Bush signed a $464 billion spending bill, but he made it clear that he wasn't entirely happy with the document, given the fact that Congress shifted funds to domestic programs not of his liking and ignored some of his requests for budget cuts. Specifically, lawmakers refused to slash four hundred million dollars from Amtrak's $1.3 billion budget.

We are addicted to oil, as the president clearly acknowledges. So let's take steps to undermine our mass transportation, of which Amtrak is a key component. Make sense? Not to me, but perhaps it would be fair to ask—given our addiction to oil, the instability of our oil supply and its suppliers, and the environmental damage caused by driving cars and trucks—why maintaining and building up our mass transportation capabilities is not as great a national priority as, say, increasing our strategic petroleum reserve.

The doubling of our strategic petroleum reserve from 727 million bbl to 1.45 billion bbl was announced by the president during his State of the Union address. The estimated cost will be some sixty billion dollars. That's today's purchase price plus the cost of financing, administration, transport, and storage. Oh yes ... and as the strategic petroleum reserve takes all that oil off the market, we may expect to pay higher prices at the pump. The doubling of the strategic petroleum reserve while enhancing transportation and energy security only marginally (given the vast reserves already in place) becomes a major windfall for the president's favorite constituents, the oil industry.

Just think what sixty billion dollars could do for the infrastructure of our passenger railroad system. It could overcome years of neglect and reduce our ever-growing dependence on cars, highways, and airlines as well as our oil imports. While shortchanging Amtrak, the administration has surreptitiously been planning a gargantuan ten-lane international superhighway linking the west coast ports of Mexico to the plains of Canada through the heart of the United States. It would end up effectively bifurcating the country at a cost of $184 billion (see the Passenger Rail Investment and Improvement Act of 2007 (S.294)).

While we ride the rails backward, England's high-speed rail link will open within a year's time and connect London to the center of Paris in two hours and fifteen minutes. According to Eurostar's chief executive, Richard Brown, "It will mark the start of a new era in travel between the UK and mainland Europe, making high speed even faster, more reliable, and less environmentally damaging as the alternative to flying" (Steve Keenan, "Eurostar Reveals St. Pancras Details," *the Times*, November 14, 2006, http://www.timesonline.co.uk/tol/travel/ holiday_type/rail_travel/article636615.ece). Not to be outdone, France opened its fastest rail line to date just this week, connecting Paris to Strasbourg. With the train traveling at two hundred miles per hour, transit time is a mere two hours and twenty minutes versus a previous time of four hours. To grasp the impact of the European achievement, by November 2003, the Train à Grande Vitesse service carried its one billionth passenger and is expected to reach the two billion mark in 2010. On a test run on February 13, 2007, the Train à Grande Vitesse's latest model achieved speeds of 344.4 miles per hour. Of particular note, the trains are all electrified. In France, 80 percent of the electric power comes from fossil fuel–free, pollutant-free nuclear power plants.

So why not here? Well, you see, Amtrak doesn't have a heavily funded foothold in Washington's K Street lobbying club comparable to—you guessed it—the oil industry, which is forever squeezing out tax breaks, depreciation credits, and royalty holidays. Ditto for construction and road building concerns, who are forever urging their friends in Congress to pave over our amber waves of grain with asphalt. There's no big money pushing Amtrak. It can't even fend for itself. The entire board of directors, with one or two exceptions, is made up of Bush appointees loyal to the administration and its values. A handful of politicians on Capitol Hill are partisans of Amtrak, such as Senators Frank Lautenberg and Trent Lott, and are egged on no doubt by constituents in their districts using Amtrak's services. But hey, those people take the train. What do you expect?

In their highly successful intervention in the leveraged buyout negotiations of the Texas power utility, TXU Corporation (the largest leveraged buyout ever), the Environmental Defense Fund was able to obtain TXU's commitment for major reductions in carbon dioxide emissions from their coal-fired power plants and in limiting construction altogether. Thus, the Environmental Defense Fund and the Natural Resources Defense Council have shown what an engaged environmental community can do to offset the influence of vested interests.

Amtrak needs help. It's time we decided to get "All aboard."

Forget a Gas Tax; We Need a Fuel Voucher Program
December 30, 2008

This past weekend, the *New York Times* brought out its heavy guns to fight for a national gasoline tax. First there was an editorial in Saturday's paper ("The Gas Tax," December 26, 2008), and then there was Thomas L. Friedman's op-ed the next day ("Win, Win, Win, Win, Win ..." December 27, 2008). In putting forth an economically regressive program, the nabobs of the *Times*, who in most cases care little about paying three or four dollars more for a gallon of gasoline for their cars, wrap themselves snugly in their well-earned mantles of elitist movers and shakers.

Of course, all the best reasons are listed to call for the urgent diminution of gasoline consumption out of economic, environmental, and geopolitical concerns even to the point where Friedman cautions our president-elect, Obama, that "[w]ithout a higher gas tax or carbon tax, [he] will lack the leverage to drive critical pieces of his foreign and domestic agenda." There is not a drop of ink now, or in recent memory as far as I can tell, on another solution that would be fairer to all Americans and would engage them in a shared sacrifice creating a universal call to arms, while mounting a communal and viable offensive against our debilitating addiction to fossil fuels.

Rather than use the term *rationing*, we might call this solution a fuel voucher program. It would in fact be a free market variation of the gas-rationing program that served the nation so well during World War II by bringing a shared sense of mission and dignity to the home front when everyone pulled together. At that time, there was a clear realization that a gas tax would penalize the part of the population that could least afford it and would thereby exacerbate differences among the nation's citizens among whom unanimity of purpose was needed to further the war effort.

I'll describe how a fuel voucher program might work. The Department of Energy or the Department of the Interior would set a maximum quantity of gasoline that could be consumed in any quarter throughout the United States. The quantity would be reduced nationally every quarter, initially in minimal amounts to permit a systematic but consistent changeover of automobile ownership from gas guzzlers to hybrid, flex-fuel capable, and electric cars so that in, say, seven or ten years, we will have reduced our daily oil consumption from the current usage of approximately twenty million bbl per day to ten million bbl per day—or by 50 percent.

Every car owner would receive a quarterly gas allocation based on that ceiling level, and the allocations would be distributed equally among the nation's car owners. Let's call these gas purchase permits. They would come in the form of magnetic debit cards, giving each private car owner the same allocation of gas. Gas purchase permits could then be used by their owners or freely traded. Drivers whose allotted amount of gas didn't meet their needs or who wanted more for whatever reason could buy all or part of someone else's allocation through online bulletin boards, through gas station markets, or even through eBay or private transactions. The key is that the gas purchase permit plan uses market incentives to permit heavier gasoline consumers to get what they need without increasing overall consumption of gasoline. Allowances could be embedded in the program for businesses and possibly for those required to drive long distances because of geographic location or employment where no mass transit is available. Operationally, this is little different from a cap and trade program, although it is on a different scale.

The fuel voucher program would address the consumption of fossil fuel–based gasoline only. All alternative fuels, be they ethanol, biomass, electric, hydrogen, cooking oil, or whatever the American imagination and ingenuity can substitute for gasoline would be open-ended, without restriction as to quantity or usage by each driver.

Along these lines, this month, the state of Hawaii together with the Hawaii Electric Power Company endorsed a program to build an alternative transportation system based on electric vehicles with swappable batteries and an intelligent battery-recharging network.

Aside from the enormous benefits that would ensue from a significant reduction of our gasoline consumption in areas already referred to above, the fuel voucher program would provide a massive boost to our economy. There are currently some 230 million vehicles plying the roads of America. Of these, less than ten million are flex-fuel, hybrid, or otherwise fuel-efficient. A fuel voucher program would provide the needed incentives to convert that massive fleet to fuel-efficient cars in a fair way and over a reasonable number of years with the government helping those with marginal incomes to trade in their cars for more fuel-efficient vehicles with tax credits directly or indirectly to the automobile manufacturers.

Brazil took but three years to transition its significant automobile industry to building 75 percent flex-fuel cars and trucks from a base of only 5 percent. In 1941, it took the partnership of our government and Detroit but eight months to convert the automobile industry from building passenger cars to assembling tanks and military equipment. It's time once more for Detroit to become the arsenal of America's future. Let flex-fuel, hybrid, and electric cars become our generation's tanks.

The Stimulus Package: Why Is Intercity Rail Service at the End of the Line?
February 4, 2009

Only yesterday, Senator Diane Feinstein was quoted as saying, "Our highways are jammed. People go to work in gridlock" (Derrick Z. Jackson, "Another Gift for the Auto Industry," *Boston Globe*, February 7, 2009, http://www.boston.com/bostonglobe/editorial_opinion/oped/articles/2009/02/07/another_gift_for_the_auto_industry/). She proposed adding twenty-five billion dollars for highway and mass transit to the economic stimulus package. Concurrently, Senator Charles Schumer is pushing to add $6.5 billion for mass transit; he is calling buses, subways, and trains the lifeblood of the largest city of the nation. Yet, as currently construed, there is but $1.1 billion set aside to improve intercity rail passenger service, and that amount is almost at the tail end of priorities listed in the House version of the bill. Given the remarkable advances achieved by rail travel in recent years and given the administration's clear focus on diminishing the nation's carbon footprint, this appears to be a particularly significant oversight and raises troubling questions about the whole process.

The driving distance between New York City and Chicago is 793 miles. Under normal driving conditions, the trip takes about fourteen hours. A bullet train service would cover the distance in some four hours from downtown to downtown. You could have lunch in Chicago and dinner in New York. With trains traveling 344 miles per hour just over the horizon, I leave the rest to your imagination.

This would be an infrastructure project we could all get enthusiastic about and for which we could roll up our sleeves with great pride. So why is it not among the forefront of the stimulus priorities? Is it because our sad Amtrak system has no constituency, no representation among the new political class—the K Street lobbyists, with their massive power, wealth, and influence? Please, President Obama, say it ain't so.

High-Speed Rail Speeding Ahead at Snail's Pace
September 3, 2009

In the months ahead, the Department of Transportation will begin awarding the eight billion dollars set aside under the federal stimulus program to those states presenting the most attractive plans for building high-speed trains. Another five billion dollars will be sought by the administration over the next five years. That's not exactly chump change, but for those counting, it's roughly equivalent to the amount showered practically overnight to a single financial entity—the $12.9 billion paid out to Goldman Sachs through AIG's counterparty redemption of near worthless derivatives and made possible by the government's infusion of cash into AIG.

Once upon a time, eight billion dollars and the prospect of an additional five billion dollars would have seemed like a munificent sum. Today, given the hundreds of billions being bandied about, it seems insufficient to the task at hand. This money is for a program that would have an extraordinarily beneficial impact on our lives, our economy, and our environment. California's governor, Arnold Schwarzenegger, commented on the proposed high-speed link from the Bay Area to Southern California, saying, "On top of stimulating the California economy, federal investment in California's rail systems will help lay a sustainable foundation for economic growth, help us meet our environmental goals and improve quality of life here in California" (Valerie Gotten, "Gov. Schwarzenegger Applies for $1.1 Billion in Recovery Funds," *California Newswire*, August 26, 2009, http://californianewswire.com/2009/08/26/CNW5338_004134.php).

Please recall that the eight billion dollars for high-speed rail was barely mentioned in the first draft of the stimulus program and was added almost as an afterthought when the concept received a much warmer following in Congress than had been anticipated (as well as after receiving the strong sponsorship of President Obama). Since then, support and enthusiasm for the program has broadened nationwide, extending to the thirteen regions that will be submitting proposals to the department in the next days. The submissions are coming from California, from the Capitol Corridor (including Virginia and North Carolina), from Chicago, from points south to St. Louis, from Arizona, from Florida, and from others. Most glaring is the paucity of national commitment to what could be a major and positive overhaul to how we travel, weaning us off of decades of addiction to endless highway and road building and the endless subsidies to air and highway funding.

Given the success and public enthusiasm for high-speed rail in Japan and China coupled with a deep sense of national pride, our efforts are long overdue in what is rapidly becoming the preferred mode of transport of the twenty-first century and beyond. This is especially so when both England and France are undertaking major expansions of their already highly successful high-speed rail infrastructure. To the popular service linking London to Paris, the British government is proposing to add service from London to Edinburgh and Glasgow; the high-speed rail would serve both Manchester and Birmingham as well. Current plans call for the link to become operative by 2030 with an expenditure of fifty-five billion dollars, according to the BBC (Lorna Gordon, "New High Speed Rail Plan Unveiled," August 26, 2009). Travel time between Glasgow and London will be reduced from four hours and ten minutes to two hours and sixteen minutes. France, with perhaps the most effective national high-speed rail network in the world, is looking to double its reach inside its own borders and to extend service links to Italy and Spain and improve links to Germany. *Le Monde* reports that more than two thousand additional kilometers of track will be put down by 2020 at a cost of ninety-eight billion dollars (M. Delberghe, "Lignes à Grande Vitesse: la France de Demain," August 11, 2009). On a proportional basis relative to size and population, that would be the equivalent of the United States committing at least $490 billion toward an analogous project.

On the issue of high-speed rail service, we are riding the caboose of history attached to a hundred-car freight train. "Lignes à Grande Vitesse: la France de Demain" freely translated is "High-Speed Rail Network: the France of Tomorrow." What about our tomorrow? When are we going to have a government that once again takes tomorrow in hand with vision, meaningful purpose, and action?

America in the Caboose While the World Barrels Ahead on High-Speed Rail
September 8, 2010

On Monday, President Obama called on Congress to approve fifty billion dollars in funding for highways, landing strips, and rail lines to stimulate the economy and create jobs, specifically to build or rebuild 150,000 miles of road, to lay and maintain four thousand miles of railroad track, and to construct 150 miles of runways. Do we really need to focus on 150,000 miles of roads? They must be popping off champagne corks in the corner offices of the oil industry and at OPEC headquarters. Of course, focusing on getting America off the gasoline habit would have been a far wiser commitment of time, effort, and money. Do we need more landing strips, encouraging us to fly, fly, fly, gulping ever-greater quantities of fossil fuels? Maybe that's not such a good idea. Then, whatever's left over goes into rail infrastructure.

In this domain, in which we once led the world, we are now eons behind. There is little else in the president's proposal that would do as much for our economy and keep us on a competitive footing with nations whose governments are not beholden to oil lobbies. There is nothing that would address so clearly the blunders of past administrations that permitted the ripping up of rail lines and tramways all over the country at the instigation of the oil interests and the once considerable influence of the automobile industry. But a fifty billion-dollar program to deal with all these objectives?

Assuming as much as half (twenty-five billion dollars) is being set aside for rail, how does that compare to other nations already far ahead of us in providing modern, up-to-date mass transportation for their citizenry or at least looking further ahead in their planning? France, will be adding another two thousand additional kilometers of track to accommodate high-speed rail by 2020 at a cost of ninety-eight billion dollars. By way of comparison, that would be the equivalent (proportionate to size and population) of the United States committing at least $490 billion to a similar project. In the time frame of one generation, China has built an infrastructure of high-speed trains that leaves us in the dust. Major hubs are connected by trains speeding along at some three hundred miles per hour, while the rail travel time between many of our major cities is now slower than it was in the 1930s and 1940s. According to Arianna Huffington's *Third World America*, it now takes eighteen hours to travel by rail between Chicago and Denver; back then, the travel time was thirteen hours. An article in the *China Daily* last year (Xinhua, "China to Increase Investment in Railway Construction," August 11, 2009) reported that China was planning to invest at least seven hundred billion yuan ($102 billion) annually from 2010 through 2012 on railway construction alone.

By comparison, we are way behind and falling further behind every year. From the very outset, our reluctance—or perhaps lack of the necessary vision—to address the ways in which a national program to rebuild our railways might impact our society has hobbled us. The stimulus program initiated last year set aside but eight billion dollars for important rail service improvement. That is a sum perhaps more appropriate to the budget of Andorra or Grenada than to that of the United States. What is it that our government doesn't get? Where is the vision that, at another time in an equally stressful economic environment, rendered unto the nation such massive capital investments and infrastructural icons as the Hoover Dam (at the time of its building in the 1930s, it was the largest dam in the world), the Tennessee Valley Authority, and the Works Progress Administration?

A massive rebuilding and expanding of our railroad infrastructure would not just be a disbursement of stimulus dollars but a far-sighted and urgently needed capital investment that would pay off in spades through greater efficiency, reduced dependence on fossil fuels, greater self-reliance, and an altogether massive improvement in the way we travel and conduct our lives. Instead of frittering away billions here and there in make-work or politically driven earmark projects, we should rebuild our rail system and bring it into the twenty-first century; that would engage the entire nation. All of us would benefit.

Booming US Gas Industry Becoming an American Energy Exporter
November 24, 2010

At this time of Thanksgiving, we can be grateful that a tectonic shift is beginning to occur in America's dependence on imported energy. In the past weeks, a number of major events have taken place that are changing the balance of energy in significant ways.

Last month, the Chinese government-owned energy company CNOC (you will recall CNOC's failed bid to take over Unocal in 2005) committed more than a billion dollars to take an important stake in the Eagle Ford shale gas acreage in Texas. In doing so, it joined the Norwegian state oil company, Statoil, which had made an investment in the Eagle Ford field as well. Major oil companies such as ExxonMobil, Shell, Chevron, and myriad other foreign entities have joined American gas producers such as Chesapeake Energy in investing tens of billions of dollars in what is becoming a treasure trove of natural gas. It ranges from Texas and Louisiana to the vast Marcellus field of western Pennsylvania, Ohio, West Virginia, and upstate New York. With new drilling techniques, the proven gas reserves of the United States have skyrocketed from bare subsistence levels by a factor of five and counting, with the shale play still in its infancy.

It has turned a market of shortage, with prices of roughly fourteen dollars per million BTUs quoted on the New York Mercantile Exchange in 2008 to a market of product glut and prices currently hovering around four dollars per million BTUs. At that price, natural gas delivers a BTU equivalency comparable to that of oil priced around $20/bbl. Today, oil is selling at over $80/bbl.

Of particular significance this Monday, Macquarie Energy and

Freeport LNG announced plans to jointly develop a two billion-dollar project to liquefy, market, and export 1.4 billion cubic feet of gas per day. Mr. Nicholas O'Kane, senior managing director of Macquarie Group (an Australian company) said that "[r]ecent developments in shale gas technology have transformed the US gas market. The U.S. has developed significant natural gas resources and is able to meet projected domestic demand and a surplus for a long time to come" ("Macquarie Energy and Freeport LNG Expansion, L.P. to Jointly Develop U.S. LNG Export Project," November 22, 2010, http://www.macquarie. com/us/about_macquarie/media_centre/20101122.html).

Clearly, the natural gas industry could play a preeminent role in liberating the nation from its dependence on energy imports. Given that natural gas, as feedstock, is significantly less polluting than coal in coal-burning energy plants, natural gas would play a major role in containing polluting emissions. That said, however, the natural gas industry will still be hard-pressed to develop to its full capability because of an oil and coal influence–addled Congress.

PART IX

Alternative Energy and the Solution
That Dare Not Speak Its Name

Color Nuclear Energy Green
June 1, 2006

I have just come back from China, and I have seen the future. It is ominously murky—literally. The enormous strides being made, the torrent of new buildings and factories, the expansive new highways, the elegant new boulevards, and even the palatial majesty of such great historical treasures as the Forbidden City are all shrouded in a mist of polluted air. The pollution is foul enough to be eroding real-estate values in Hong Kong.

China's deteriorating environment is spilling over near and far and is a major contributor to integrated Hong Kong's declining attractiveness to expatriate managers and professionals. So significant is the pollution that particles are reaching as far as California. We all know by now that air pollution isn't a localized affair. What isn't so well known is how pressing the danger is, given the headlong leap into industrial development by nations that represent as much as half the world's population (China, India, Korea, swaths of Southeast Asia, and Russia). We are left with a Hobson's choice—a choice that's no choice at all but one that must be made. From what I have seen, it is essential that it be made thoughtfully before it has to be made hastily.

It was gratifying to learn that others better placed and with wide experience share and are now broadcasting views reappraising the need for conversion to nuclear power. This is especially welcome in the case of an unlikely yet most influential and welcome convert to the cause of nuclear energy: Patrick Moore, cofounder of Greenpeace, the environmental watchdog group. Moore has not only written a strong defense of nuclear power plants but also joined forces with Christie Whitman, former head of the Environmental Protection Agency, as the cochair of a new industry-funded initiative, the Clean and Safe Energy Coalition, to support increased use of nuclear energy.

A few years ago, no one would have believed such a turnaround was possible for a man who, as he now says, took it as gospel "that nuclear energy was synonymous with nuclear holocaust" (Patrick Moore, "Outlook: Nuclear Energy," *Washington Post*, April 17, 2006, http:// www.washingtonpost.com/wp-dyn/content/discussion/2006/04/13/ DI2006041301125.html). Moore still has colleagues who accuse him of selling out to the forces of darkness. But growing numbers of green leaders are joining him in switching sides, including James Lovelock, who conceived the Gaia theory of the Earth as a living organism, and Stewart Brand, founder of the Whole Earth Catalog. Sometimes, new converts pay a price; the late British bishop, Hugh Montefiore, founder of Friends of the Earth, was forced to resign from its board after he wrote a pronuclear article in a church newsletter.

Moore's reasoning for this change, laid out in an op-ed piece in the *Washington Post* in April ("Going Nuclear," April 16, 2006), is simple and persuasive. He writes, "Nuclear energy may just be the energy source that can save our planet from another possible disaster: catastrophic climate change." He says the more than six hundred coal-fired power plants in the United States alone churn out 36 percent of the nation's emissions of the greenhouse gas carbon dioxide. That's nearly two billion tons and 10 percent of the world total. It's also the equivalent of the exhaust from three hundred million cars. While these plants are producing 60 percent of the nation's electricity, 103 nuclear plants are producing another 20 percent of our power without spewing the seven hundred million tons of carbon dioxide that coal-fired plants would have emitted. If the ratio of coal to nuclear power could be reversed, he argues, it "would go a long way toward cleaning the air."

Rebutting conventional perceptions, Moore argues that nuclear facilities aren't expensive, their initial investment notwithstanding. He says they are among the least costly sources of power when calculated over the generating life of the plant. Nor are they dangerous. He says Chernobyl was an "inherently bad design" and that what alarmists failed to notice or acknowledge about Three Mile Island was that the containment shell did its job, and no fatalities resulted. The problem of nuclear waste, he says, will be greatly reduced by new techniques for recycling spent fuel. While the danger is genuine that nuclear fuel can be diverted to make bombs, "[J]ust because nuclear technology can be put to evil purposes is not an argument to ban its use." In the past two decades, Moore points out, African machetes have killed far more people than the number who died at Hiroshima and Nagasaki. He goes on to say, "If we banned everything that can be used to kill people, we would never have harnessed fire."

Of course, Moore tells his green friends, wind and solar power have their place. But because wind and the sun are not reliable, they can never be our primary sources of energy. Natural gas is a fossil fuel and comparatively expensive, while hydroelectric power sources are already being exploited at near-capacity rates. Thus, in the end, "nuclear is, by elimination, the only viable substitute for coal. It's that simple."

Too bad the *New York Times* can't bring itself to add a stronger voice in favor of nuclear power. In a recent editorial entitled "The Greening of Nuclear Power" (Editorial, May 13, 2006), the *Times* somewhat grudgingly endorsed the notion of giving nuclear power "a fresh look," but it seemed more intent on criticizing the Bush administration for signing a pact that shares nuclear power technology with India than on championing the environmental cause.

India's emissions of carbon dioxide could be reduced by 170 million tons per year. That's the equivalent of what an industrialized country such as the Netherlands emits in the same period. If India succeeds in its plan to supply 25 percent of its galloping electricity needs with nuclear power by 2050, it would have an important impact not only on gas emissions but also on fossil fuel consumption. We must also consider the benefits of having India's much-touted technological brain trust working to develop clean and safe solutions to the problem of nuclear waste disposal.

China, of course, is not unaware of its pollution dilemma and its potential for catastrophe. It is intent on cutting emissions pollution and has opted to harness nuclear energy to head off its crisis. China plans to build up to forty new nuclear power plants by the year 2020. Six are under construction already. The United States hasn't built one since the 1970s. But now, with the likes of Mr. Moore on board, let's go.

Nuclear Waste: "Not in My Backyard!" Then in Whose?
July 7, 2006

The enveloping miasma of climate change and its risk to us and to future generations calls for dynamic action to forestall and, I hope, prevent the disasters ahead. It calls for a clear understanding that this is not a local, regional, national, continental, or even hemispheric issue but one that is totally global in its origins, its reach, and its ultimate impact. It will affect each and every one of us in some important way. Because of its universality, we cannot conquer it alone, although we can accomplish much by deed and example. Clearly, though, its global dimension demands a global response, and the time for meaningful cooperation on a world scale is slipping away.

In my opinion—and some will disagree—the most effective and quickest way to reduce fossil fuel emissions, other than massively curtailing consumption, is to embrace the enormous potential of nuclear power. The question before us, then, is how to expedite the construction of nuclear facilities and get them up and running in the shortest time possible. Certainly, one of the major constraints is the storage and disposal of nuclear waste. This is not the only concern delaying nuclear power plant construction, but it, more than anything else, seems to be the elephant in the room that is holding back the broad and expeditious application of nuclear energy. Concurrent to arranging for nuclear waste storage sites, we need to develop advanced recycling technologies that do not produce separated plutonium. This would significantly diminish nuclear proliferation concerns while recycling used fuel would dramatically reduce the amount of waste requiring permanent disposal.

Understandably, the cry of "not in my backyard"—even when the backyard is thousands of miles away at Nevada's Yucca Mountain—has been raised to a deafening level and drowns out reasoned arguments. This scenario is replicating itself in virtually every corner of the world where nuclear power is being contemplated or expanded.

Yet France, where nearly 80 percent of electricity is generated by nuclear power, finds no such objections. One has to wonder why the French, who are not otherwise celebrated for their quiet acquiescence, accede to a set of conditions that would have American communities up in arms. The answer is not clear, because the entire issue is shielded, in large measure, by a decree of national security, which is meant to block debate. You see, France sends thousands of tons of nuclear waste to Russia each year, where it is stored at the Mayak nuclear facility located in the Chelyabinsk region. Though we know some details of the arrangement, much is still kept from public view. That's a pity. France's arrangement just might provide the kernel of a solution to the global problem of nuclear waste. If the Franco-Russian program could be applied globally, it could offer a solution that transcends borders, is effective, is environmentally sound, and is secure.

There are vast reaches of the world where nuclear waste disposal would have a truly minimal, even nonexistent, social impact and present the least possible environmental concern. Siberia, the Australian outback, the Gobi Desert, and the Canadian Shield, among others, come to mind. These are stretches of land that could provide an urgently needed backyard to allow the world to get on with its pressing need to expand the use of economical, carbon-free nuclear energy.

The International Atomic Energy Agency, working under the auspices of the United Nations, already oversees the inspection and monitoring of nuclear power and fissionable materials around the world. The International Atomic Energy Agency has, in its way, become the world watchdog on nuclear matters. Could the agency not also take on the oversight of international nuclear waste sites that would be accessible to all the world's nuclear power plants? The International Atomic Energy Agency or some similar agency could be given full control of both storage and security at the sites. Admittedly, working out the details of agency oversight of nuclear waste depots would take some doing, but given the importance of the issue, it needs to be done. Such a program could be very profitable for any country agreeing to undertake nuclear waste storage.

The Russian government, for example, recently passed a law to allow additional storage of nuclear waste on Russian soil. The Ministry of Atomic Energy, or Minatom, claims that ten thousand to twenty thousand tons of high-level nuclear waste could be imported over the next decade for storage and reprocessing, and the ministry expects to earn twenty billion dollars from the waste storage business. Russia is considering two separate sites: Chelyabinsk-65 (for reprocessing) and the Novaya Zemlya archipelago in the Northern Arkhangelsk region (dust off your atlas).

Australia, with some 30 percent of the world's uranium reserves, is currently meeting 20 percent of the world's need. With nuclear expansion in China and India, this offtake will grow considerably in the years ahead. Business proposals aimed at Australia, which has ideal geological conditions for waste storage, are proliferating. The Australian government is not unaware of these overtures, which promise to be highly profitable.

Now for a suggestion closer to home—and forgive me if I duck the slings and arrows that will come my way. Rather than drilling the Arctic National Wildlife Refuge with the wide and intrusive footprint Arctic National Wildlife Refuge oil development would entail, what if we set aside a very significantly smaller landmass as our own Novaya Zemlya archipelago to serve as a national depot for nuclear waste? We could then get on with building nuclear energy plants here at home and start taking a big bite out of our fossil fuel emissions. The caribou and polar bears would still have ample room to roam and happily carry on. Do not forget, they, too, have a vested interest in stopping and reversing global warming.

The Energy Entrepreneur Pioneers Take on the Oil Industry Goliath
August 24, 2006

A news report based on an article in Britain's *Guardian* newspaper hit the wire services earlier this week heralding a "free energy" technology. According to the *Observer* (David Smith, "Scientists Flock to Test 'Free Energy' Discovery," August 20, 2006, http://www.guardian. co.uk/technology/2006/aug/20/news.theobserversuknewspages), Sean McCarthy, who heads Steorn, a small high-technology company in Dublin, Ireland, stated that no one was more surprised than he when his firm hit upon a way to generate energy from the interaction of magnetic fields. The jury is still out on whether the breakthrough is fool's gold or the 24-karat variety, but McCarthy is sufficiently convinced of the validity of the discovery that he took out an ad in the *Economist* inviting the scientific community to investigate his company's findings.

McCarthy is one of a new breed of entrepreneurs who are challenged by the dangers our energy usage presents to our lives and our planet. He and his peers have a common goal: Drive a stake through the heart of our fossil fuel dependency, freeing us at long last from our morbid and expensive addiction. Many of these entrepreneurs have already achieved success and mastered challenges in other fields from Silicon Valley to the world of finance. They aren't motivated so much by profit but by the realization that energy—its usage as well as the politics of its production—present a fundamental threat to our lives, our children's lives, and our planet's future. For these entrepreneurs, it's giveback time.

They are people like Vinod Khosla, an especially gifted venture capitalist who invested early on in the likes of Amazon and Google. Kholsa, who was featured in a recent *Washington Post* article, is passionate in his belief that Americans can grow their way out of their dependence on the oil patch cabal. He is convinced of biofuels' efficacy, and more tellingly, he is willing to put his money where his mouth is. In keeping with his conviction that ethanol and similar biofuels are a viable alternative to oil, he threw down the gauntlet earlier this summer to Jeroen van der Veer, Shell's chief executive officer. Kholsa offered to supply significant quantities of alternative fuels like ethanol were Shell to commit to creating a distribution system that would make ethanol generally available to consumers throughout the country. Here's the kicker: Kholsa would guarantee a fixed price for five to seven years at an amount that would permit Shell or some similar large organization to sell ethanol for $1.99 per gallon across the United States. The price of $1.99 per gallon would also incorporate a fair profit margin for Shell. Last I heard (in July), Kholsa had found no takers. Will he? I doubt it, given the massive profits Shell and its oil patch brethren make on selling fossil fuels from the well to the gas tank.

Ultimately, Kholsa feels the government needs to do its part to make us more energy independent and energy secure. First, it must require or extend incentives to auto companies to manufacture more flex-fuel cars; second, it must require distributors to add ethanol fuel pumps at their gas stations; and third, it must be prepared to vary whatever subsidy programs currently exist (i.e., for corn) to ensure continued economic viability should the oil patch drop pricing to destructive levels—say, below Kholsa's $1.99 marker—placing investment (in production facilities, distribution networks, etc.) for alternative fuels at risk. He envisages a time in the not-so-distant future when most of our vehicle fuels will come from our farms, switch grass, and woody crops like hybrid willow and poplar, thereby making us both energy secure and able to enjoy the ancillary benefit of containing carbon emissions.

Then we have the likes of T. J. Rodgers, a committed libertarian who shuns any manner of government support. His company, SunPower, has been integrating computer chip technology into solar cells that directly convert sunlight into electricity. Rodgers's technical advances permit up to 50 percent greater efficiency than his current competition in the solar power field. SunPower is gearing up to produce thirty-five million of its six-inch black silicon wafers. That should be enough to generate one hundred million watts of solar power each year.

These are but a few examples of the new breed of energy pioneers. Their interest in finding the silver bullet to destroy the fossil fuel, carbon-belching monster once and for all is giving a whole new meaning to entrepreneurship. Whether their efforts will be successful remains to be seen, but we are fortunate that they, with their competence and resources, are motivated to take on the oil barons and their ilk.

The Importance of Nuclear Energy to the Nation's Future: Lafayette, We Need You Again
January 3, 2007

Our consumption of oil, given the threats it poses to our national security, its impact on our economy, and most importantly, its affect on our environment, evidences one of the sad shortcomings of our governance and public discourse. Not a single nuclear energy plant has been built in this country since the 1970s. There are valid reasons for this hiatus: the experience of Three Mile Island; the lingering memory of the Chernobyl disaster; the costs of construction and the arduous licensing process; the conundrum of nuclear waste disposal, nuclear proliferation issues; and on and on and on.

Yet, for all of the negatives of nuclear power, others have found nuclear energy to be a viable alternative to their growing dependence on fossil fuels. It is viewed by many nations as the cleanest, cheapest solution to the world's energy needs. Nuclear energy has no polluting emissions and provides clean energy to our increasingly vulnerable and deteriorating environment with reliable generating capacity to fuel the world's growing economies. In due course, it will become a major source of electrical power for plug-in hybrids, which, together with flex-fuel vehicles, will inevitably go a long way toward replacing gas-guzzling automobiles. Nuclear energy will play a major role in reducing the role of oil, which today powers 98 percent of the world's cars, trucks, and planes.

Consider that countries such as China, India, and Brazil (to name a few once viewed as developing nations) are emerging as sophisticated economies that are surpassing us in growth by factors of three and four and are amassing significant current account balances, as was reported in the *New York Times* by Floyd Norris ("Maybe Developing Nations Are Not Emerging But Have Emerged," December 30, 2006).

Earlier this month, two important events were announced. In Beijing in the presence of Secretary of Energy Samuel Bodman, United States–based Westinghouse Electric signed a multibillion-dollar agreement to supply four nuclear power plants to China. It will be a first major step in China's ambition to be at the forefront of a global trend toward increased use of nuclear power. After the signing, Secretary of Energy Bodman was quoted as saying, "It is my hope that this very serious commitment by the Chinese government will help persuade the nuclear power industry in the [United States] that now is the time to commit to building new nuclear power plants in our country to expand our own sources of clean, emissions-free electric power and further diversify our energy portfolio" (Emma Graham-Harrison, "Westinghouse Wins Massive China Nuclear Deal," *Washington Post*, December 16, 2006, http://www.washingtonpost.com/wp-dyn/content/article/2006/12/16/AR2006121600236_pf.html). In sharp contrast to our timidity, China plans to build some thirty new nuclear plants by 2020, raising its installed capacity to forty gigawatts—just about enough to power Spain.

Only a few days later on December 18, President Bush signed a treaty that will allow India to purchase US nuclear reactors and fuel for the first time in thirty years. The deal reverses a US policy that precluded nuclear cooperation with India because it had developed nuclear weapons despite never having signed the Non-Proliferation Treaty. Under the agreement, India will allow inspection of its civilian nuclear facilities. Before the treaty becomes operative, three additional approvals are needed from the International Atomic Energy Agency, the forty-five–nation Nuclear Suppliers Group, and a second time by the US Congress, but the intent and direction are clear.

As the world's largest democracy, India's nuclear ambitions rival that of China. India's demand for electricity is expected to double as early as 2015, and in the face of this staggering growth, it is India's goal to generate 25 percent of its electricity needs through nuclear energy by 2050. India projects that, in reaching this goal, its annual abatement of greenhouse gas pollution will be equal to the total yearly carbon emissions produced by the economy of the Netherlands.

So here we have two of the fastest growing economies in the world, whose gross national products will soon begin to rival ours, who are linking their futures to the development of nuclear power generation for economic, energy security, and environmental reasons. Our capabilities are helping them make that possible. It is high time we began to help ourselves. The issue of nuclear energy needs be revisited with heightened seriousness in public discourse and Congressional focus. If Congress and our government cannot set us on a course to deal with this issue in a constructive and goal-oriented way, perhaps we should ask the French for help. After all, nearly 80 percent of the French power grid is supplied by nuclear-generated electricity, as opposed to little over 20 percent in the United States. Lafayette, we need you again.

Monsieur le Président Bush, Parlez-Vous Français?
May 21, 2007

Monsieur le Président Bush, parlez-vous Français? If not and should you be inclined to learn, please don't start with the word *weasel*. There are other words in translation that will be more useful to your French lexicon. The following would be helpful:

- Global Warming: France's recently elected President Nicolas Sarkozy (bringing France probably as close to a French edition of an American Republican as we are going to see in our lifetime) proclaimed in his inaugural address last week that fighting global warming will be his highest priority. How unlike the policy of his confrère across the sea, for whom scrapping the Kyoto Treaty has been the order of the day since day one nearly seven years ago.

- Mass Transportation: France has built and enhanced its railway system to become one of the foremost mass transportation systems in the world. Train service spans the nation and is viable, energy efficient, and run in large measure through greenhouse gas-free electricity that is generated by nuclear power. Here future innovation in rail transport is supported with test runs of rail service reaching nearly 350 miles per hour. This stands in stark contrast with our country, where rail transport is starved for funding and our own monsieur le président fights for cuts in the financing of our Amtrak system.

- Alternative Energy Sources: France has a national economy in which the electricity grid is powered not by coal-, gas-, and oil-fired plants but rather by nuclear power with plants located throughout the country. Nuclear power is clean, efficient, and cheaper by far at today's fossil fuel stock prices, not to mention that it is virtually self-reliant. Yes, there are problems of waste disposal, but there are also solutions. In the nearly seven years of Bush's presidency, no viable steps toward expanding nuclear capabilities have been taken, and there has been no effort at meaningful use of the president's bully pulpit to educate us about the benefits, the economic viability, and the environmental pluses of nuclear energy when compared to fossil fuel sources of energy. While France continues on its way to becoming self-reliant in energy, we haven't built a nuclear plant in decades.

- Effectively Reducing Greenhouse Gas Emissions: Paris as a city embraces its nation's values and provides leadership in policy and action. In France's capital, targets have been set to reduce traffic by 40 percent and greenhouse gases by 60 percent by the year 2020. A number of initiatives are already in place or are in the process of becoming so. There will be a refocusing on and an extension of tramways. There will be designated civilized thoroughfares with priority lanes for buses and bicycles. The banks of the Seine will become pedestrian. Areas throughout the city will be restricted to pedestrian traffic only. The beltway around Paris will have lanes that allow quick passage for buses, taxis, and emergency vehicles. Public parking facilities are being eliminated, reduced, or turned over to the motorized scooters and bicycles, which already pepper the Parisian streetscape.

Our monsieur le président's actions on greenhouse gases belie his intentions. Only last week as he talked to us from the White House

Rose Garden, we were advised that he was ordering federal agencies to work together to devise regulations to reduce greenhouse gases. This working together will take until 2008 to come up with findings—in essence, providing them at the end of his mandate and thereby flipping the issue to the next presidency. All the while, he shows where his true interests lie by maintaining the fifty-four–cent duty on imported ethanol.

Voilà, Monsieur le Président Bush. Perhaps it's time to order up that plate of French fries and for the rest of us to brush up on those old French lessons.

An Essential and Viable Energy Fix and the Renaissance of Detroit
April 4, 2008

On December 29, 1940, Nazi Germany had conquered much of Europe and allied with Italy and Japan. It was collaborating closely with the Soviet Union and mortally threatening Britain, the last frontline holdout of democracy. On that day in one of his venerable fireside chats, Franklin D. Roosevelt highlighted the phrase that America would become the "arsenal of democracy" (Franklin D. Roosevelt, "Arsenal of Democracy," speech, December 29, 1940), wiping away any sense of complacency from a then-isolationist America. It was a symbolic call to arms. He called on Americans to become the "spearhead of resistance to world conquest." He focused on the "splendid cooperation between the government and industry and labor" and on "how important the manufacture of weapons and vehicles is to being strong as a nation." Franklin D. Roosevelt then continued in words whose sense of urgency could be applicable to our current enslavement to fossil fuels and to the accelerating threat of global warming, saying, "Emphatically we must get these weapons to them, get them to them in sufficient volume and quickly enough, so that we and our children will be saved the agony and suffering of war which others have had to endure."

Then in 1940, Detroit, the city that became metaphorically the arsenal of democracy, changed almost overnight from being the world's most important builder of passenger cars and vehicles to building the tanks and motorized equipment and armaments that carried this nation and its "greatest generation" ("The Greatest Generation" is a term coined by journalist Tom Brokaw to describe the generation that grew up in the United States during the deprivation of the Great Depression and then went on to fight in World War II; http://en.wikipedia.org/wiki/Greatest_Generation) to ultimate victory in close cooperation with the Washington of that era. That was then, and this is now. As destiny called upon the greatest generation, so too it now beckons to us and to our progeny. September 11 taught us that we are at war and that the ongoing risks to our environment, our economy, our national security, and our national self-respect cry out for definitive action now! Our addiction to driving fossil-fuel-burning, carbon emissions–spewing vehicles has turned these conveyances into the wardens of our self-imposed imprisonment. We must turn this around lest we become the vassals of the oil producers and our children choke on despoiled and poisoned air.

Our politicians tell us that there is no silver bullet. The oil industry tells us that our consumption of oil will continue to grow exponentially. This administration continues to slumber away, content with the riches being visited on their cronies in the oil industry both here and abroad. Well, they are wrong. Renault Nissan and California-based Project Better Place are working together with the government of Israel to make the country independent from oil by 2020. Denmark has already signed on to implement the sinews of this major electric car initiative.

In broad outline, Renault Nissan will build cars powered by lithium-ion batteries that run purely on electricity and deliver performance on par with a 1.6-liter gasoline engine. These electric car models will become available as of 2011. A key component will be the preparation and development of a national infrastructure to access electric power. Project Better Place will arrange for the installation of five hundred thousand charging hookups throughout Israel. It is estimated that electric power charging costs for the lifetime of this car will approximate the cost of fueling an equivalent gasoline-powered vehicle for some two years at current gasoline prices.

Denmark plans to provide the power supply for electric cars with wind power. Israel is planning huge mirrors in the Negev Desert to capture the solar energy needed for its electric cars. With an extensive grid of plug-in locations, there will be no need for lengthy charging periods so charging up shouldn't take much more time than tanking up does currently.

Will it work? Yes. The cars described will be limited in size and range (about 120 miles). But since when has evolving greater size and broader scale been an American limitation? Conceptually, this plan sets the broad outline of what could be replicated in the United States. Consider that the price of energy is pushing us toward recession and stagflation and that Detroit and the American auto industry's business is at the lowest ebb in years with United States–based automakers' share of their home market dropping to only 48.4 percent of cars sold. What a boon it would be to have a renaissance of our historic Detroit arsenal with our government and the automobile industry working together once again on a program critical to the nation's future—together to begin replacing our gas-guzzling, poison-spewing cars with their new electric-powered counterparts on a massive national scale, bringing us back to the spirit of Franklin D. Roosevelt and the "greatest generation."

Certainly, this program would be fought tooth and nail by the oil industry and those beholden to it. This administration won't touch it. Yet given the political season in which we find ourselves, we can fairly ask what we can expect from those now running for high office? How welcome their comments would be.

Obama's Forceful Call to Arms: Defining the Nation's Energy Future
December 16, 2008

In an extraordinary press conference yesterday introducing his energy and environmental team, the president-elect, Barack Obama, put forward his energy program. In doing so, he conveyed a sense that finally our government-to-be is about to lead us out of our long and hapless wanderings in the desert of fossil fuel enslavement. His was a vision, a conviction, and a will to topple our shameful and destructive dependence on oil once and for all, to end our dependence on fossil fuels once and for all, whether priced high or low. The president-elect said, it "will be a leading priority of my presidency" (John M. Broder and Andrew C. Revkin, "Hard Task for New Team on Energy and

Climate," *New York Times*, December 15, 2008, http://www.nytimes.com/2008/12/16/us/politics/16energy.html).

The language and the presentation were exactly what was needed, what many in this nation have been waiting for these past eight years and beyond. It was a call to arms from the bully pulpit, which was used brilliantly to invest the declamation with a shared sense of mission under a leadership that is determined, forthright, and totally engaged on this issue. Phrases that once risked becoming vacuous shibboleths—such as "new energy frontier," "environmental quality," "transforming our economy," "ending our dependence on hostile regimes," "in the face of opposition from special interests," "challenge of climate change," "new energy economy," "based on renewable resources," "turning to wind, solar, and agriculture," "there is not a contradiction between economic growth and sound environmental practices"—all took on an entirely new and ringing dimension.

On this issue, with its existential dimension for the future of the nation and the planet, perhaps, just perhaps, we have found our modern, slimmed-down version of Winston Churchill. We wish him well. We pray for his success.

Climate Change and Nuclear Energy: America's Missed Opportunity for Clean Energy and Thousands of Jobs
December 13, 2009

With 10 percent unemployment and a government determined to stimulate economic growth and put people back to work, what better use could we have for our stimulus programs than building a series of nuclear facilities around the country? Billions from the stimulus pool are already being designated to accelerate the cleanup of nuclear sites at Hanford, Washington; Oak Ridge, Tennessee; and the Savannah River site in South Carolina. At the Savannah site alone, cleanup has created some 1,400 new jobs and drawn workers from all over the country.

Would it not make sense to go one step further and expand an energy infrastructure that is clean, efficient, and not foreign supply–dependent? We hear much about the job-creating possibilities of new clean energy technologies. They should go forward at full speed. But in nuclear power, we have a preeminent technology being sought out by others and vast knowledge in an energy field that is at the top of the agenda for many nations in a world that needs efficient and clean energy solutions. Here we are doing close to nothing to bring about a nuclear renaissance in our own communities even when it could be at the core of dealing with climate change and a key stimulus to our labor market.

The paucity of our efforts and the lack of national vision on this issue were underlined by Indian Prime Minister Monmohan Singh's visit to Washington two weeks ago. His visit refocused attention on India's and America's efforts to tie up the details of the highly important and symbolic binational nuclear cooperation agreement. India is planning to build seven additional nuclear power plants by 2020, and access to American nuclear technology is key to India's plans. American and Indian negotiators are working diligently on the energy cooperative agreement approved last year by the legislatures of both countries.

There are still details to be worked out, including:

- assurances that low-enriched uranium sold by the US companies for use in Indian reactors does not end up reprocessed as weapons-grade fuel;

- guarantees from nuclear-armed India that the fuel would not be used for military purposes;

- assurances that India, which is not a signatory of the Nuclear Non-Proliferation Treaty, will not pass on its nuclear know-how; and

- issues of liability protection.

The cooperation between the United States and India to help India broaden its commitment to nuclear energy exposes a major failure of American national policy. Here is India, an ancient civilization transformed into a vibrant emerging economy, seeking help from its somnolent sister democracy. Our nation hasn't had the determination or volition to build a new nuclear facility since the late 1970s; that's a generation-long hiatus while India plans seven new nuclear plants by 2020, while China has twenty under construction and will have built thirty-two by 2020 and three hundred more by 2050. France is ratcheting up its electrical grid to 100 percent nuclear in the next few years.

Our stimulus monies could not be better focused than on building a series of nuclear power plants around the country. In France, many towns and cities compete to have facilities located in or near them because of the employment opportunities they bring and the economic infrastructure they encourage. How many of our towns and cities would be so inclined? It would be interesting to find out.

Yes, of course, there are myriad problems attendant to nuclear energy expansion, but they can be dealt with as other nations have done. A first and important step would be to reverse President Jimmy Carter's almost unilateral indefinite deferral of our plans to reprocess and recycle used nuclear fuel because of concerns that reprocessing could contribute to the proliferation of nuclear weapons. President Carter expected other nations to follow his lead, but they did not, because they recognized that Carter's policy offered no viable path to prevent proliferation.

Mr. David Rossin, who was assistant secretary for nuclear energy in the US Department of Energy from 1986 to 1987 and president of the American Nuclear Society from 1992 to 1993, points out, "French and British experts and diplomats have strong memories about the way the [United States] undermined their nuclear fuel cycle in the first 100 days of [President Carter's] administration, without national public debate nor international counsel" (David Rossin, "The French Were Late on Iran's Nukes But Are Right," *Wall Street Journal*, October 4, 2009, http://online.wsj.com/article/SB1000142405274870447150457444739 0499032188.html). In doing so, Carter severely hampered the nation's ability to deal with the nuclear fuel cycle. Since then, France, for one, has significantly increased the capacity of its reprocessing facilities. At the very least, it is time to review in depth the Department of Energy's initiative to promote new reactor technology using proliferation-resistant reprocessed fuel.

At this moment—with emissaries from all over the world gathering in Copenhagen and on the heels of the Environmental Protection Agency's dire ruling that greenhouse gases pose a danger to human health and the environment, given the ominous issues of energy, both strategic and environmental, and given the economic demands of a world economy that is becoming ever more fully integrated—this is a failing of national proportions. It is a reflection of failed or incompetent leadership or, worse, a government no longer able to function effectively in a new world in which other national entities work for the greater good of their citizens rather than for the parochial interests of the well-connected few. Nuclear energy is essential to a green future and to our economic competitiveness. We cannot afford to have another generation go by without engaging it fully and putting it at the forefront of our national energy policy.

Oil Spewing in the Gulf: Now Is the Time for the National Renewable Energy Trust
May 25, 2010

The disastrous oil spill in the gulf is assuming near biblical proportions and destroying large swaths of the environment and the livelihood of thousands upon thousands of our fellow citizens. The disaster has exacerbated our loss of trust in the oil industry to develop our natural resources—that is, our national patrimony on federal lands or at sea—in a way that benefits all Americans rather than simply the bottom lines of the oil companies. As presently constituted, the oil/concession system itself is an abomination that has profited no one but the oil companies at great cost to the nation as a whole. To see the environmental expense of the industry as currently constituted, one need go no further than the front page of any newspaper on this day.

It is long past time for the nation's citizens to reclaim their national patrimony: the oil, gas, and shale oil deposits on federal lands and the continental shelf. The revenues from oil and gas deposits should be channeled toward developing alternative energy sources as a cornerstone of a viable program for breaking our increasingly dangerous dependency on fossil fuels. Such a program could be modeled after a program of the world's third largest energy exporter (after Saudi Arabia and Russia), Norway's Petroleum Directorate. The stated objective of the directorate is to create the greatest value for Norwegian society from Norway's oil and gas deposits. This has been accomplished safely with enormous benefits to all Norwegians. We could do the same by creating a national renewable energy trust to explore and develop, in a viable and safe way, our energy deposits on national lands and on the continental shelf. Such a program would be a boon to the nation, especially if proceeds were dedicated to a massively funded alternative energy program.

As a nation, we are not without examples of major government initiatives that parallel the private sector. In the depths of the Depression, President Roosevelt sought different solutions and different thinking, with courage and imagination, to deal with the crippling economic conditions facing the nation. He asked Congress to mandate the creation of a "corporation clothed with the power of government but possessed of the flexibility and initiative of private enterprise" (Tennessee Valley Authority, "Short History of TVA," tva.com, http://www.tva.com/abouttva/history.htm).

On May 18, 1933, Congress established the Tennessee Valley Authority to revitalize the economically devastated Tennessee Valley with power generation, river navigation, flood control, reforestation, and erosion control. The Tennessee Valley Authority's success in all these areas was and continues to be outstanding. To this day, the Tennessee Valley Authority pursues an aggressive clean air program and is on track to meet its commitments to achieve 80 to 85 percent of 1977 sulfur dioxide emission levels by the end of this year. The Tennessee Valley Authority has consistently set a standard for public responsibility against which private companies could be measured.

Another example of hands-on government in times of national need is when the nation's railroads were nationalized during World War I and administered by the US Railroad Administration to great effect, making a major contribution to the war effort.

The Norwegian Petroleum Directorate is a source of particular pride to the Norwegian people. Isn't it time for us to harness our national patrimony for the well-being of the nation and future generations? The time for a national renewable energy trust is now.

Natural Gas Replacing Coal-Fired Power Plants: A Major Step toward Diminishing Carbon Dioxide Emissions
July 14, 2010

Last week at an Aspen Institute Ideas Festival session, Marvin E. Odum, the president of Shell Oil, was in a dialogue with Andrea Mitchell, NBC chief foreign affairs correspondent and host of MSNBC's *Andrea Mitchell Reports*. The primary theme of the day was, of course, the gulf oil disaster, how it might have been prevented, steps to be taken in the future, and other related topics of urgent and immediate importance.

In the course of the discussion, Mr. Odum brought into focus another important issue: the role that natural gas should play in the abatement of carbon dioxide emissions.

Odum made the audience aware of the newly defined and abundant deposits of the natural gas termed *shale gas*, which are accessed by the novel techniques of horizontal drilling and hydraulic fracturing. He went on to discuss the potential of this new resource abundance were it to be employed as a substitute for coal, replacing coal-fired power generating plants in significant measure, and what it would achieve in the abatement of greenhouse gas emissions. According to Mr. Odum, converting from coal- to gas-fired electricity plants would eliminate 50 to 70 percent of current carbon dioxide emissions, depending on the coal-burning systems being replaced; it is, therefore, an issue that must come to the forefront of our current energy policy.

Mr. Odum advised that Shell has just committed five billion dollars to taking an important stake in the Marcellus Shale, a staggeringly rich shale gas field—it contains some five hundred trillion cubic feet of gas—that lies within the Appalachian Basin extending through eastern Ohio, West Virginia, Pennsylvania, and into New York State. Mr. Odum further noted that Shell was fully aware of the environmental issues related to shale gas drilling such as the risk of shallow freshwater aquifer contamination. The company is nevertheless confident that the environmental impact issues can be managed through careful and fully transparent procedures to the satisfaction of government and oversight agencies.

Coincidentally, just over a month ago, the Massachusetts Institute of Technology's Energy Initiative issued a singularly informative report, "The Future of Natural Gas: An Interdisciplinary Study." It is required reading for anyone interested in the subject of fossil fuel consumption and its environmental impact or for anyone who wishes to have a deeper, more hands-on understanding of an element that will unquestionably be at core of the nation's energy future. Its dimensions and importance were made clear from the very outset, as Massachusetts Institute of Technology's Energy Initiative director, Ernst J. Moniz, introduced the report, saying, "Much has been said about natural gas as a bridge to a low-carbon future, with little underlying analysis to back up this contention. The analysis in this study provides the confirmation—

natural gas truly is a bridge to a low-carbon future." The report is a comprehensive review that brings into clear focus the future importance of natural gas as an element of the fossil fuel equation. The study shows a baseline global estimate of recoverable gas resources reaching some 16,200 trillion cubic feet—enough to last more than 160 years at current global consumption rates.

The report, which was conducted by a study group of thirty Massachusetts Institute of Technology faculty members, researchers, and graduate students, is publicly available on the Massachusetts Institute of Technology's website (http://web.mit.edu/mitei/research/studies/report-natural-gas.pdf). It is well worth the reader's time to access this important study wherever there is an interest in the future of fossil fuel consumption and its environmental impact.

Afterword

This book *Oil and Finance: The Epic Corruption* focuses on those issues widely misunderstood and fraught with misinformation. In many ways, it is a condemnation of a system that is barely functioning, responsive not to the general weal nor to the basic economic laws of supply and demand but rather to the influence, lucre, and access of the few and their special interests.

Too many people and interests have too much at stake in the status quo—both financially and in terms of their power and influence. We can count on them to fight tooth and nail against any reform. Oil is the lifeblood of most Middle Eastern governments, and as I have detailed herein, it is also the lifeblood of terrorism. Any attempt to weaken oil's stranglehold on our economy, our environment, and our national security will be treated by oil's beneficiaries as an act of aggression, even an act of war.

One might conclude after reading this book that, when it comes to the global oil market, the more things change, the more they stay the same. Year after year, OPEC, big oil, the traders using underregulated exchanges and their enablers in our government, and the media preside over an almost unthinkable theft from American and world petroleum consumers. We are robbed of billions of dollars every day by those oil interests in their pursuit of price objectives at massive cost and grave risk to the world's economy. Wall Street and the significant resources of the financial sector play their roles in the distortion of the oil market through vast speculation that is unhindered by somnolent government oversight agencies. Nor does it seem to matter much who is in power.

President Obama, who campaigned persuasively on promises of change, has been no more effective in checking ever-rising oil costs than was his oil patch–friendly predecessor, George W. Bush. Could it be that the corruption and complacency are now too deeply entrenched to be reversed?

The unwillingness or inability to act has resulted in a distorted cost of oil. Price levels flirting with $100/bbl are an outrage, especially given that the world's inventories of oil are filled to overflowing. Incredibly, oil is now priced higher by a factor of more than seven than it was ten years ago. No commodity of such fundamental importance to the economy has had anything near a similar escalation in price. Clearly, the price determination and marketing of oil has left all ballast of the laws of supply and demand and continues to do so.

Ideas have been put forward herein on how we might deal with a number of these issues. Of course, we need farseeing policies and to urgently embrace alternative clean energy in all its forms, ranging from solar power to electric vehicles and on to safe nuclear energy. It is time for citizens of all political persuasions to fight political complacency. The public cannot afford to remain ignorant of the conditions and machinations underpinning the ongoing oil extortion while our governments sit idly by, international agencies remain mute, and our press stays unfocused such is the power of money to achieve silence. Rather than simply grumbling helplessly at the gas pump, Americans must learn to ask, *cui bono?* Who benefits, how, and what are the consequences? Americans must be made aware of how oil prices and policies are manipulated, and they must learn more about where that money goes. They must understand that the withdrawal from our oil addiction—like withdrawals from all addictions—may be painful, but the result will be a healthier economy and society.

Index

Hess, Leon, 85, 175, 176
Hess Corporation, 175
Hess Oil, 85
Hezbollah, 44
high-speed rail, 55, 257, 261–262, 263, 264
highway/road building, addiction to, 262, 263
Hobson's choice, 18, 268
Hong Kong exchange, 86
Hoover Dam, 264
Hopkins, Kathryn, 201
housing market, 186, 214, 216, 218, 226, 227
Houston TX, 42, 46, 59, 60
Hoyos, Carola, 7, 9, 58, 80
Hubbert, M. King, 153, 161, 162, 164
Hubbert curve theory, 160
Huffington, Arianna, 221, 264
HuffingtonPost.com, 162, 200, 245
hurricane activity, 145, 154, 165
Hurricane Katrina, 3, 57, 90, 165, 166, 235, 237
Hurricane Rita, 57
Hussein, Saddam, 14, 98, 99
Hutchison, Kay Bailey, 23, 24
hybrid vehicles, 118, 253, 254, 260
hydroelectric power, 14, 22, 171, 270

I

Ibero-American summit, 33
Illinois, 104. *See also* Chicago IL
imaging software, 75
import licenses/permits, 42, 43–44, 104
Independent, 179
India
    carbon dioxide emissions, 270
    demand for electricity, 276–277
    effect on economy of with embargo of Iran, 102
    greenhouse gas pollution, 277
    industrial development of, 268
    nuclear cooperation with US, 270, 276, 283
    nuclear expansion, 130, 272

oil fields in, 163
riots in, 77
Saudi resources as essential to, 27
as sophisticated economy, 276
suspension of futures trading in foodstuffs markets, 176
technological brain trust, 270
Indian NDTV, 5, 27
Indonesia, 52, 66
initial public offering (IPO), 218, 222
inland waterways/port facilities, 55, 142
Intercontinental Exchange, 65, 71
International Atomic Energy Agency, 272, 276
International Energy Agency, 6, 18, 21, 22, 28, 31, 75, 83, 90, 95, 116, 139, 170, 240
international exchanges, 70
International Herald Tribune, 45
International Machinists and Aerospace Workers, 68
International Policy Network, 126
International Swap and Derivatives Association, 229
investor sentiment, 82
IPO (initial public offering), 218, 222
Iran
    backing of Shiites, 18, 25
    bulwark against, 32
    de Margerie's gas project with, 30
    and the *Front Page*, 101
    natural gas production, 96
    nuclear program, 66, 144
    nuclear standoff with, 90
    oil exports, 95, 102
    on oil prices, 93
    oil production, 90, 95, 238
    OPEC member, xxiii
    Pakistani nuclear components to, 12
    pressing for reduction in production quotas, 5, 6, 7, 42
    prospective sanctions in, 154
    reputation as troublemaker, 96
    response to UN threat of sanctions, 243

9 781462 018109